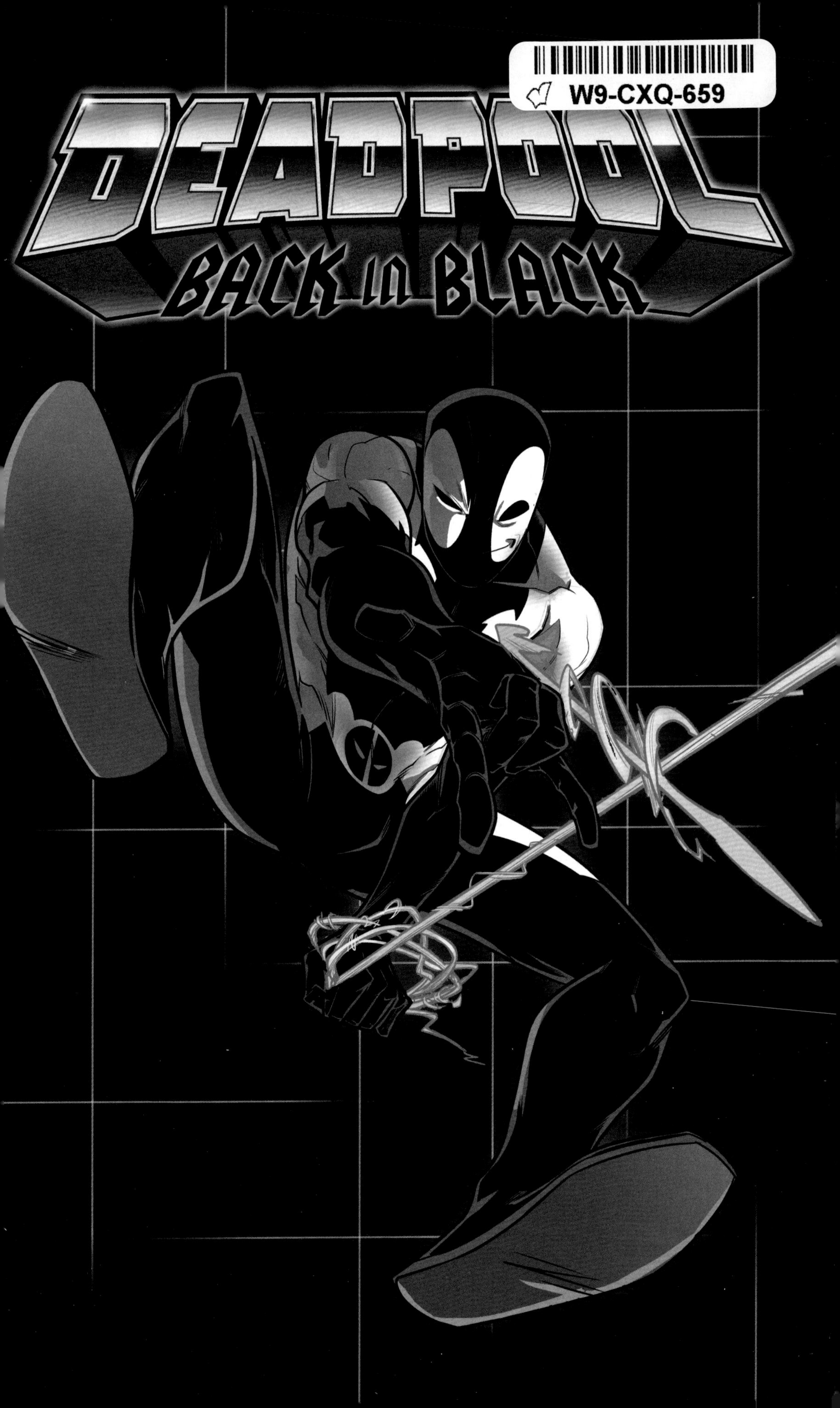
DEADPOOL
BACK in BLACK

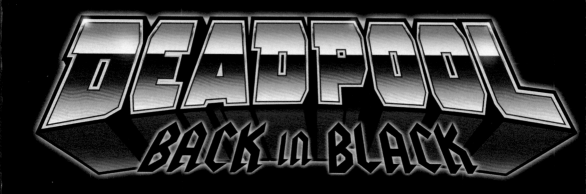

DEADPOOL
BACK IN BLACK

CULLEN BUNN
WRITER

SALVA ESPIN
ARTIST

RUTH REDMOND
COLORIST

VC's JOE SABINO
LETTERER

SALVA ESPIN WITH **RUTH REDMOND** (#1-2) & **GURU-eFX** (#3-5)
COVER ART

HEATHER ANTOS
ASSISTANT EDITOR

JORDAN D. WHITE
EDITOR

DEADPOOL CREATED BY ROB LIEFELD & FABIAN NICIEZA

JENNIFER GRÜNWALD
COLLECTION EDITOR

CAITLIN O'CONNELL
ASSISTANT EDITOR

KATERI WOODY
ASSOCIATE MANAGING EDITOR

MARK D. BEAZLEY
EDITOR, SPECIAL PROJECTS

JEFF YOUNGQUIST
VP PRODUCTION & SPECIAL PROJECTS

DAVID GABRIEL
SVP PRINT, SALES & MARKETING

ADAM DEL RE
BOOK DESIGNER

AXEL ALONSO
EDITOR IN CHIEF

JOE QUESADA
CHIEF CREATIVE OFFICER

DAN BUCKLEY
PUBLISHER

ALAN FINE
EXECUTIVE PRODUCER

DEADPOOL: BACK IN BLACK. Contains material originally published in magazine form as DEADPOOL: BACK IN BLACK #1-5. First printing 2017. ISBN# 978-1-302-90188-2. Published by MARVEL WORLDWIDE, INC., a subsidiary of MARVEL ENTERTAINMENT, LLC. OFFICE OF PUBLICATION: 135 West 50th Street, New York, NY 10020. **Printed in Canada.** ALAN FINE, President, Marvel Entertainment; DAN BUCKLEY, President, TV, Publishing & Brand Management; JOE QUESADA, Chief Creative Officer; TOM BREVOORT, SVP of Publishing; DAVID BOGART, SVP of Business Affairs & Operations, Publishing & Partnership; C.B. CEBULSKI, VP of Brand Management & Development, Asia; DAVID GABRIEL, SVP of Sales & Marketing, Publishing; JEFF YOUNGQUIST, VP of Production & Special Projects; DAN CARR, Executive Director of Publishing Technology; ALEX MORALES, Director of Publishing Operations; SUSAN CRESPI, Production Manager; STAN LEE, Chairman Emeritus. For information regarding advertising in Marvel Comics or on Marvel.com, please contact Vit DeBellis, Integrated Sales Manager, at vdebellis@marvel.com. For Marvel subscription inquiries, please call 888-511-5480. **Manufactured between 12/30/2016 and 2/6/2017 by SOLISCO PRINTERS, SCOTT, QC, CANADA.**

10 9 8 7 6 5 4 3 2 1

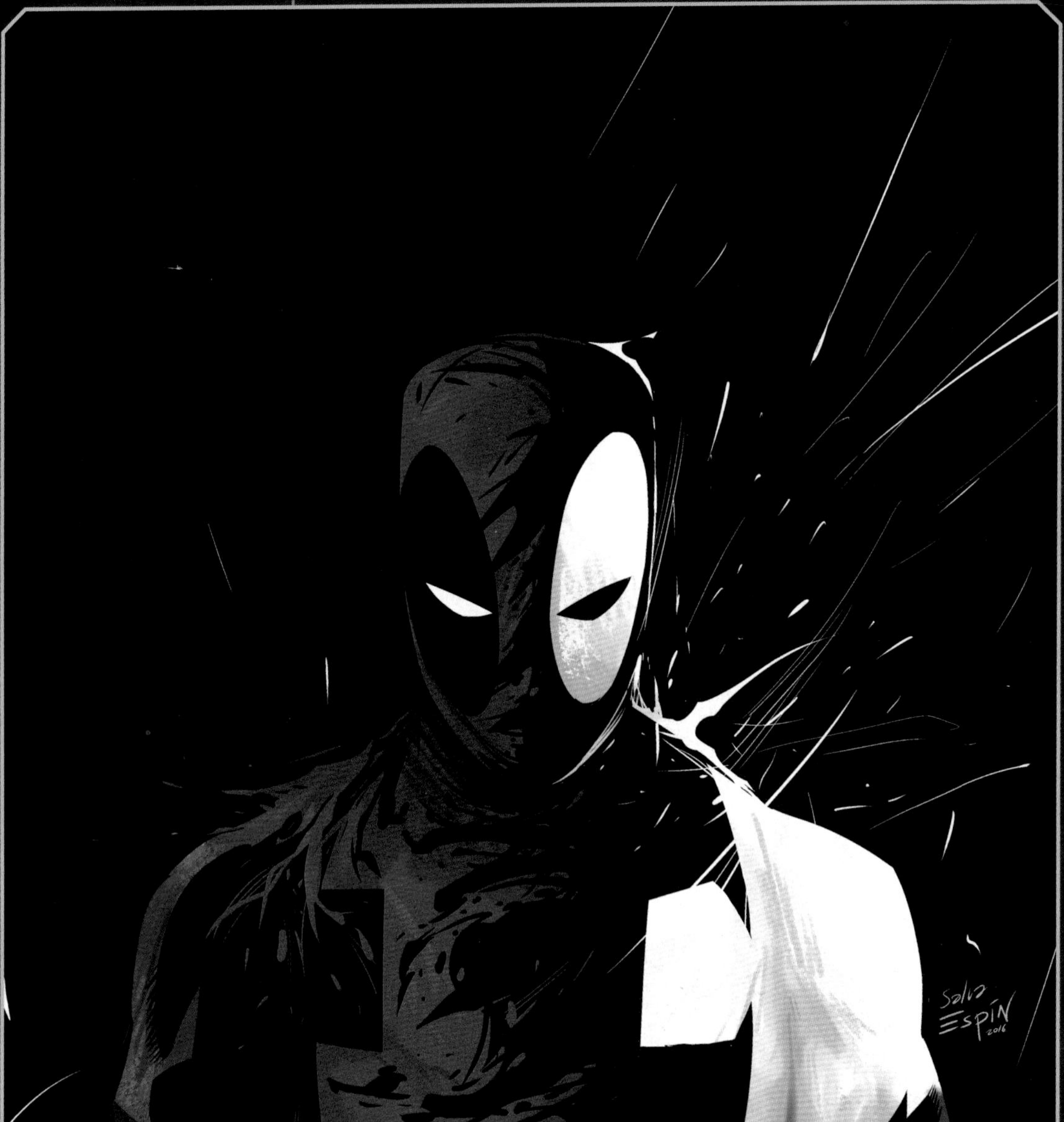
Salva
ESPÍN
2016

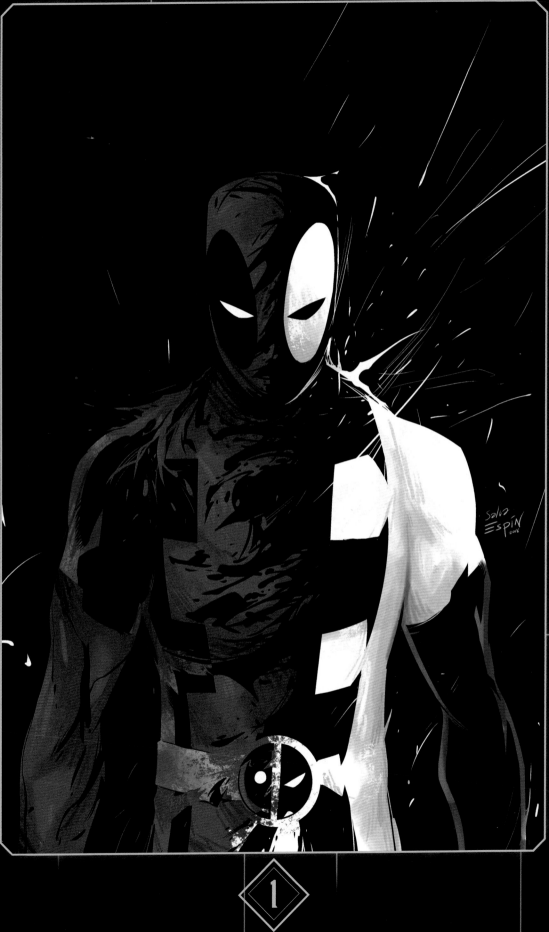

1

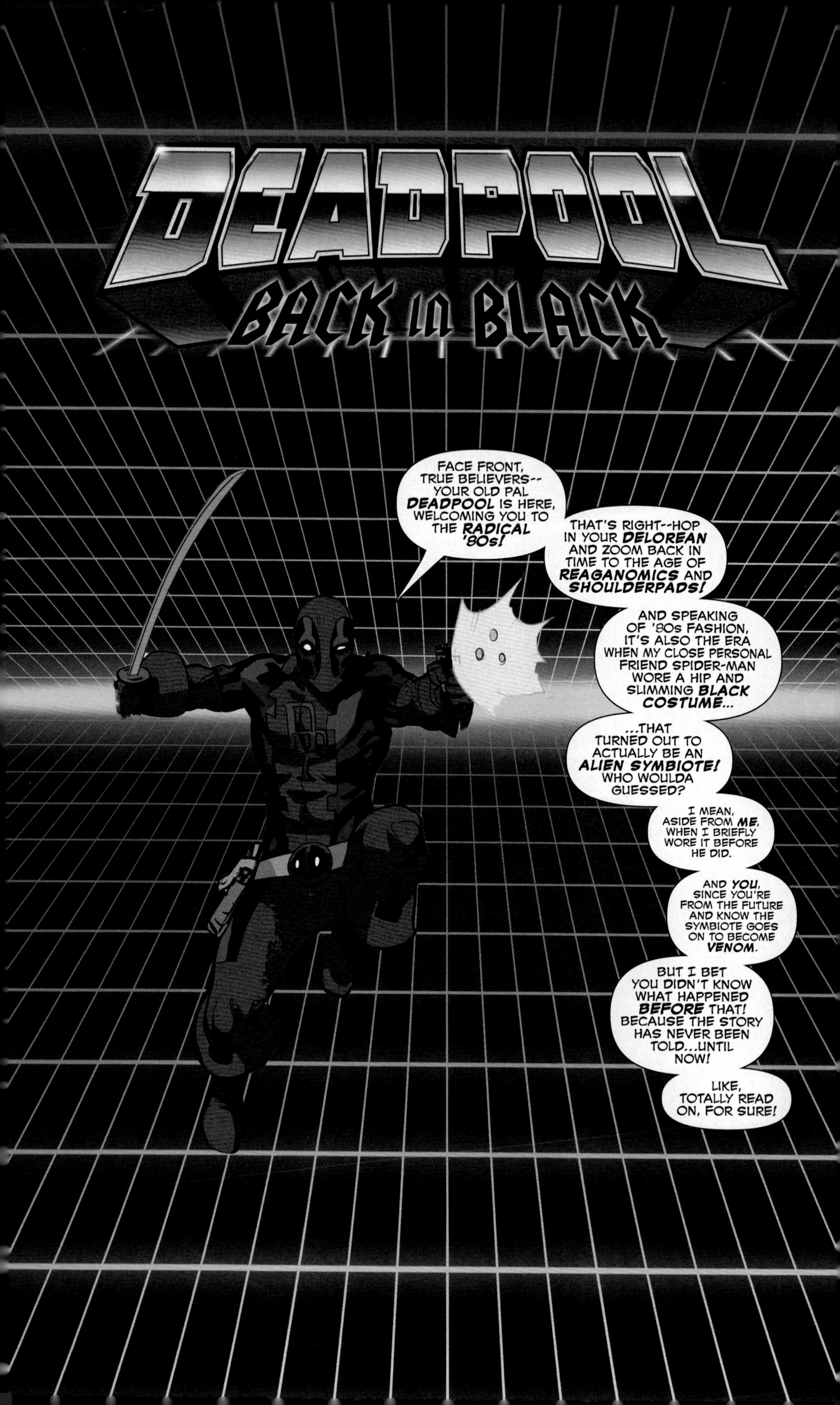
DEADPOOL
BACK IN BLACK
FACE FRONT, TRUE BELIEVERS--YOUR OLD PAL DEADPOOL IS HERE, WELCOMING YOU TO THE RADICAL '80s!
THAT'S RIGHT--HOP IN YOUR DELOREAN AND ZOOM BACK IN TIME TO THE AGE OF REAGANOMICS AND SHOULDERPADS!
AND SPEAKING OF '80s FASHION, IT'S ALSO THE ERA WHEN MY CLOSE PERSONAL FRIEND SPIDER-MAN WORE A HIP AND SLIMMING BLACK COSTUME...
...THAT TURNED OUT TO ACTUALLY BE AN ALIEN SYMBIOTE! WHO WOULDA GUESSED?
I MEAN, ASIDE FROM ME, WHEN I BRIEFLY WORE IT BEFORE HE DID.
AND YOU, SINCE YOU'RE FROM THE FUTURE AND KNOW THE SYMBIOTE GOES ON TO BECOME VENOM.
BUT I BET YOU DIDN'T KNOW WHAT HAPPENED BEFORE THAT! BECAUSE THE STORY HAS NEVER BEEN TOLD...UNTIL NOW!
LIKE, TOTALLY READ ON, FOR SURE!

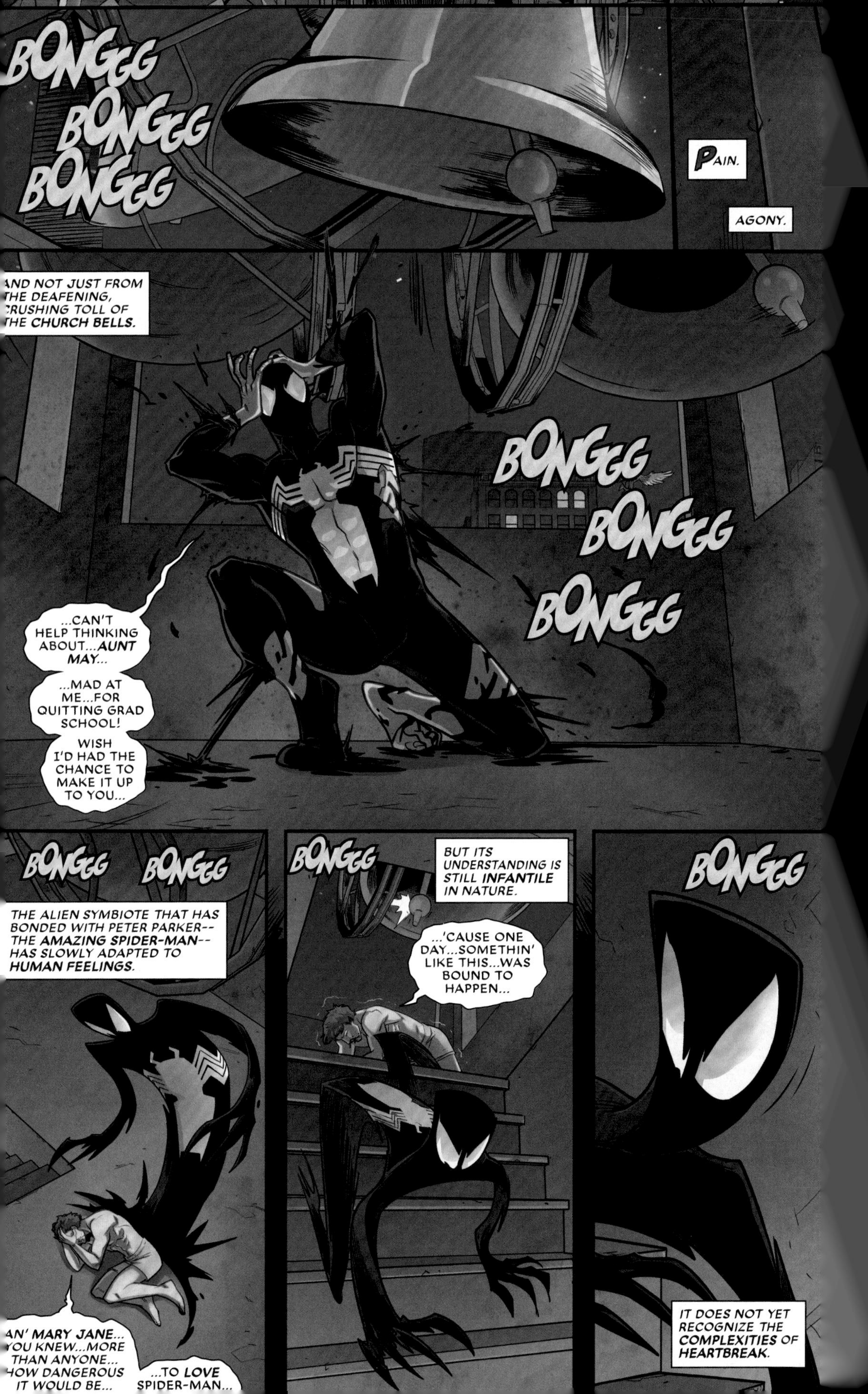

BONGGG
BONGGG
BONGGG
PAIN.
AGONY.
AND NOT JUST FROM THE DEAFENING, CRUSHING TOLL OF THE CHURCH BELLS.
BONGGG
BONGGG
BONGGG
...CAN'T HELP THINKING ABOUT...AUNT MAY...
...MAD AT ME...FOR QUITTING GRAD SCHOOL!
WISH I'D HAD THE CHANCE TO MAKE IT UP TO YOU...
BONGGG
BONGGG
THE ALIEN SYMBIOTE THAT HAS BONDED WITH PETER PARKER--THE AMAZING SPIDER-MAN--HAS SLOWLY ADAPTED TO HUMAN FEELINGS.
AN' MARY JANE... YOU KNEW...MORE THAN ANYONE... HOW DANGEROUS IT WOULD BE...
...TO LOVE SPIDER-MAN...
BONGGG
BUT ITS UNDERSTANDING IS STILL INFANTILE IN NATURE.
...'CAUSE ONE DAY...SOMETHIN' LIKE THIS...WAS BOUND TO HAPPEN...
BONGGG
IT DOES NOT YET RECOGNIZE THE COMPLEXITIES OF HEARTBREAK.

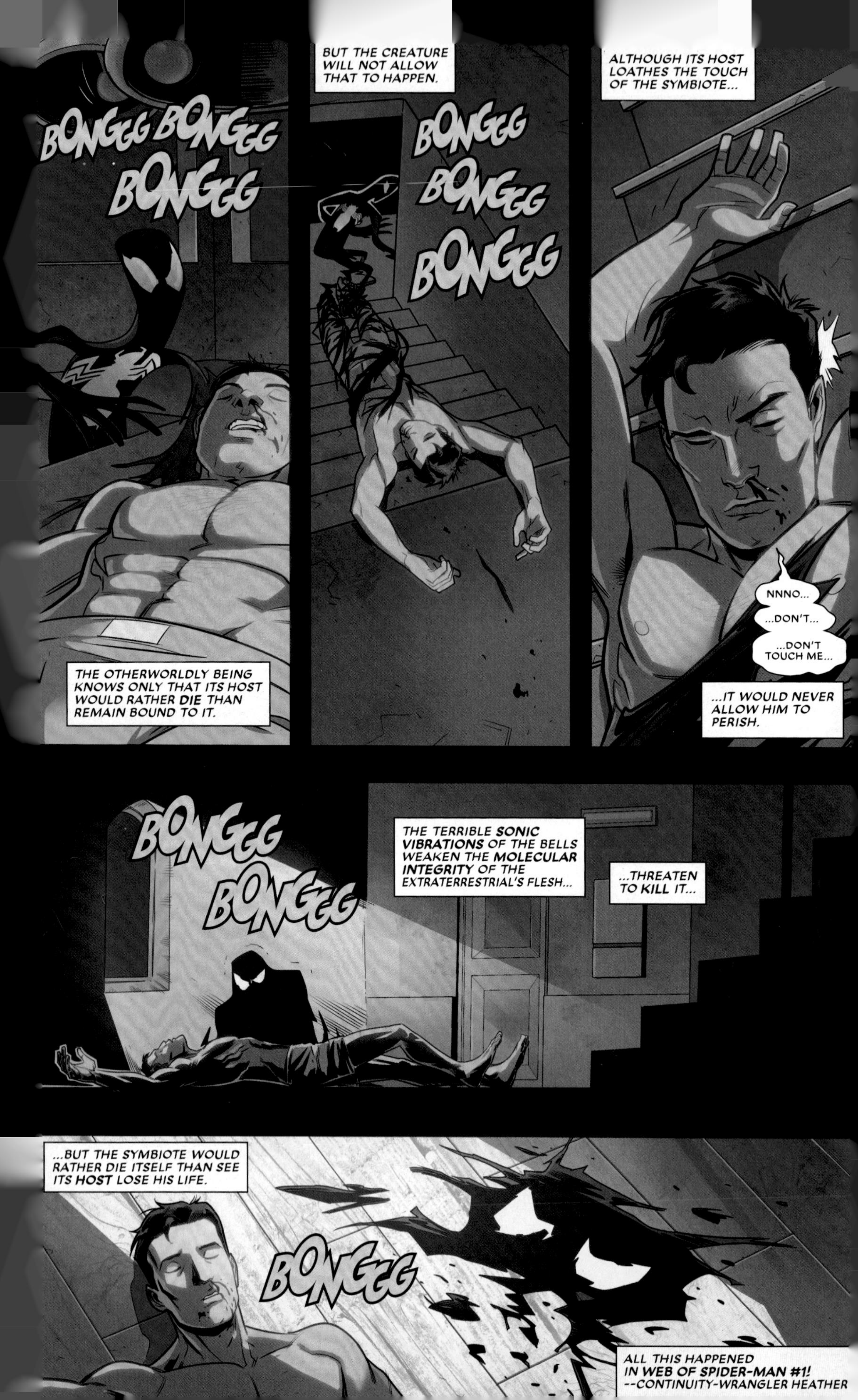
BONGGG BONGGG
BONGGG
THE OTHERWORLDLY BEING KNOWS ONLY THAT ITS HOST WOULD RATHER DIE THAN REMAIN BOUND TO IT.
BUT THE CREATURE WILL NOT ALLOW THAT TO HAPPEN.
BONGGG
BONGGG
BONGGG
ALTHOUGH ITS HOST LOATHES THE TOUCH OF THE SYMBIOTE...
NNNO...
...DON'T...
...DON'T TOUCH ME...
...IT WOULD NEVER ALLOW HIM TO PERISH.
BONGGG
BONGGG
THE TERRIBLE SONIC VIBRATIONS OF THE BELLS WEAKEN THE MOLECULAR INTEGRITY OF THE EXTRATERRESTRIAL'S FLESH...
...THREATEN TO KILL IT...
...BUT THE SYMBIOTE WOULD RATHER DIE ITSELF THAN SEE ITS HOST LOSE HIS LIFE.
BONGGG
ALL THIS HAPPENED IN WEB OF SPIDER-MAN #1! --CONTINUITY-WRANGLER HEATHER

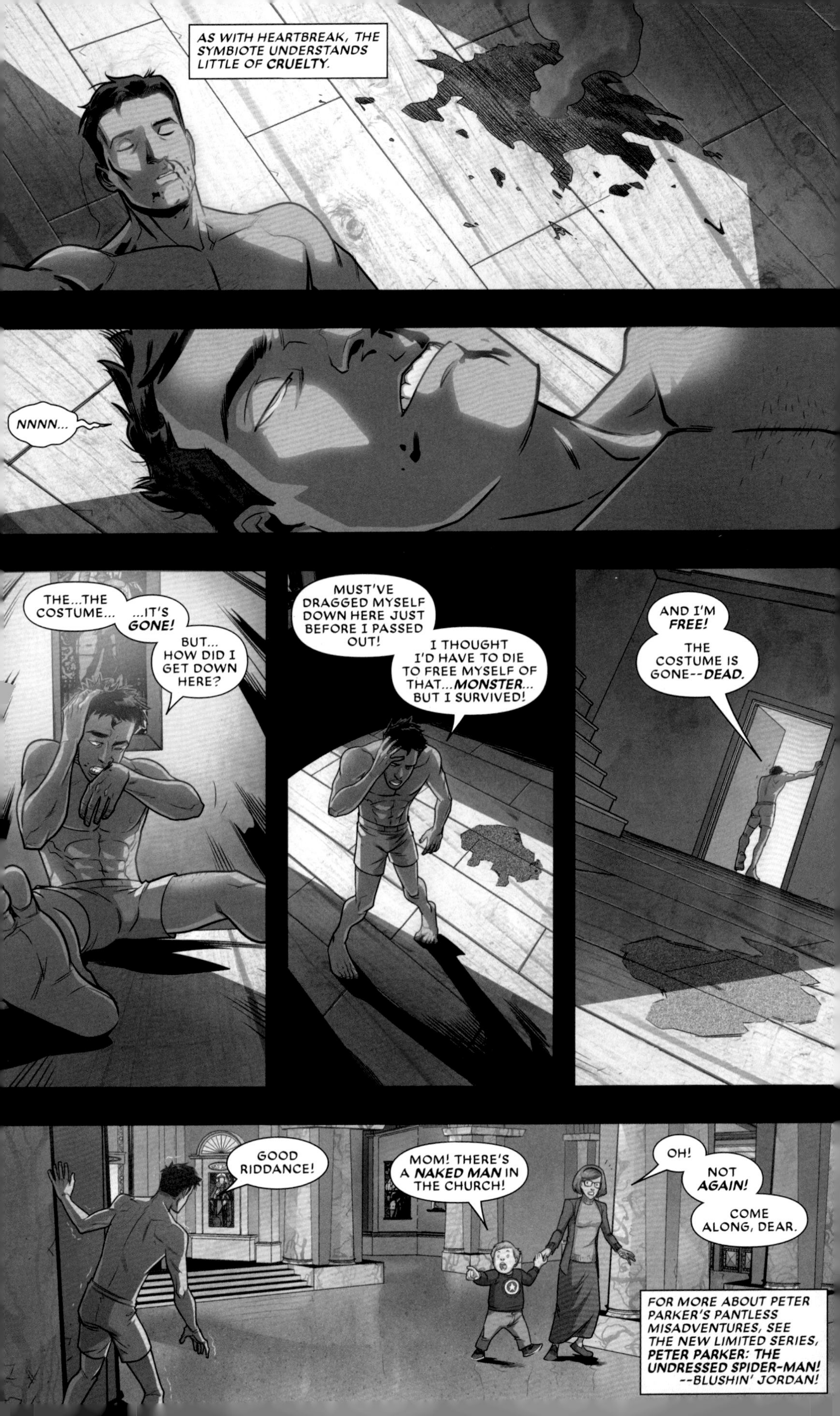
AS WITH HEARTBREAK, THE SYMBIOTE UNDERSTANDS LITTLE OF CRUELTY.
NNNN...
THE...THE COSTUME...
...IT'S GONE!
BUT... HOW DID I GET DOWN HERE?
MUST'VE DRAGGED MYSELF DOWN HERE JUST BEFORE I PASSED OUT!
I THOUGHT I'D HAVE TO DIE TO FREE MYSELF OF THAT...MONSTER... BUT I SURVIVED!
AND I'M FREE!
THE COSTUME IS GONE--DEAD.
GOOD RIDDANCE!
MOM! THERE'S A NAKED MAN IN THE CHURCH!
OH!
NOT AGAIN!
COME ALONG, DEAR.
FOR MORE ABOUT PETER PARKER'S PANTLESS MISADVENTURES, SEE THE NEW LIMITED SERIES, PETER PARKER: THE UNDRESSED SPIDER-MAN! --BLUSHIN' JORDAN!

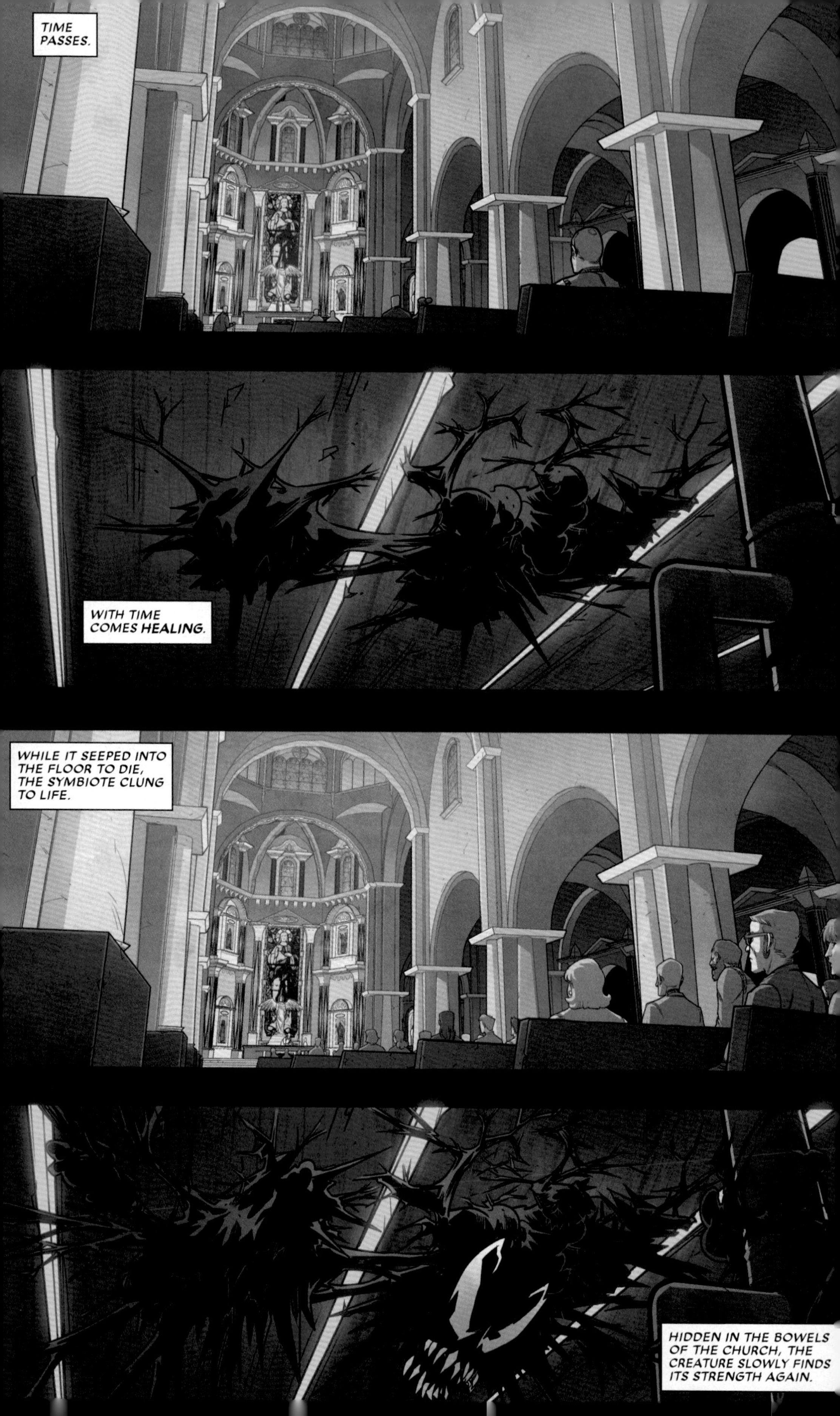
TIME PASSES.
WITH TIME COMES HEALING.
WHILE IT SEEPED INTO THE FLOOR TO DIE, THE SYMBIOTE CLUNG TO LIFE.
HIDDEN IN THE BOWELS OF THE CHURCH, THE CREATURE SLOWLY FINDS ITS STRENGTH AGAIN.

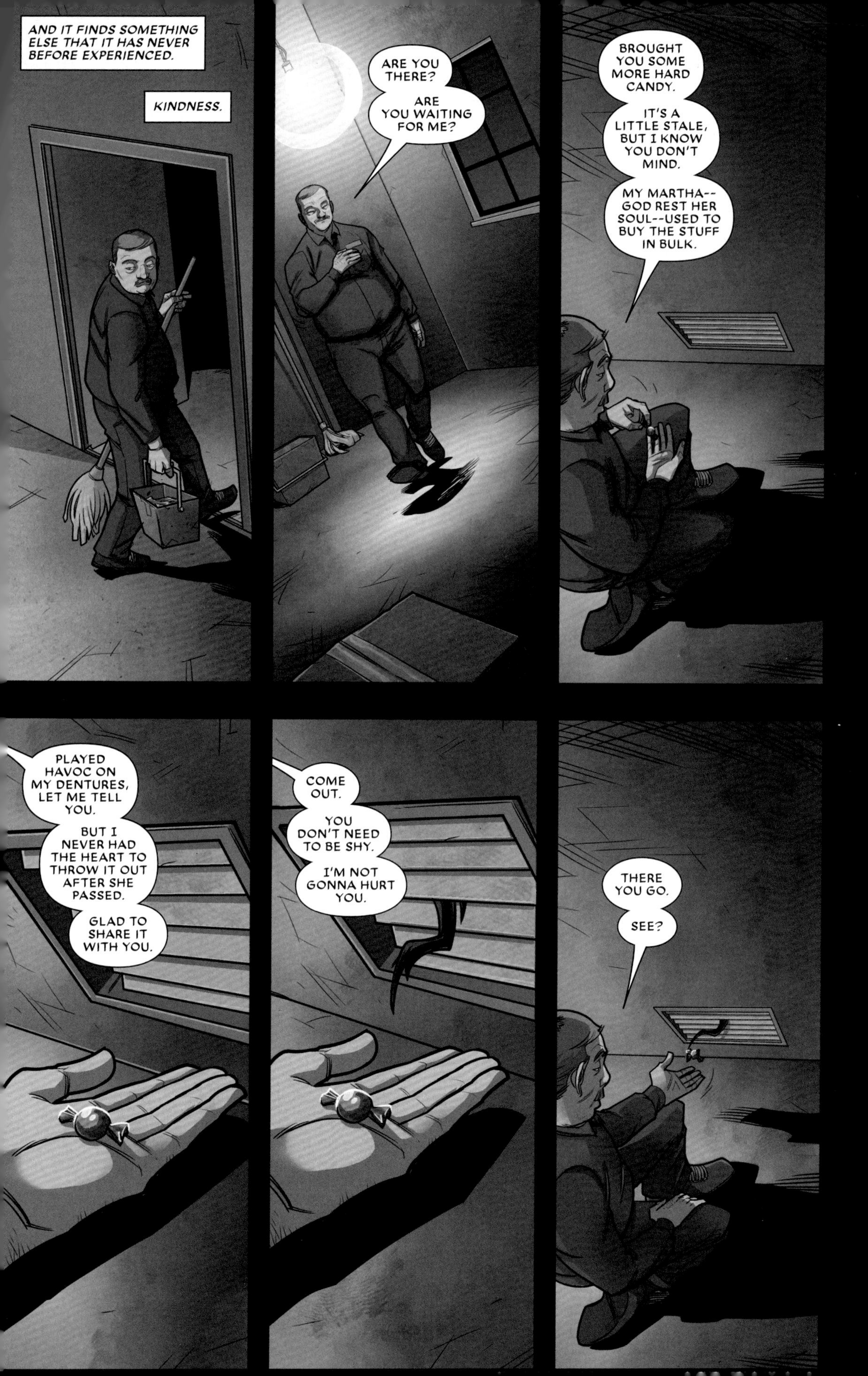
AND IT FINDS SOMETHING ELSE THAT IT HAS NEVER BEFORE EXPERIENCED.
KINDNESS.
ARE YOU THERE?
ARE YOU WAITING FOR ME?
BROUGHT YOU SOME MORE HARD CANDY.
IT'S A LITTLE STALE, BUT I KNOW YOU DON'T MIND.
MY MARTHA--GOD REST HER SOUL--USED TO BUY THE STUFF IN BULK.
PLAYED HAVOC ON MY DENTURES, LET ME TELL YOU.
BUT I NEVER HAD THE HEART TO THROW IT OUT AFTER SHE PASSED.
GLAD TO SHARE IT WITH YOU.
COME OUT.
YOU DON'T NEED TO BE SHY.
I'M NOT GONNA HURT YOU.
THERE YOU GO.
SEE?

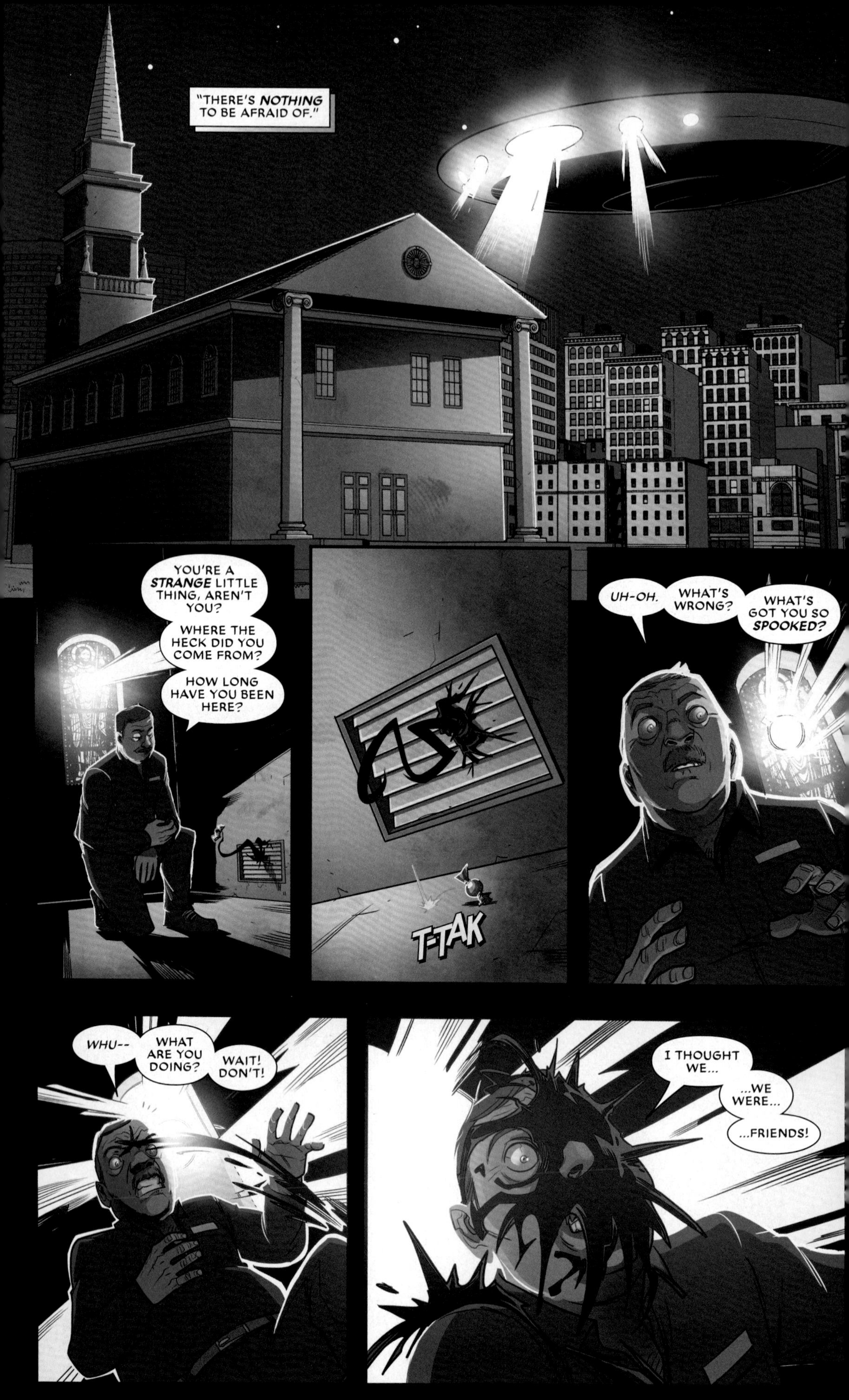

"THERE'S NOTHING TO BE AFRAID OF."
YOU'RE A STRANGE LITTLE THING, AREN'T YOU?
WHERE THE HECK DID YOU COME FROM?
HOW LONG HAVE YOU BEEN HERE?
T-TAK
UH-OH.
WHAT'S WRONG?
WHAT'S GOT YOU SO SPOOKED?
WHU--
WHAT ARE YOU DOING?
WAIT! DON'T!
I THOUGHT WE...
...WE WERE...
...FRIENDS!

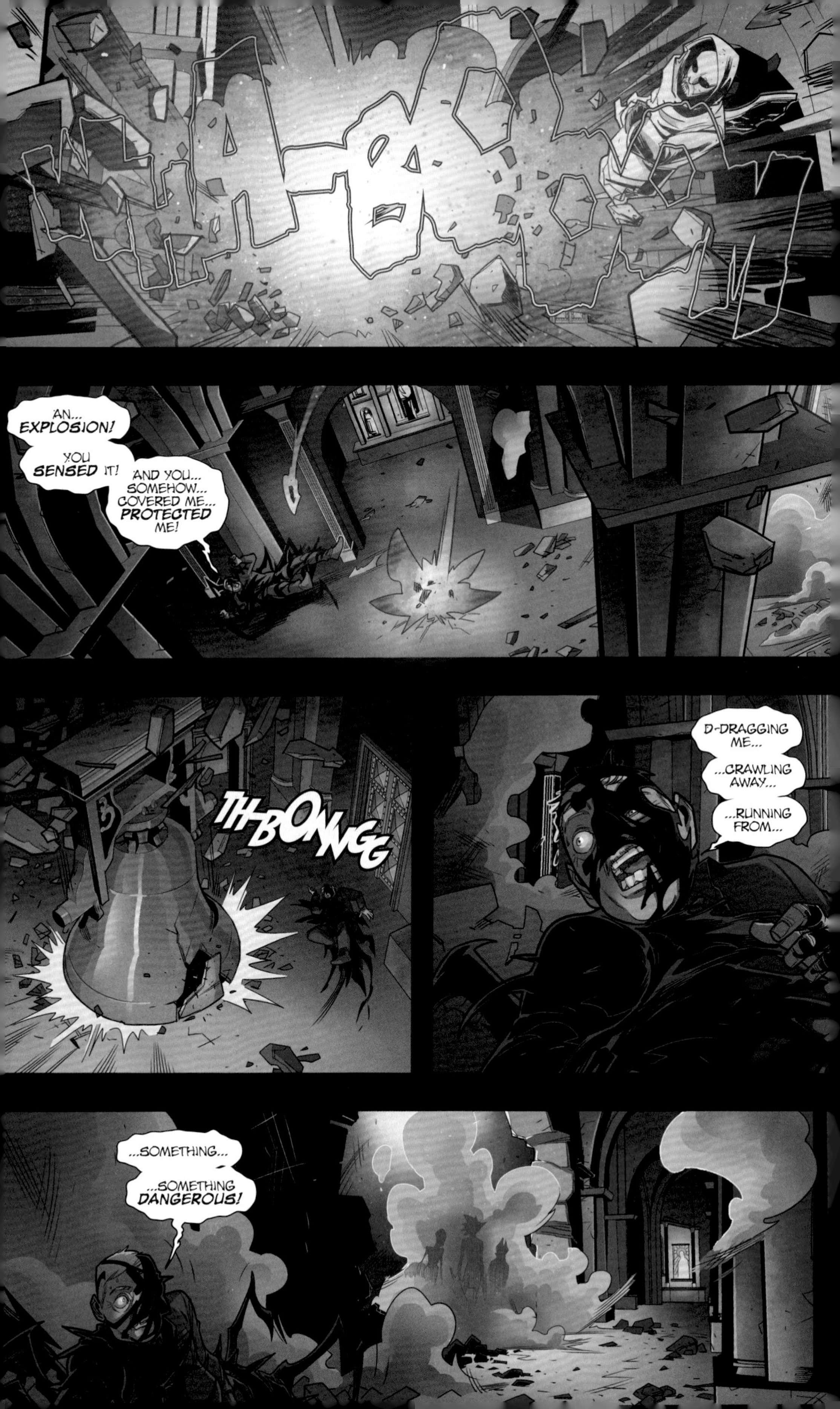
AN... EXPLOSION!
YOU SENSED IT!
AND YOU... SOMEHOW... COVERED ME... PROTECTED ME!
TH-BONNGG
D-DRAGGING ME...
...CRAWLING AWAY...
...RUNNING FROM...
...SOMETHING...
...SOMETHING DANGEROUS!

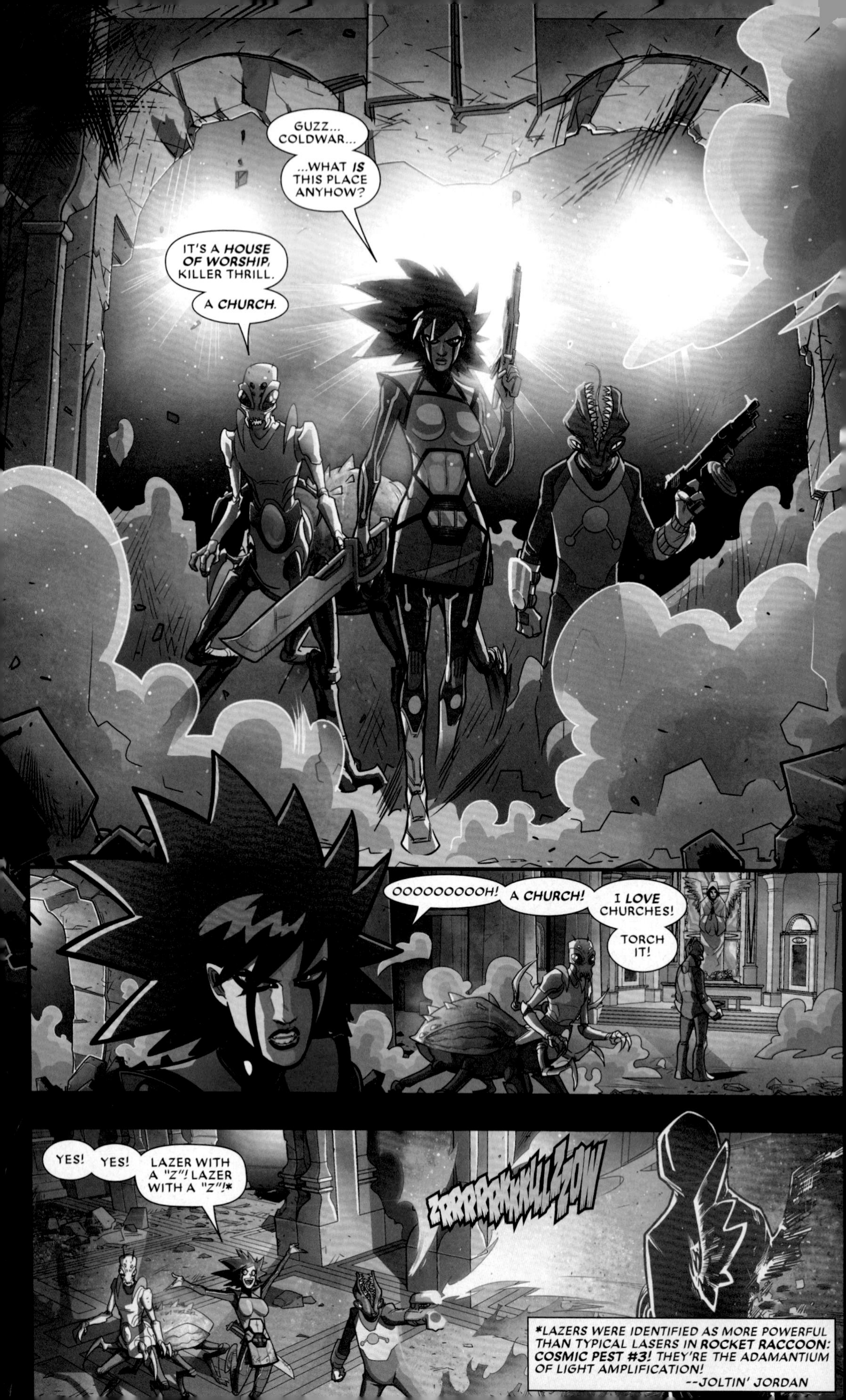
GUZZ... COLDWAR...
...WHAT *IS* THIS PLACE ANYHOW?
IT'S A *HOUSE OF WORSHIP,* KILLER THRILL.
A *CHURCH*.
OOOOOOOOOH!
A *CHURCH!*
I *LOVE* CHURCHES!
TORCH IT!
YES!
YES!
LAZER WITH A "Z"! LAZER WITH A "Z"!*
*LAZERS WERE IDENTIFIED AS MORE POWERFUL THAN TYPICAL LASERS IN **ROCKET RACCOON: COSMIC PEST #3!** THEY'RE THE ADAMANTIUM OF LIGHT AMPLIFICATION!
--JOLTIN' JORDAN

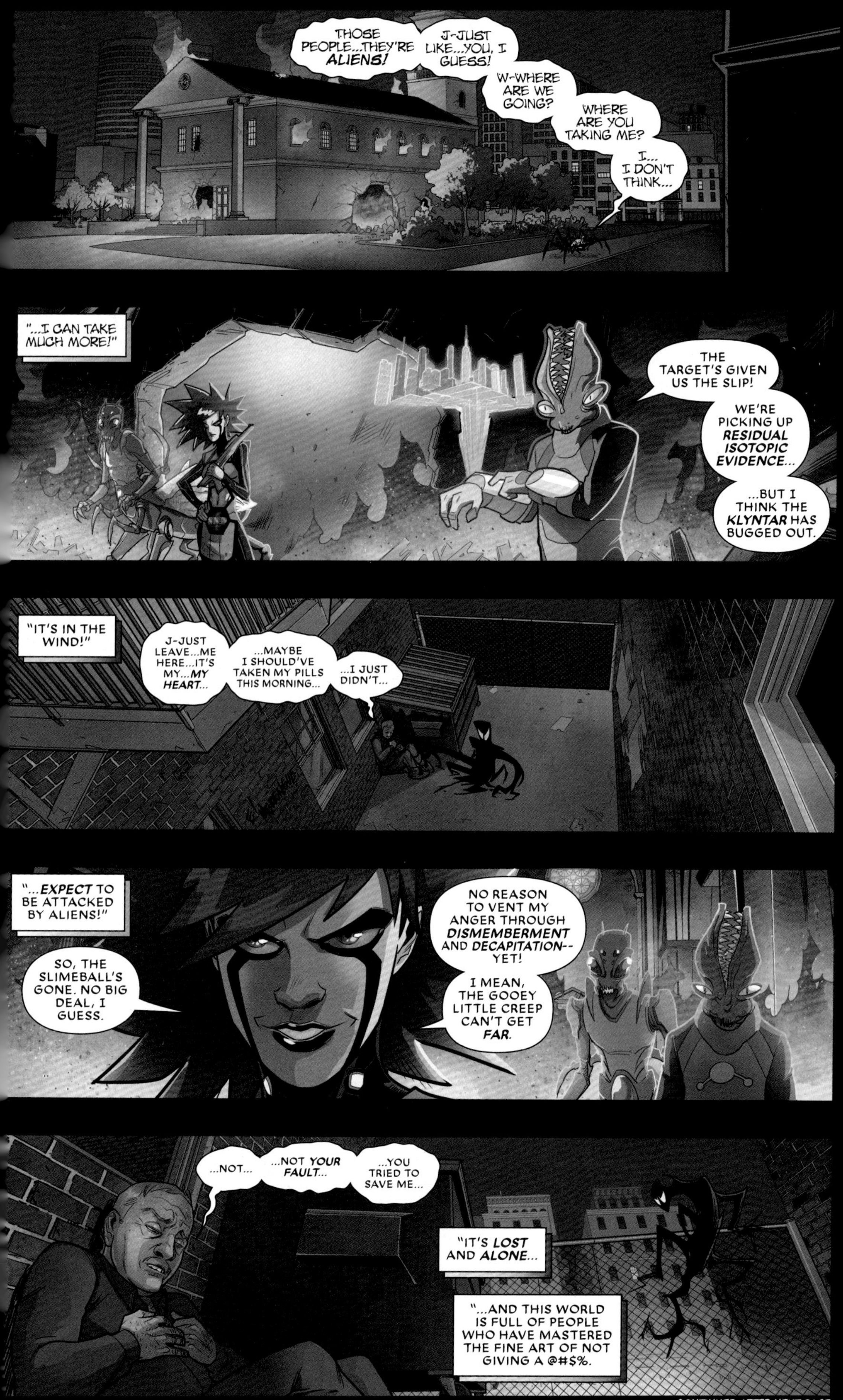
THOSE PEOPLE...THEY'RE ALIENS!
J-JUST LIKE...YOU, I GUESS!
W-WHERE ARE WE GOING?
WHERE ARE YOU TAKING ME?
I... I DON'T THINK...
"...I CAN TAKE MUCH MORE!"
THE TARGET'S GIVEN US THE SLIP!
WE'RE PICKING UP RESIDUAL ISOTOPIC EVIDENCE...
...BUT I THINK THE KLYNTAR HAS BUGGED OUT.
"IT'S IN THE WIND!"
J-JUST LEAVE...ME HERE...IT'S MY...MY HEART...
...MAYBE I SHOULD'VE TAKEN MY PILLS THIS MORNING...
...I JUST DIDN'T...
"...EXPECT TO BE ATTACKED BY ALIENS!"
SO, THE SLIMEBALL'S GONE. NO BIG DEAL, I GUESS.
NO REASON TO VENT MY ANGER THROUGH DISMEMBERMENT AND DECAPITATION--YET!
I MEAN, THE GOOEY LITTLE CREEP CAN'T GET FAR.
...NOT...
...NOT YOUR FAULT...
...YOU TRIED TO SAVE ME...
"IT'S LOST AND ALONE...
"...AND THIS WORLD IS FULL OF PEOPLE WHO HAVE MASTERED THE FINE ART OF NOT GIVING A @#$%.

CONTINUED AFTER NEXT PAGE

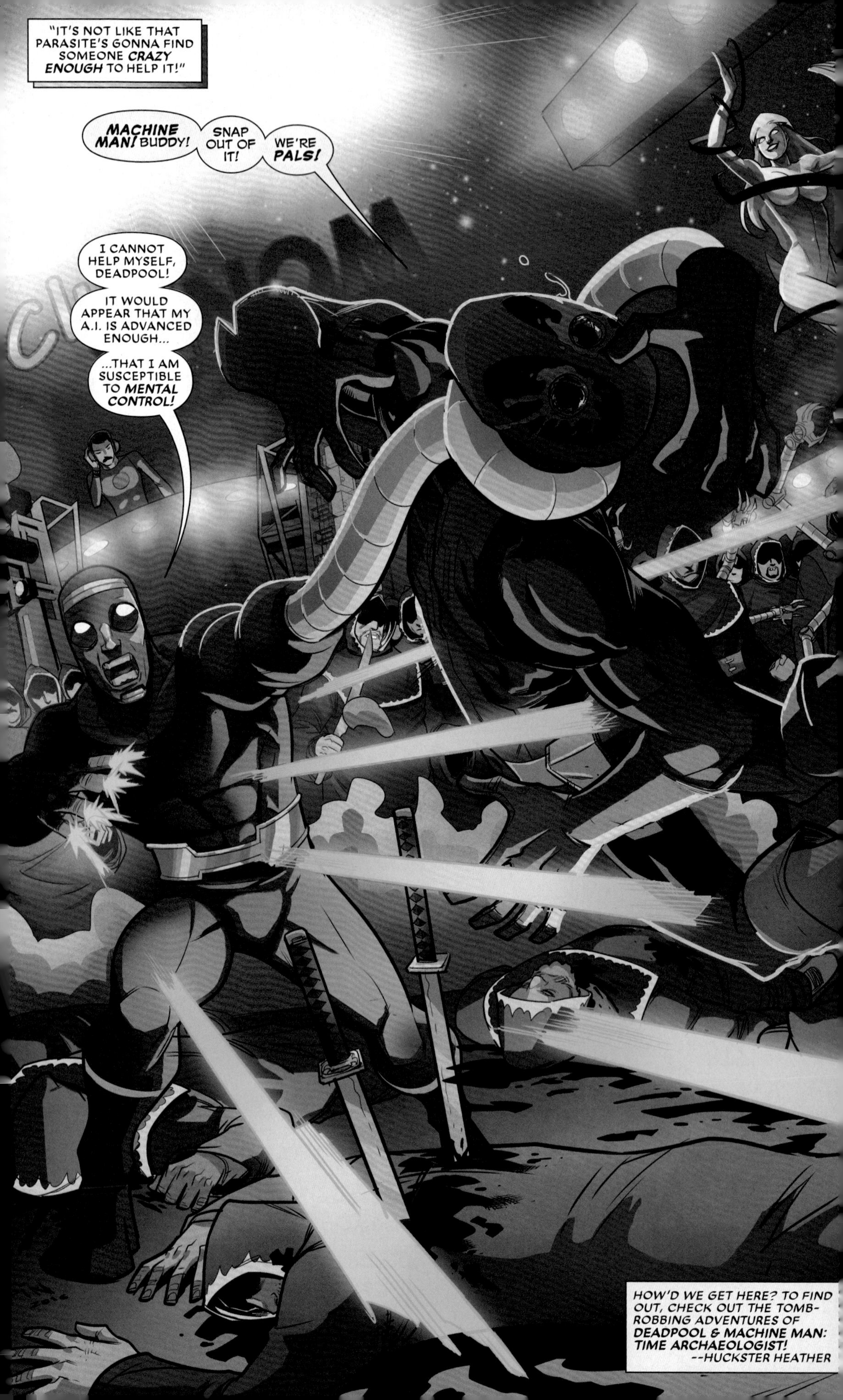
"IT'S NOT LIKE THAT PARASITE'S GONNA FIND SOMEONE CRAZY ENOUGH TO HELP IT!"
MACHINE MAN! BUDDY!
SNAP OUT OF IT!
WE'RE PALS!
I CANNOT HELP MYSELF, DEADPOOL!
IT WOULD APPEAR THAT MY A.I. IS ADVANCED ENOUGH...
...THAT I AM SUSCEPTIBLE TO MENTAL CONTROL!
HOW'D WE GET HERE? TO FIND OUT, CHECK OUT THE TOMB-ROBBING ADVENTURES OF DEADPOOL & MACHINE MAN: TIME ARCHAEOLOGIST!
--HUCKSTER HEATHER

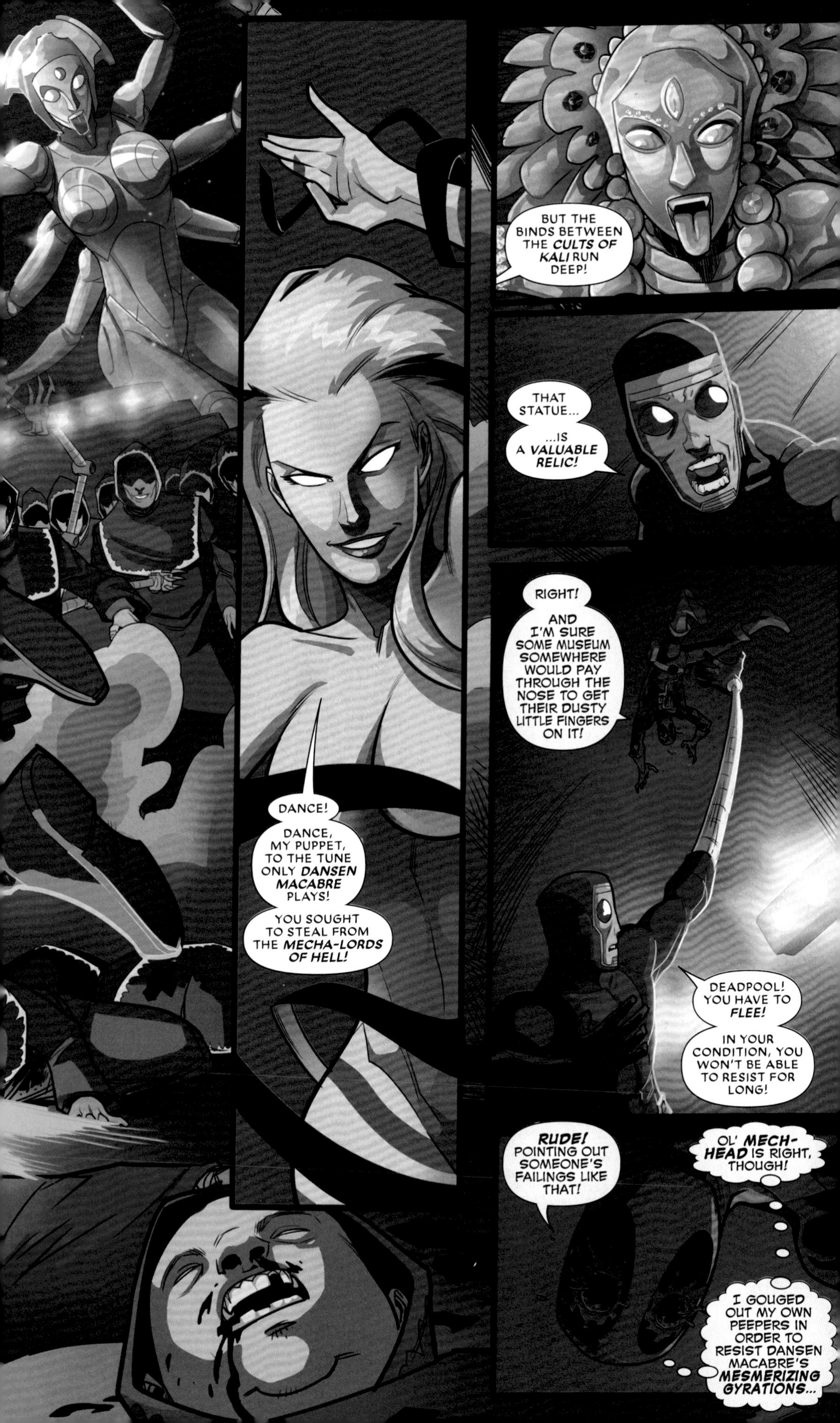

BUT THE BINDS BETWEEN THE CULTS OF KALI RUN DEEP!
THAT STATUE...
...IS A VALUABLE RELIC!
DANCE!
DANCE, MY PUPPET, TO THE TUNE ONLY DANSEN MACABRE PLAYS!
YOU SOUGHT TO STEAL FROM THE MECHA-LORDS OF HELL!
RIGHT!
AND I'M SURE SOME MUSEUM SOMEWHERE WOULD PAY THROUGH THE NOSE TO GET THEIR DUSTY LITTLE FINGERS ON IT!
DEADPOOL! YOU HAVE TO FLEE!
IN YOUR CONDITION, YOU WON'T BE ABLE TO RESIST FOR LONG!
RUDE! POINTING OUT SOMEONE'S FAILINGS LIKE THAT!
OL' MECH-HEAD IS RIGHT, THOUGH!
I GOUGED OUT MY OWN PEEPERS IN ORDER TO RESIST DANSEN MACABRE'S MESMERIZING GYRATIONS...

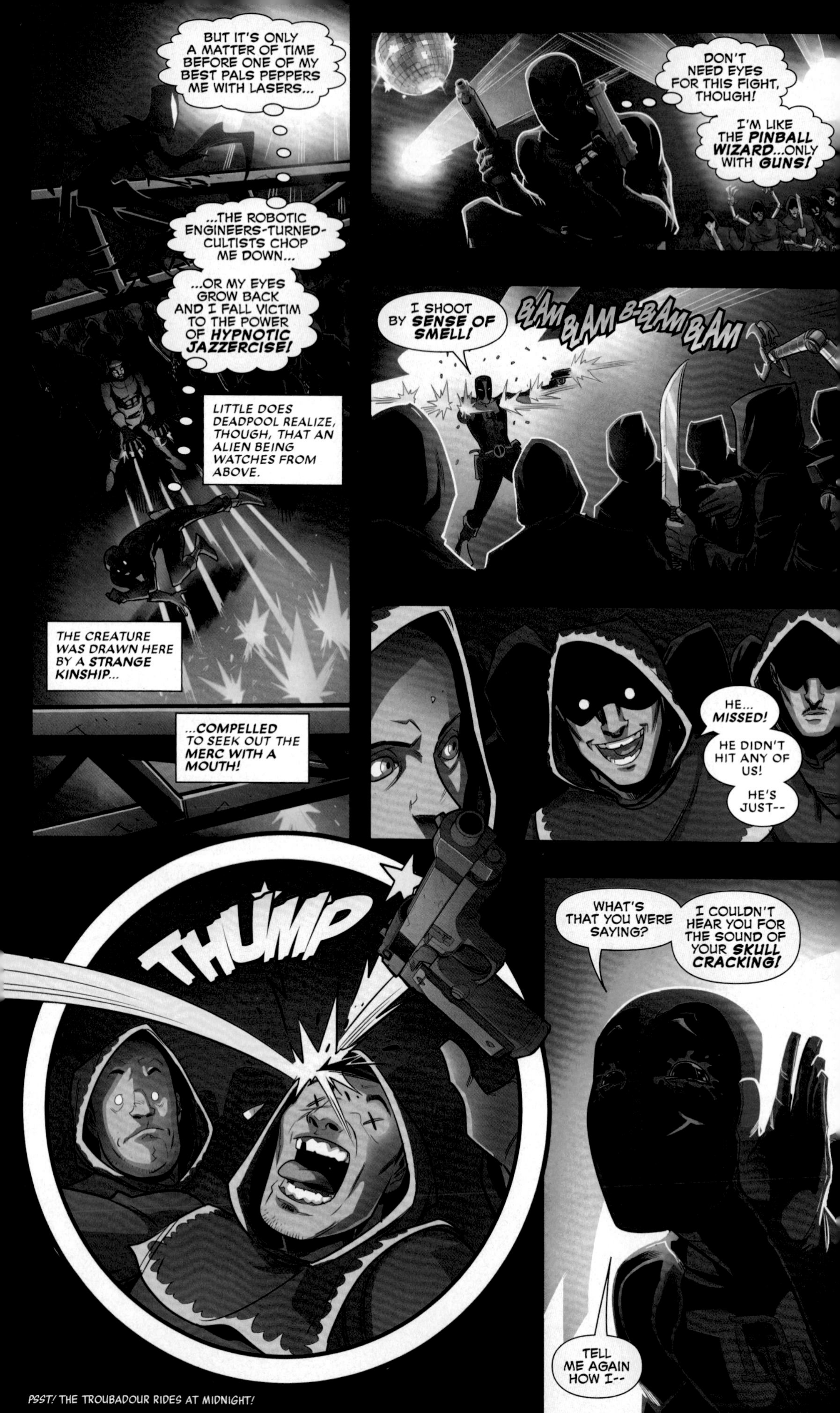
BUT IT'S ONLY A MATTER OF TIME BEFORE ONE OF MY BEST PALS PEPPERS ME WITH LASERS...
...THE ROBOTIC ENGINEERS-TURNED-CULTISTS CHOP ME DOWN...
...OR MY EYES GROW BACK AND I FALL VICTIM TO THE POWER OF HYPNOTIC JAZZERCISE!
LITTLE DOES DEADPOOL REALIZE, THOUGH, THAT AN ALIEN BEING WATCHES FROM ABOVE.
THE CREATURE WAS DRAWN HERE BY A STRANGE KINSHIP...
...COMPELLED TO SEEK OUT THE MERC WITH A MOUTH!
DON'T NEED EYES FOR THIS FIGHT, THOUGH!
I'M LIKE THE PINBALL WIZARD...ONLY WITH GUNS!
I SHOOT BY SENSE OF SMELL!
BLAM BLAM B-BLAM BLAM
HE... MISSED!
HE DIDN'T HIT ANY OF US!
HE'S JUST--
THUMP
WHAT'S THAT YOU WERE SAYING?
I COULDN'T HEAR YOU FOR THE SOUND OF YOUR SKULL CRACKING!
TELL ME AGAIN HOW I--

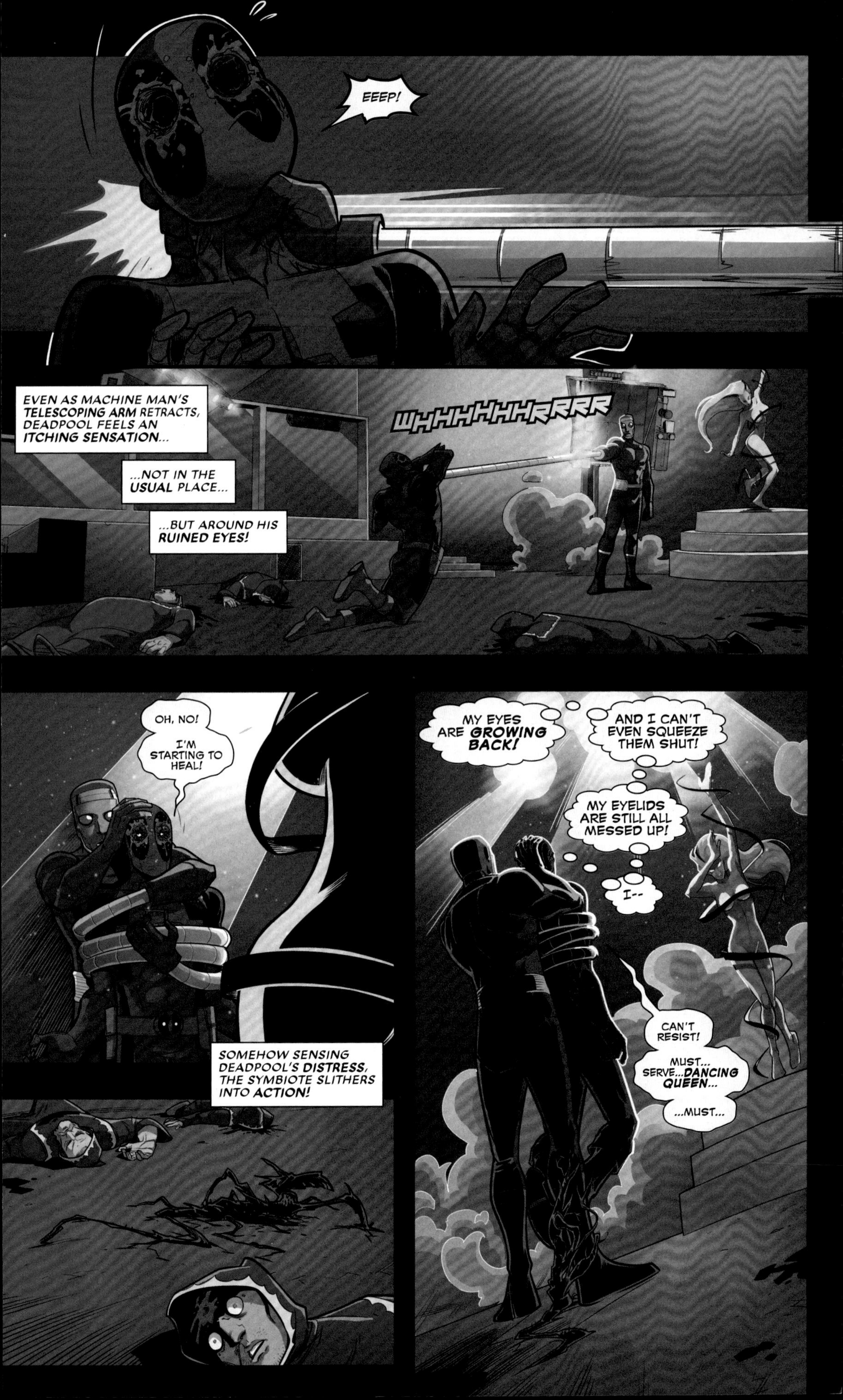
EEEP!
EVEN AS MACHINE MAN'S TELESCOPING ARM RETRACTS, DEADPOOL FEELS AN ITCHING SENSATION...
...NOT IN THE USUAL PLACE...
...BUT AROUND HIS RUINED EYES!
WHHHHHHRRRR
OH, NO!
I'M STARTING TO HEAL!
SOMEHOW SENSING DEADPOOL'S DISTRESS, THE SYMBIOTE SLITHERS INTO ACTION!
MY EYES ARE GROWING BACK!
AND I CAN'T EVEN SQUEEZE THEM SHUT!
MY EYELIDS ARE STILL ALL MESSED UP!
I--
CAN'T RESIST!
MUST... SERVE...DANCING QUEEN...
...MUST...

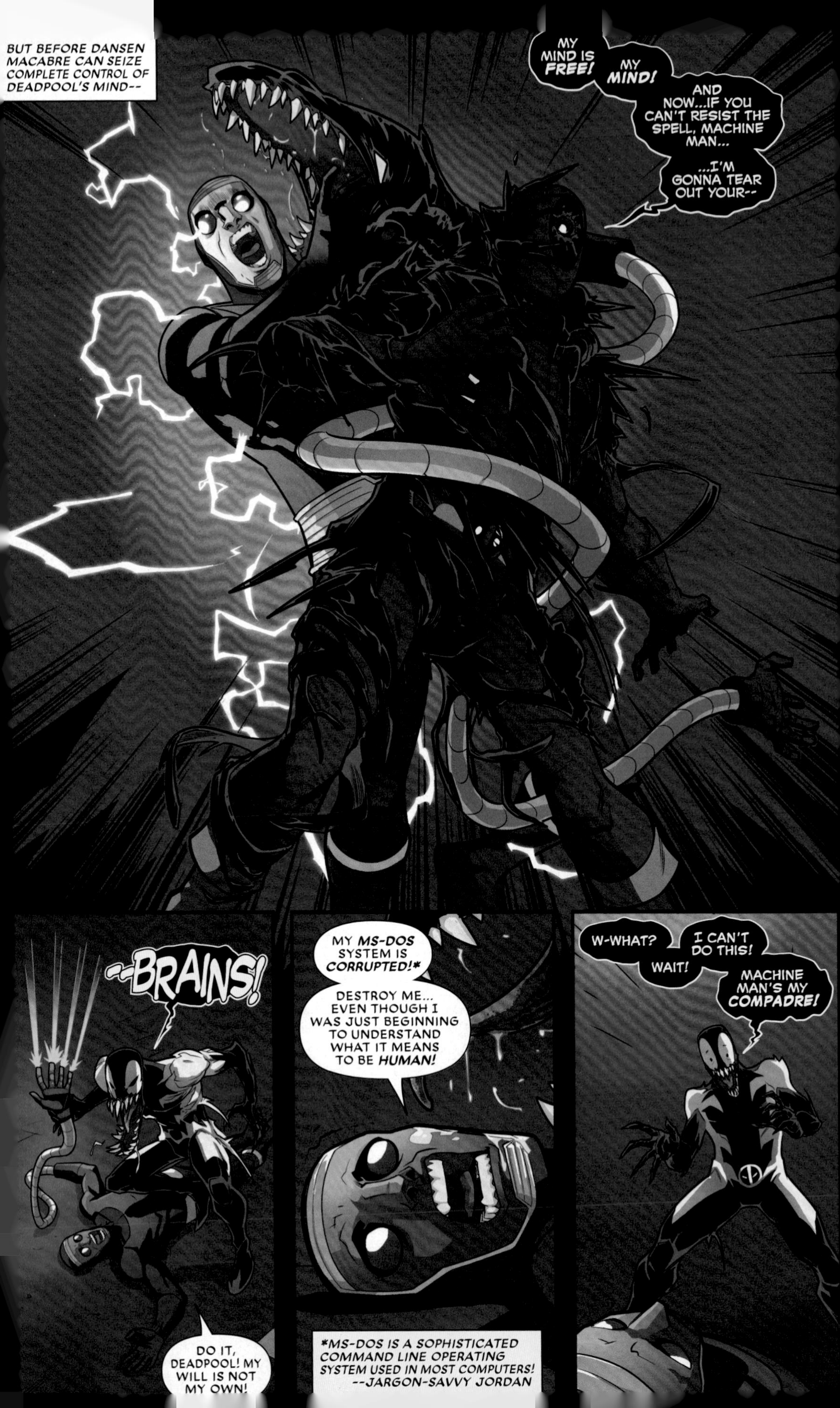
BUT BEFORE DANSEN MACABRE CAN SEIZE COMPLETE CONTROL OF DEADPOOL'S MIND--
MY MIND IS FREE!
MY MIND!
AND NOW...IF YOU CAN'T RESIST THE SPELL, MACHINE MAN...
...I'M GONNA TEAR OUT YOUR--
--BRAINS!
DO IT, DEADPOOL! MY WILL IS NOT MY OWN!
MY MS-DOS SYSTEM IS CORRUPTED!*
DESTROY ME... EVEN THOUGH I WAS JUST BEGINNING TO UNDERSTAND WHAT IT MEANS TO BE HUMAN!
*MS-DOS IS A SOPHISTICATED COMMAND LINE OPERATING SYSTEM USED IN MOST COMPUTERS! --JARGON-SAVVY JORDAN
W-WHAT?
I CAN'T DO THIS!
WAIT!
MACHINE MAN'S MY COMPADRE!

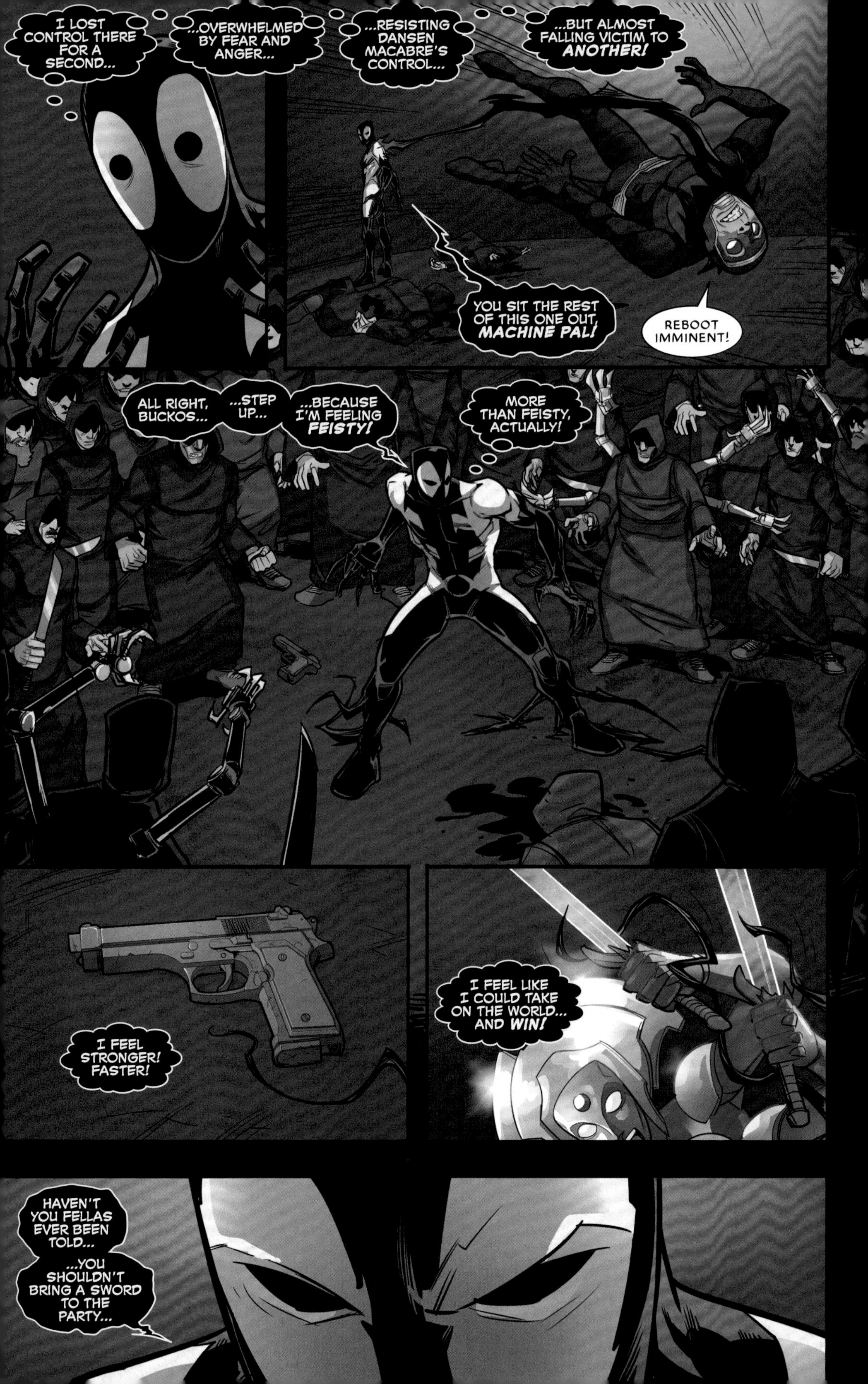

I LOST CONTROL THERE FOR A SECOND...
...OVERWHELMED BY FEAR AND ANGER...
...RESISTING DANSEN MACABRE'S CONTROL...
...BUT ALMOST FALLING VICTIM TO ANOTHER!
YOU SIT THE REST OF THIS ONE OUT, MACHINE PAL!
REBOOT IMMINENT!
ALL RIGHT, BUCKOS...
...STEP UP...
...BECAUSE I'M FEELING FEISTY!
MORE THAN FEISTY, ACTUALLY!
I FEEL STRONGER! FASTER!
I FEEL LIKE I COULD TAKE ON THE WORLD... AND WIN!
HAVEN'T YOU FELLAS EVER BEEN TOLD...
...YOU SHOULDN'T BRING A SWORD TO THE PARTY...

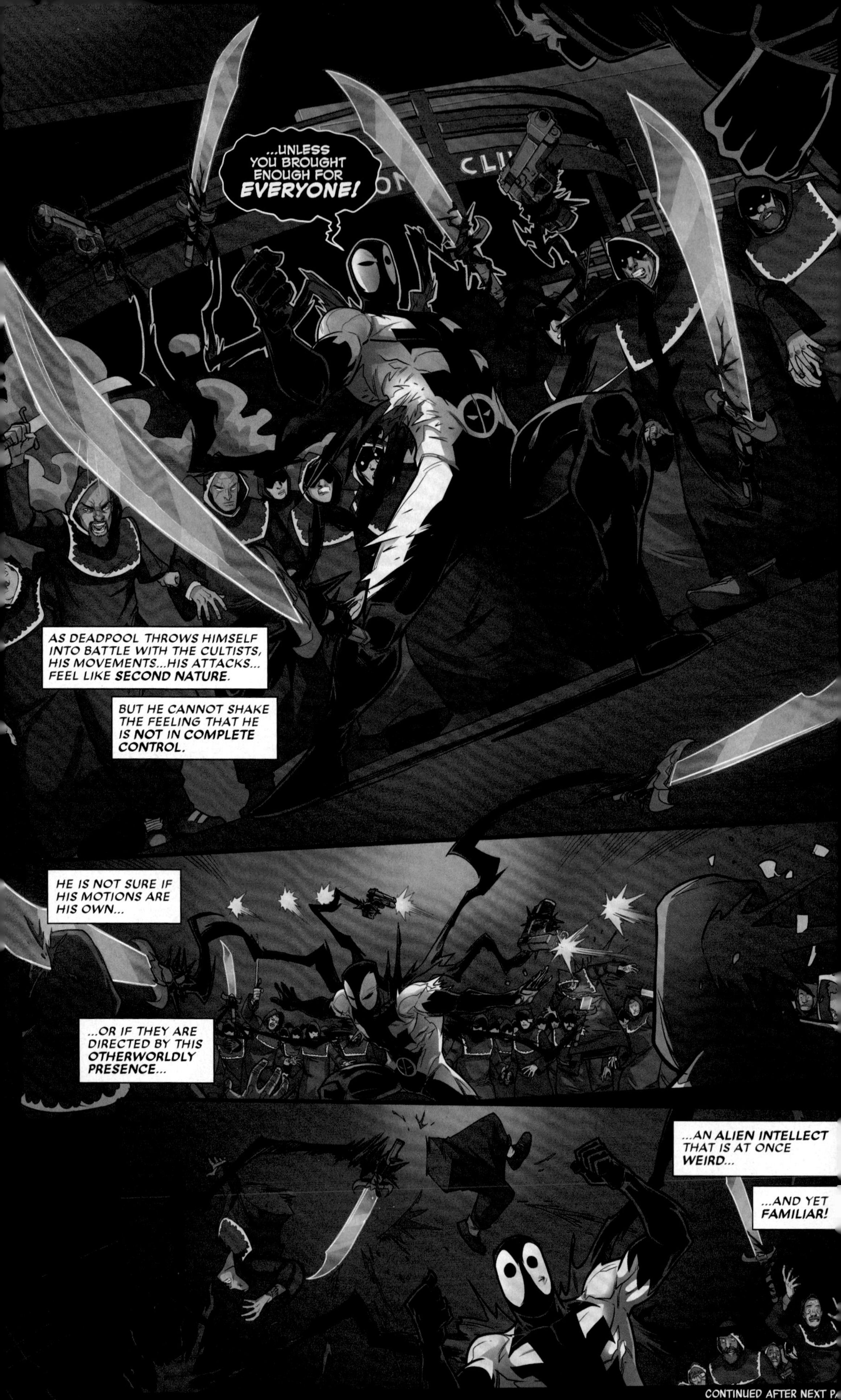

...UNLESS YOU BROUGHT ENOUGH FOR EVERYONE!
AS DEADPOOL THROWS HIMSELF INTO BATTLE WITH THE CULTISTS, HIS MOVEMENTS...HIS ATTACKS... FEEL LIKE SECOND NATURE.
BUT HE CANNOT SHAKE THE FEELING THAT HE IS NOT IN COMPLETE CONTROL.
HE IS NOT SURE IF HIS MOTIONS ARE HIS OWN...
...OR IF THEY ARE DIRECTED BY THIS OTHERWORLDLY PRESENCE...
...AN ALIEN INTELLECT THAT IS AT ONCE WEIRD...
...AND YET FAMILIAR!

CONTINUED AFTER NEXT P

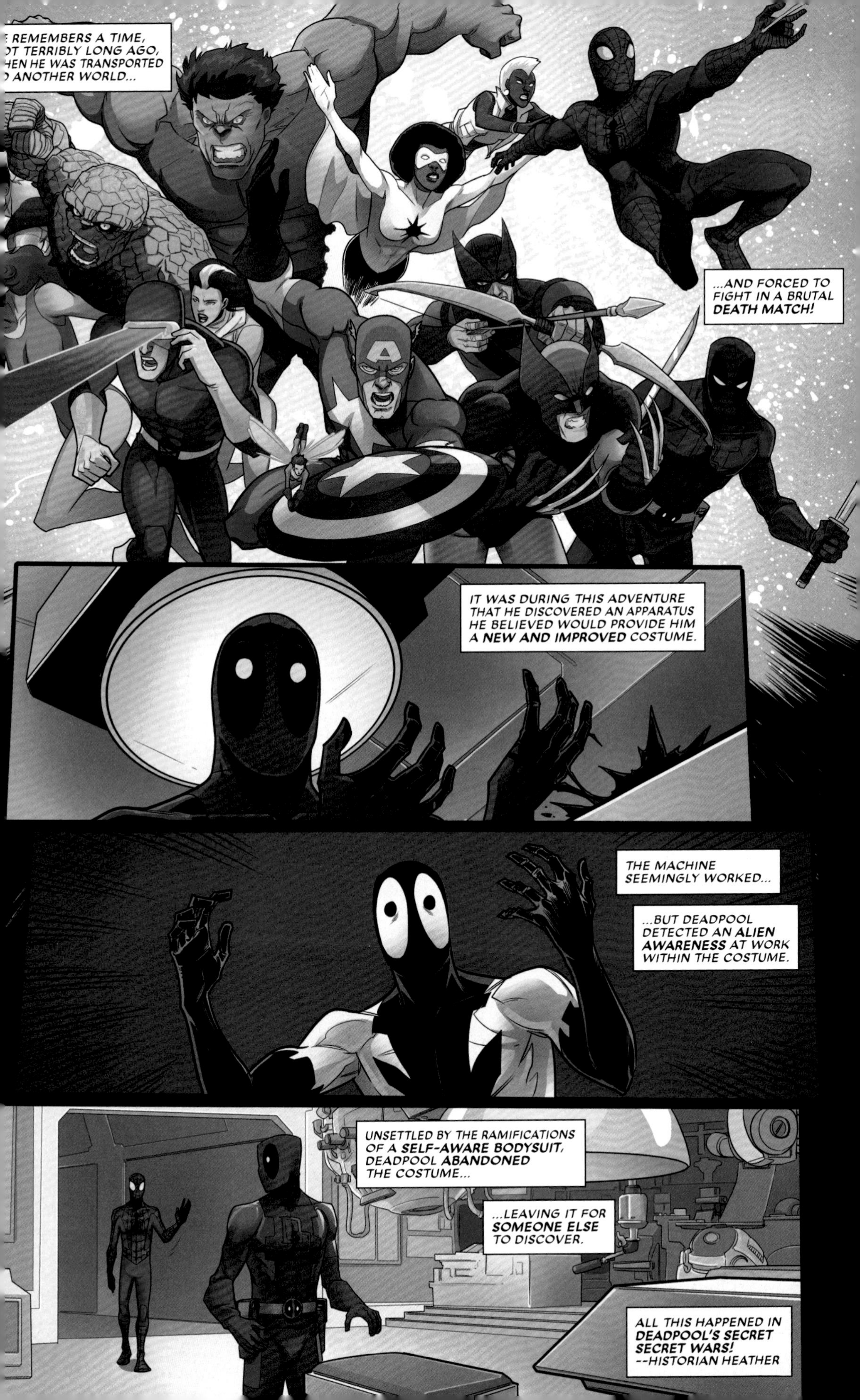

E REMEMBERS A TIME, OT TERRIBLY LONG AGO, HEN HE WAS TRANSPORTED O ANOTHER WORLD...
...AND FORCED TO FIGHT IN A BRUTAL DEATH MATCH!
IT WAS DURING THIS ADVENTURE THAT HE DISCOVERED AN APPARATUS HE BELIEVED WOULD PROVIDE HIM A NEW AND IMPROVED COSTUME.
THE MACHINE SEEMINGLY WORKED...
...BUT DEADPOOL DETECTED AN ALIEN AWARENESS AT WORK WITHIN THE COSTUME.
UNSETTLED BY THE RAMIFICATIONS OF A SELF-AWARE BODYSUIT, DEADPOOL ABANDONED THE COSTUME...
...LEAVING IT FOR SOMEONE ELSE TO DISCOVER.
ALL THIS HAPPENED IN DEADPOOL'S SECRET SECRET WARS! --HISTORIAN HEATHER

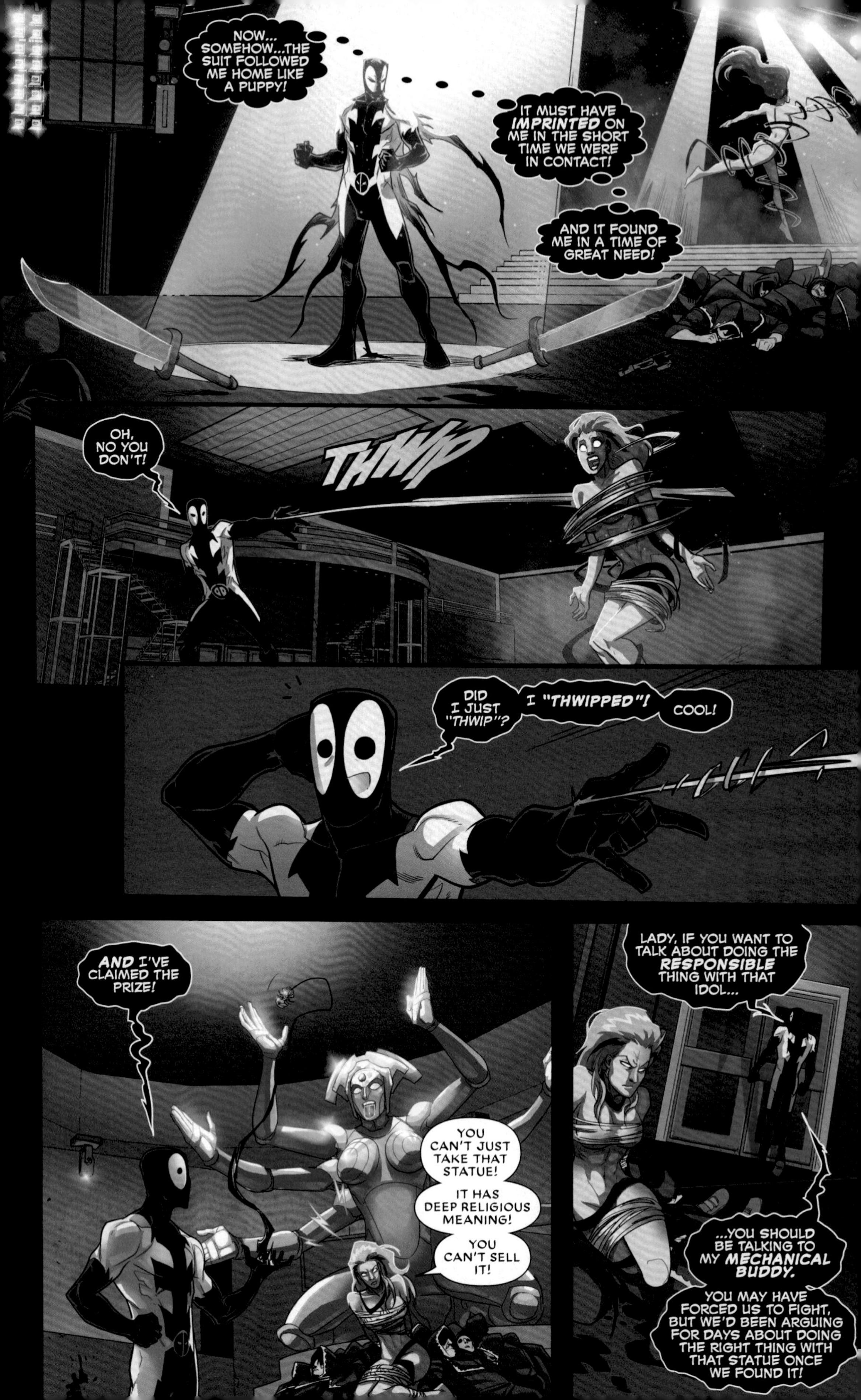

NOW... SOMEHOW...THE SUIT FOLLOWED ME HOME LIKE A PUPPY!
IT MUST HAVE IMPRINTED ON ME IN THE SHORT TIME WE WERE IN CONTACT!
AND IT FOUND ME IN A TIME OF GREAT NEED!
OH, NO YOU DON'T!
THWIP
DID I JUST "THWIP"?
I "THWIPPED"!
COOL!
AND I'VE CLAIMED THE PRIZE!
YOU CAN'T JUST TAKE THAT STATUE!
IT HAS DEEP RELIGIOUS MEANING!
YOU CAN'T SELL IT!
LADY, IF YOU WANT TO TALK ABOUT DOING THE RESPONSIBLE THING WITH THAT IDOL...
...YOU SHOULD BE TALKING TO MY MECHANICAL BUDDY.
YOU MAY HAVE FORCED US TO FIGHT, BUT WE'D BEEN ARGUING FOR DAYS ABOUT DOING THE RIGHT THING WITH THAT STATUE ONCE WE FOUND IT!

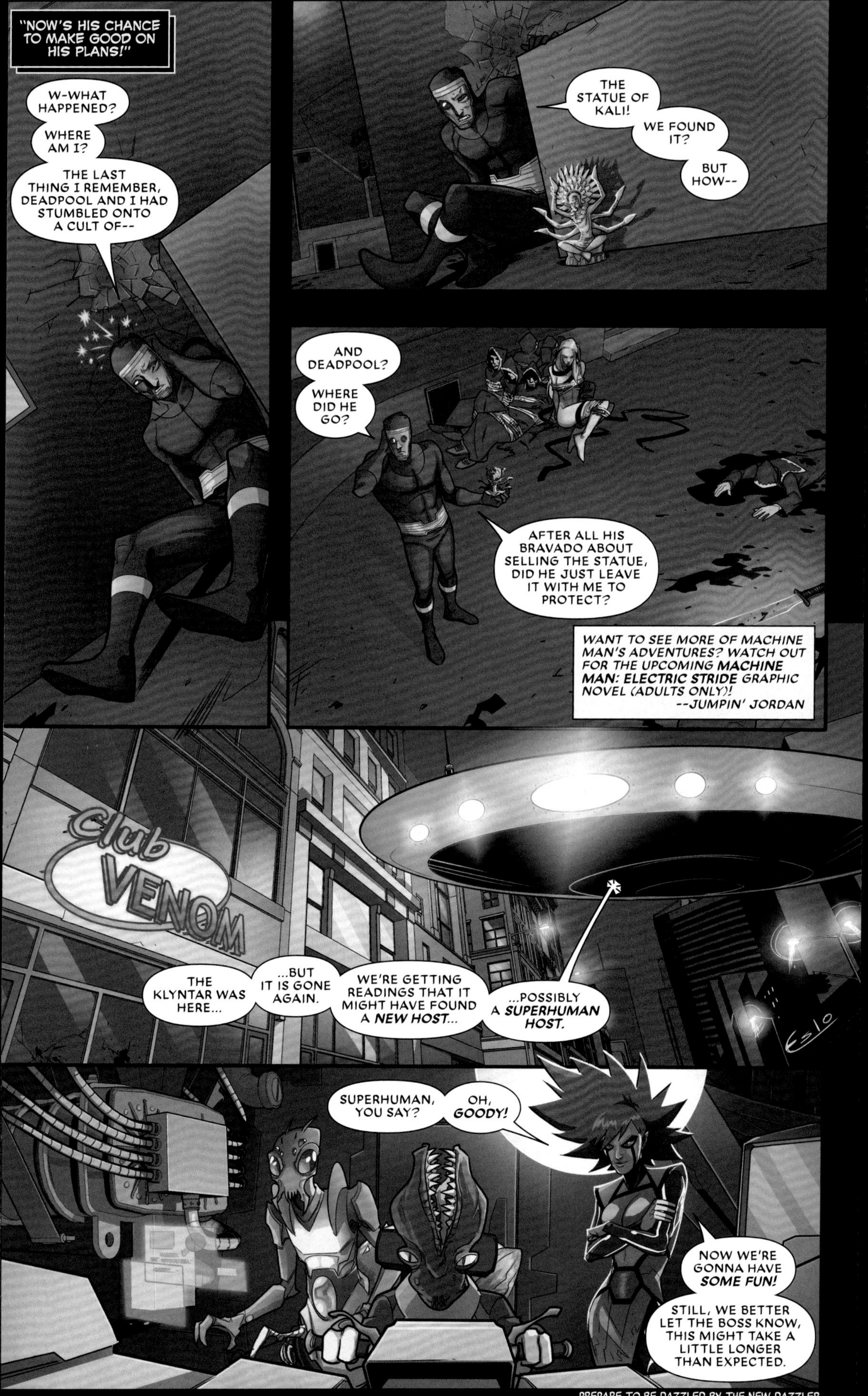
"NOW'S HIS CHANCE TO MAKE GOOD ON HIS PLANS!"
W-WHAT HAPPENED?
WHERE AM I?
THE LAST THING I REMEMBER, DEADPOOL AND I HAD STUMBLED ONTO A CULT OF--
THE STATUE OF KALI!
WE FOUND IT?
BUT HOW--
AND DEADPOOL?
WHERE DID HE GO?
AFTER ALL HIS BRAVADO ABOUT SELLING THE STATUE, DID HE JUST LEAVE IT WITH ME TO PROTECT?
WANT TO SEE MORE OF MACHINE MAN'S ADVENTURES? WATCH OUT FOR THE UPCOMING MACHINE MAN: ELECTRIC STRIDE GRAPHIC NOVEL (ADULTS ONLY)! --JUMPIN' JORDAN
Club VENOM
THE KLYNTAR WAS HERE...
...BUT IT IS GONE AGAIN.
WE'RE GETTING READINGS THAT IT MIGHT HAVE FOUND A NEW HOST...
...POSSIBLY A SUPERHUMAN HOST.
SUPERHUMAN, YOU SAY?
OH, GOODY!
NOW WE'RE GONNA HAVE SOME FUN!
STILL, WE BETTER LET THE BOSS KNOW, THIS MIGHT TAKE A LITTLE LONGER THAN EXPECTED.

PREPARE TO BE DAZZLED BY THE NEW DAZZLER

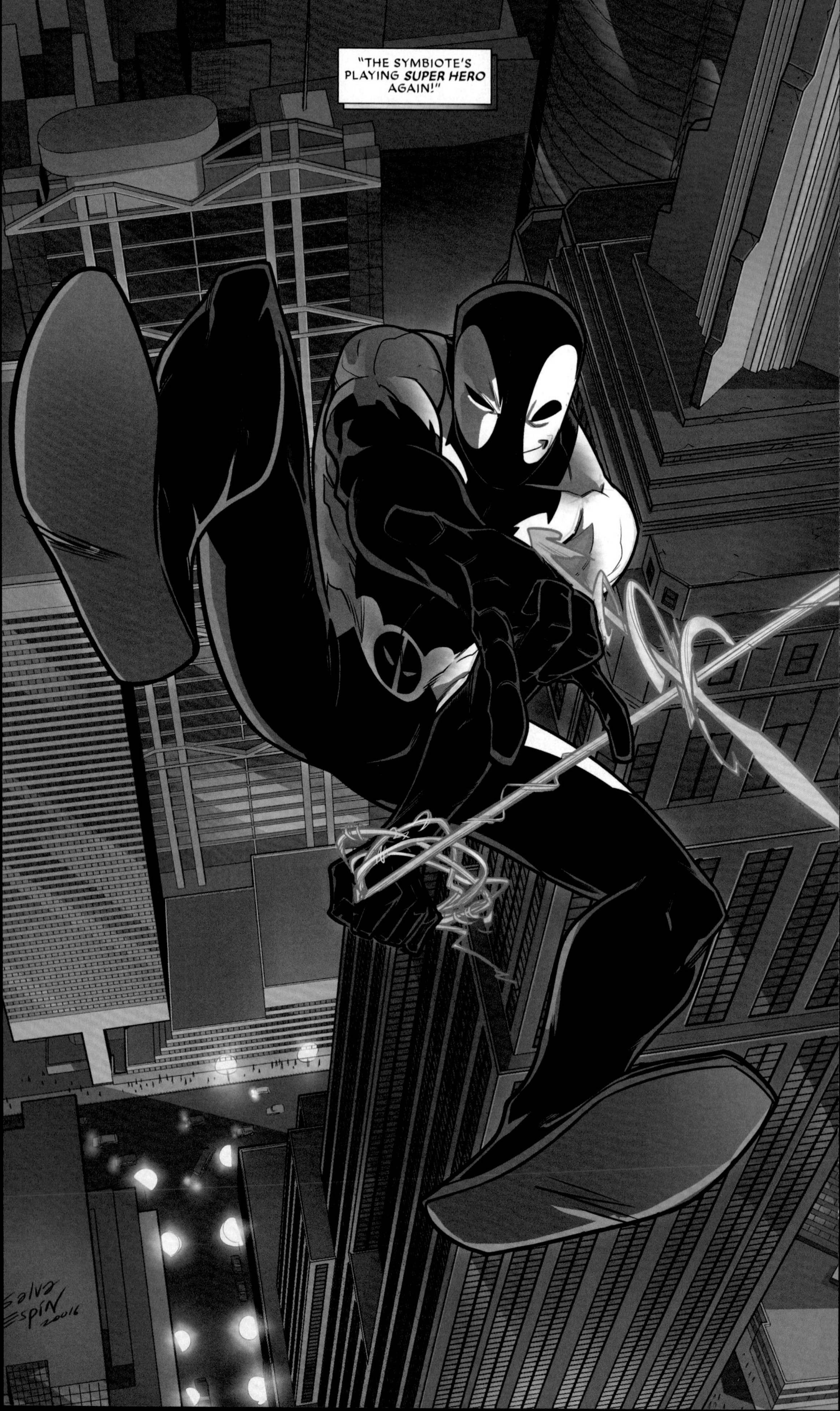
"THE SYMBIOTE'S PLAYING SUPER HERO AGAIN!"

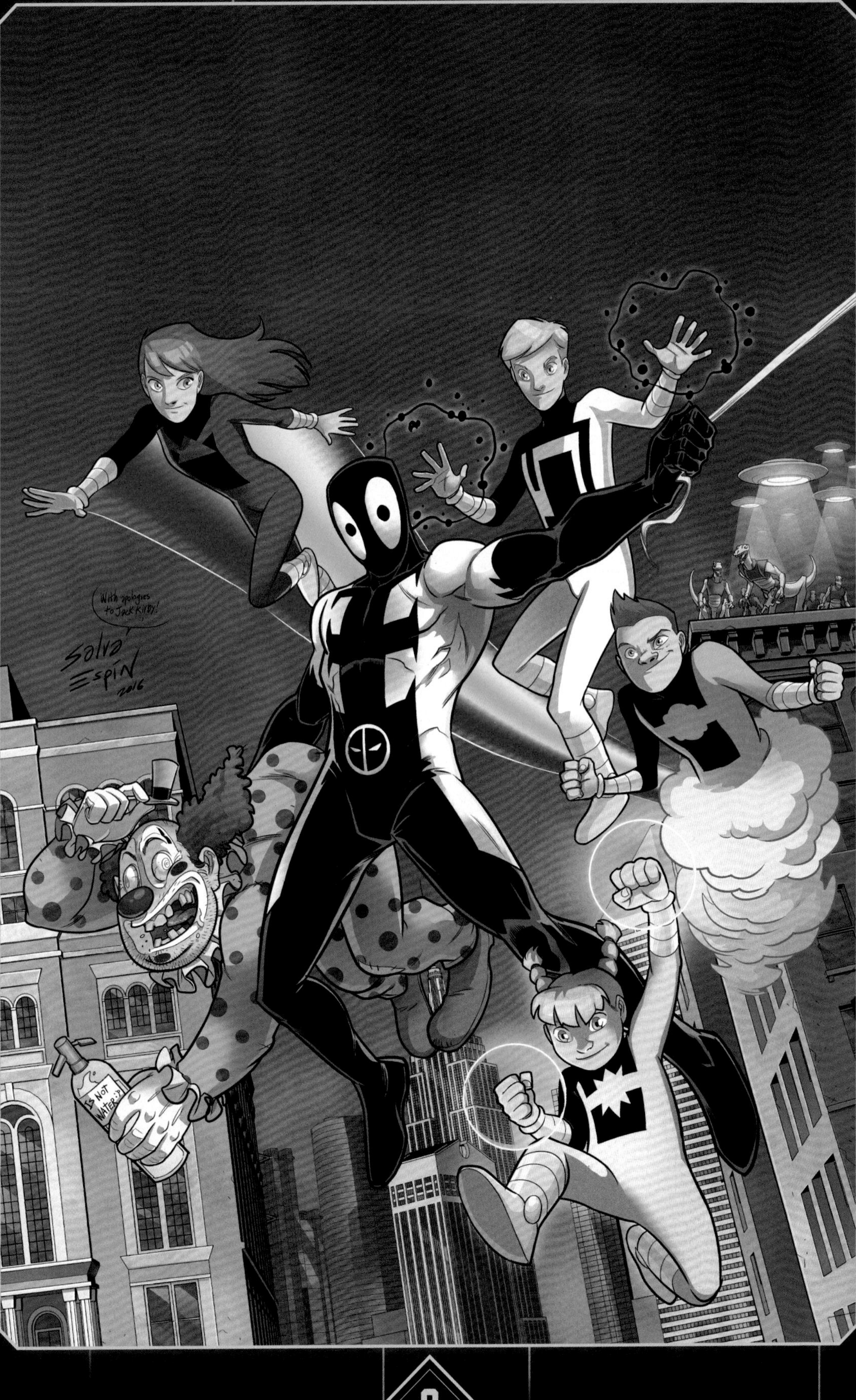
With apologies to Jack Kirby!
Salva Espín 2016
Is NOT WATER :P

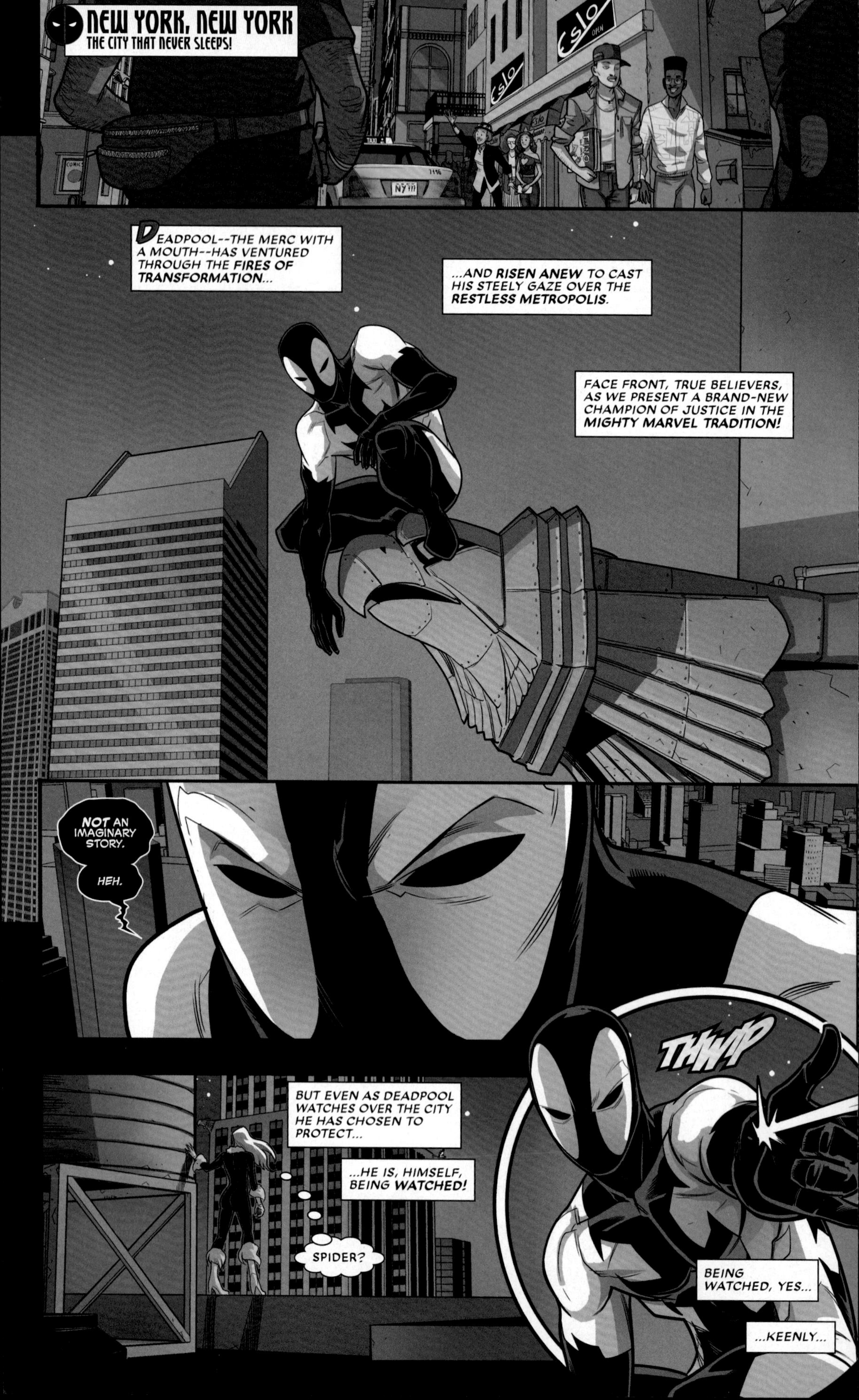
NEW YORK, NEW YORK
THE CITY THAT NEVER SLEEPS!
DEADPOOL--THE MERC WITH A MOUTH--HAS VENTURED THROUGH THE FIRES OF TRANSFORMATION...
...AND RISEN ANEW TO CAST HIS STEELY GAZE OVER THE RESTLESS METROPOLIS.
FACE FRONT, TRUE BELIEVERS, AS WE PRESENT A BRAND-NEW CHAMPION OF JUSTICE IN THE MIGHTY MARVEL TRADITION!
NOT AN IMAGINARY STORY.
HEH.
BUT EVEN AS DEADPOOL WATCHES OVER THE CITY HE HAS CHOSEN TO PROTECT...
...HE IS, HIMSELF, BEING WATCHED!
SPIDER?
THWIP
BEING WATCHED, YES...
...KEENLY...

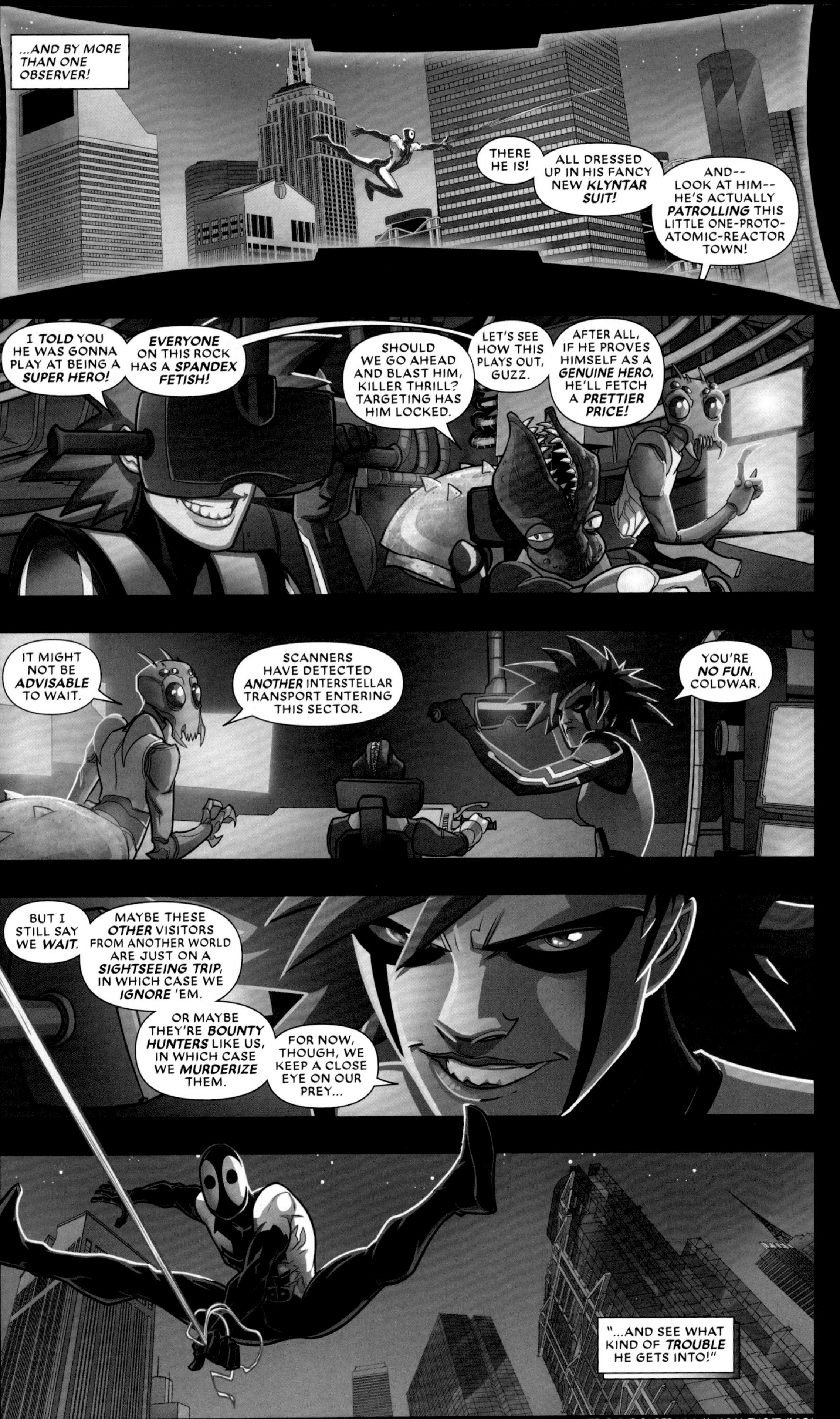

...AND BY MORE THAN ONE OBSERVER!
THERE HE IS!
ALL DRESSED UP IN HIS FANCY NEW KLYNTAR SUIT!
AND-- LOOK AT HIM-- HE'S ACTUALLY PATROLLING THIS LITTLE ONE-PROTO-ATOMIC-REACTOR TOWN!
I TOLD YOU HE WAS GONNA PLAY AT BEING A SUPER HERO!
EVERYONE ON THIS ROCK HAS A SPANDEX FETISH!
SHOULD WE GO AHEAD AND BLAST HIM, KILLER THRILL? TARGETING HAS HIM LOCKED.
LET'S SEE HOW THIS PLAYS OUT, GUZZ.
AFTER ALL, IF HE PROVES HIMSELF AS A GENUINE HERO, HE'LL FETCH A PRETTIER PRICE!
IT MIGHT NOT BE ADVISABLE TO WAIT.
SCANNERS HAVE DETECTED ANOTHER INTERSTELLAR TRANSPORT ENTERING THIS SECTOR.
YOU'RE NO FUN, COLDWAR.
BUT I STILL SAY WE WAIT.
MAYBE THESE OTHER VISITORS FROM ANOTHER WORLD ARE JUST ON A SIGHTSEEING TRIP, IN WHICH CASE WE IGNORE 'EM.
OR MAYBE THEY'RE BOUNTY HUNTERS LIKE US, IN WHICH CASE WE MURDERIZE THEM.
FOR NOW, THOUGH, WE KEEP A CLOSE EYE ON OUR PREY...
"...AND SEE WHAT KIND OF TROUBLE HE GETS INTO!"

FEAR THE GILDED LILY IN ALPHA FLIGHT #20!

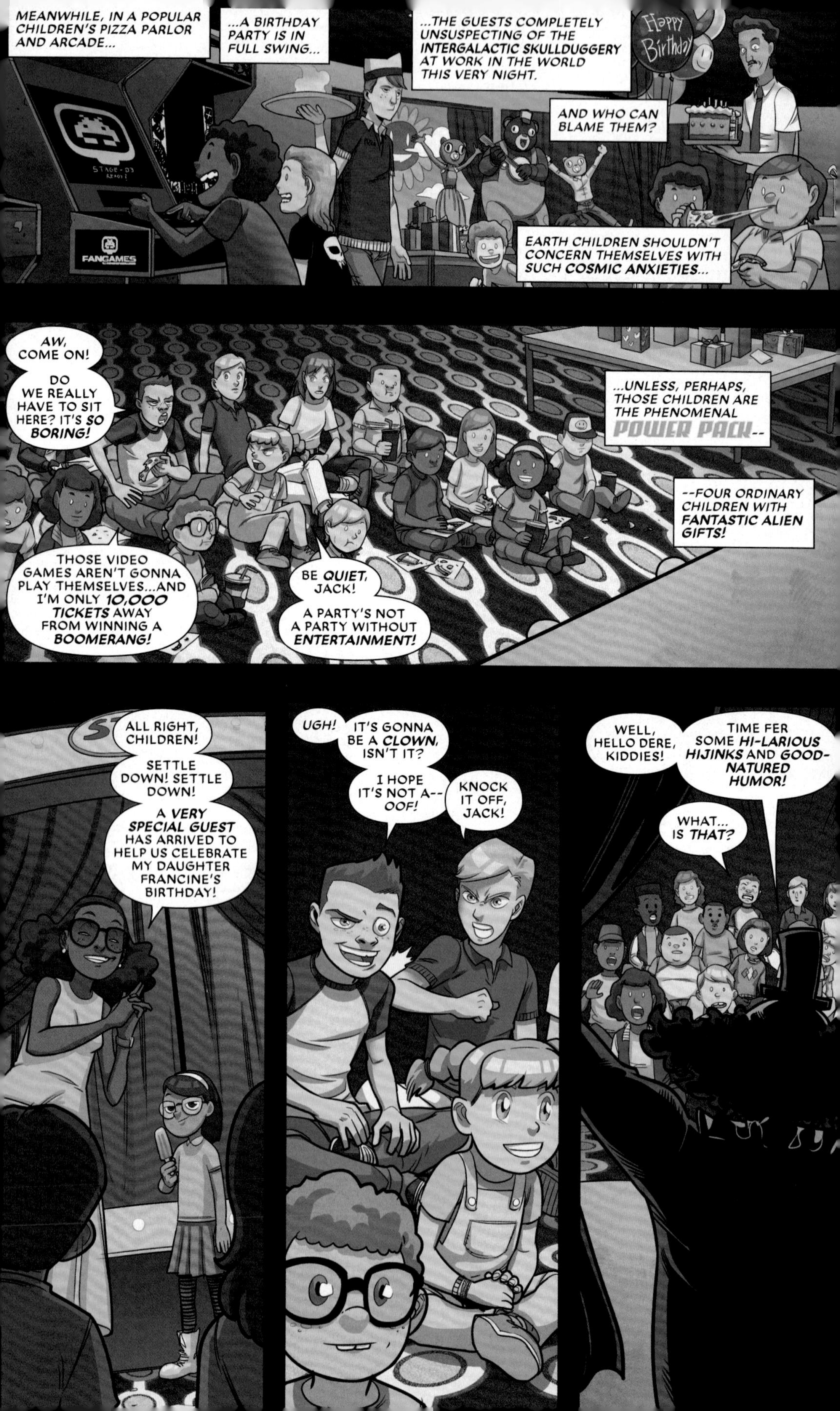
MEANWHILE, IN A POPULAR CHILDREN'S PIZZA PARLOR AND ARCADE...
...A BIRTHDAY PARTY IS IN FULL SWING...
...THE GUESTS COMPLETELY UNSUSPECTING OF THE INTERGALACTIC SKULLDUGGERY AT WORK IN THE WORLD THIS VERY NIGHT.
Happy Birthday
AND WHO CAN BLAME THEM?
EARTH CHILDREN SHOULDN'T CONCERN THEMSELVES WITH SUCH COSMIC ANXIETIES...
FANGAMES
STAGE-03
AW, COME ON!
DO WE REALLY HAVE TO SIT HERE? IT'S SO BORING!
...UNLESS, PERHAPS, THOSE CHILDREN ARE THE PHENOMENAL POWER PACK--
--FOUR ORDINARY CHILDREN WITH FANTASTIC ALIEN GIFTS!
THOSE VIDEO GAMES AREN'T GONNA PLAY THEMSELVES...AND I'M ONLY 10,000 TICKETS AWAY FROM WINNING A BOOMERANG!
BE QUIET, JACK!
A PARTY'S NOT A PARTY WITHOUT ENTERTAINMENT!
ALL RIGHT, CHILDREN!
SETTLE DOWN! SETTLE DOWN!
A VERY SPECIAL GUEST HAS ARRIVED TO HELP US CELEBRATE MY DAUGHTER FRANCINE'S BIRTHDAY!
UGH!
IT'S GONNA BE A CLOWN, ISN'T IT?
I HOPE IT'S NOT A-- OOF!
KNOCK IT OFF, JACK!
WELL, HELLO DERE, KIDDIES!
TIME FER SOME HI-LARIOUS HIJINKS AND GOOD-NATURED HUMOR!
WHAT... IS THAT?

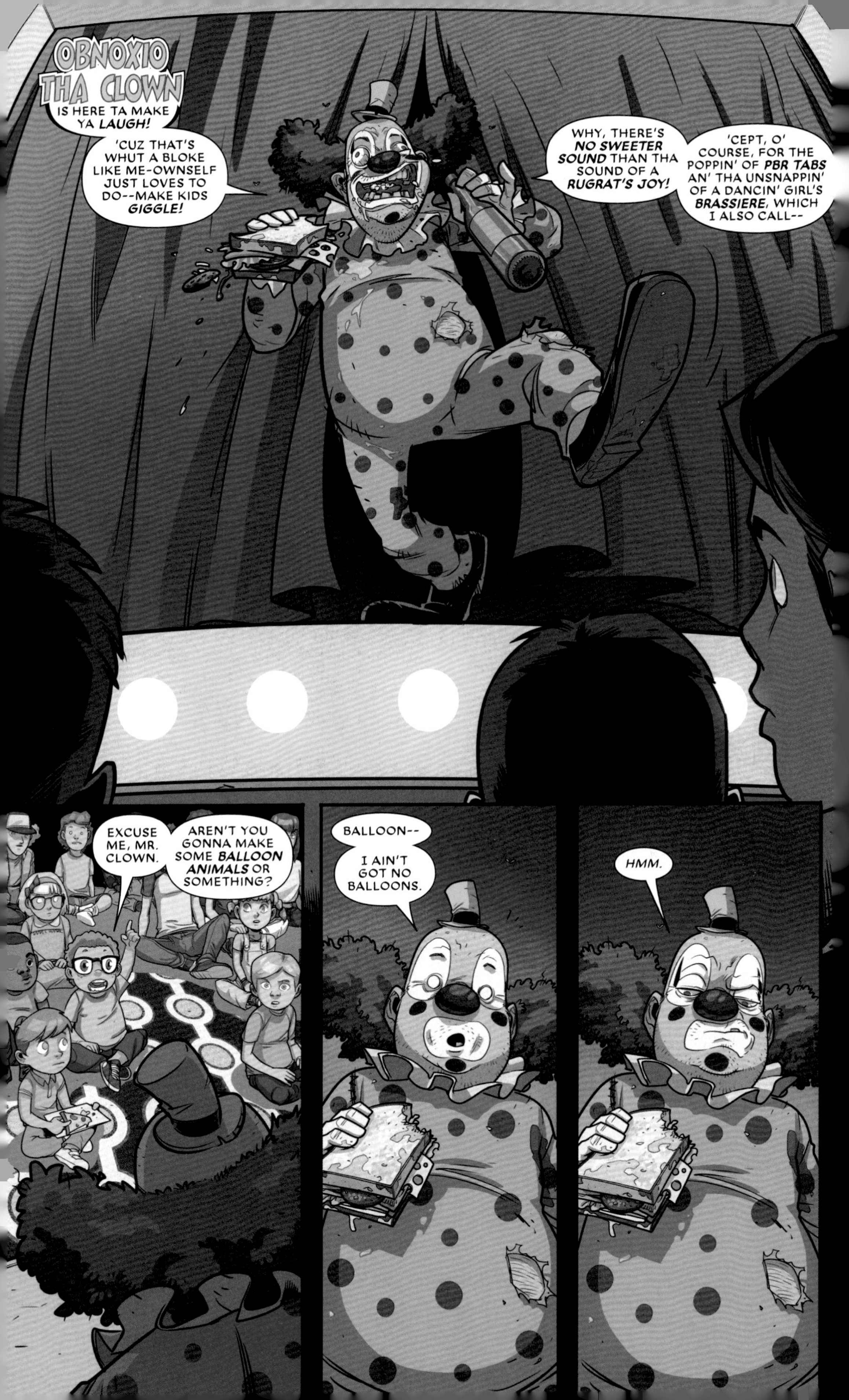
OBNOXIO THA CLOWN IS HERE TA MAKE YA LAUGH!
'CUZ THAT'S WHUT A BLOKE LIKE ME-OWNSELF JUST LOVES TO DO--MAKE KIDS GIGGLE!
WHY, THERE'S NO SWEETER SOUND THAN THA SOUND OF A RUGRAT'S JOY!
'CEPT, O' COURSE, FOR THE POPPIN' OF PBR TABS AN' THA UNSNAPPIN' OF A DANCIN' GIRL'S BRASSIERE, WHICH I ALSO CALL--
EXCUSE ME, MR. CLOWN.
AREN'T YOU GONNA MAKE SOME BALLOON ANIMALS OR SOMETHING?
BALLOON--
I AIN'T GOT NO BALLOONS.
HMM.

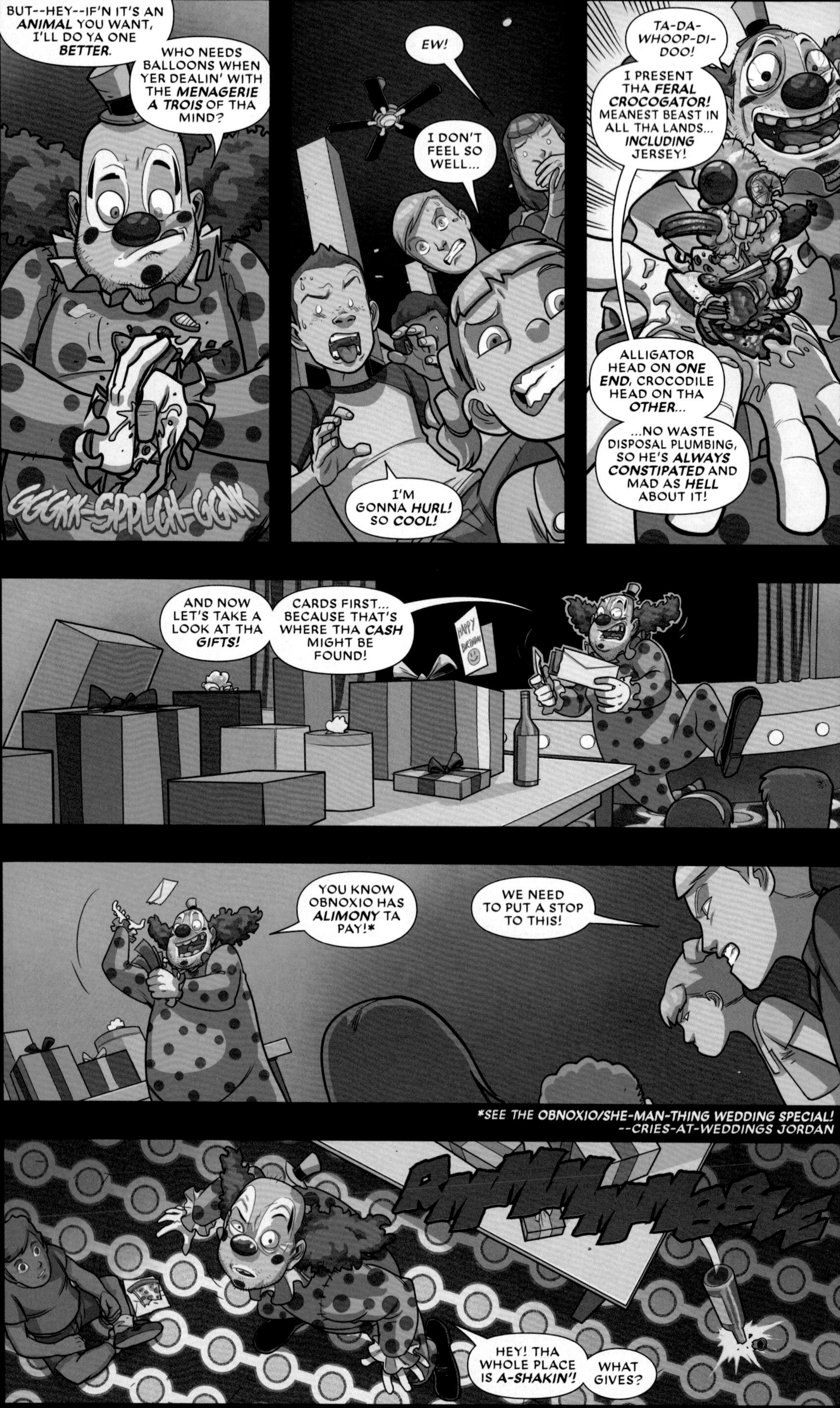
BUT--HEY--IF'N IT'S AN ANIMAL YOU WANT, I'LL DO YA ONE BETTER.
WHO NEEDS BALLOONS WHEN YER DEALIN' WITH THE MENAGERIE A TROIS OF THA MIND?
GGGKK-SPPLCH-GGNK
EW!
I DON'T FEEL SO WELL...
I'M GONNA HURL! SO COOL!
TA-DA-WHOOP-DI-DOO!
I PRESENT THA FERAL CROCOGATOR! MEANEST BEAST IN ALL THA LANDS... INCLUDING JERSEY!
ALLIGATOR HEAD ON ONE END, CROCODILE HEAD ON THA OTHER...
...NO WASTE DISPOSAL PLUMBING, SO HE'S ALWAYS CONSTIPATED AND MAD AS HELL ABOUT IT!
AND NOW LET'S TAKE A LOOK AT THA GIFTS!
CARDS FIRST... BECAUSE THAT'S WHERE THA CASH MIGHT BE FOUND!
HAPPY BIRTHDAY
YOU KNOW OBNOXIO HAS ALIMONY TA PAY!*
WE NEED TO PUT A STOP TO THIS!
*SEE THE OBNOXIO/SHE-MAN-THING WEDDING SPECIAL! --CRIES-AT-WEDDINGS JORDAN
HEY! THA WHOLE PLACE IS A-SHAKIN'!
WHAT GIVES?

CONTINUED AFTER NEXT PAGE

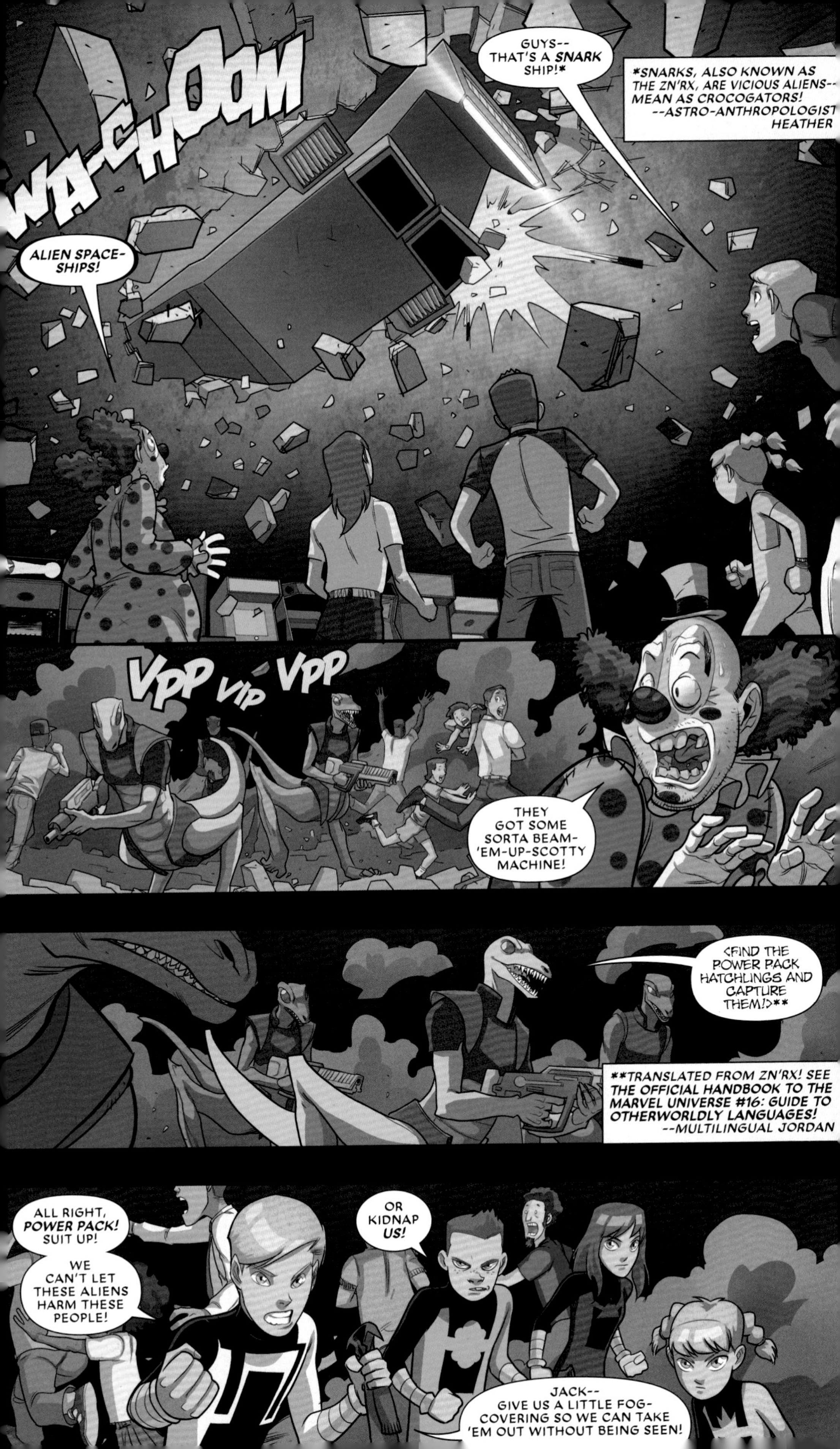
WA-CHOOM
GUYS-- THAT'S A SNARK SHIP!*
*SNARKS, ALSO KNOWN AS THE ZN'RX, ARE VICIOUS ALIENS-- MEAN AS CROCOGATORS! --ASTRO-ANTHROPOLOGIST HEATHER
ALIEN SPACE-SHIPS!
VPP VIP VPP
THEY GOT SOME SORTA BEAM-'EM-UP-SCOTTY MACHINE!
<FIND THE POWER PACK HATCHLINGS AND CAPTURE THEM!>**
**TRANSLATED FROM ZN'RX! SEE THE OFFICIAL HANDBOOK TO THE MARVEL UNIVERSE #16: GUIDE TO OTHERWORLDLY LANGUAGES! --MULTILINGUAL JORDAN
ALL RIGHT, POWER PACK! SUIT UP!
WE CAN'T LET THESE ALIENS HARM THESE PEOPLE!
OR KIDNAP US!
JACK-- GIVE US A LITTLE FOG-COVERING SO WE CAN TAKE 'EM OUT WITHOUT BEING SEEN!

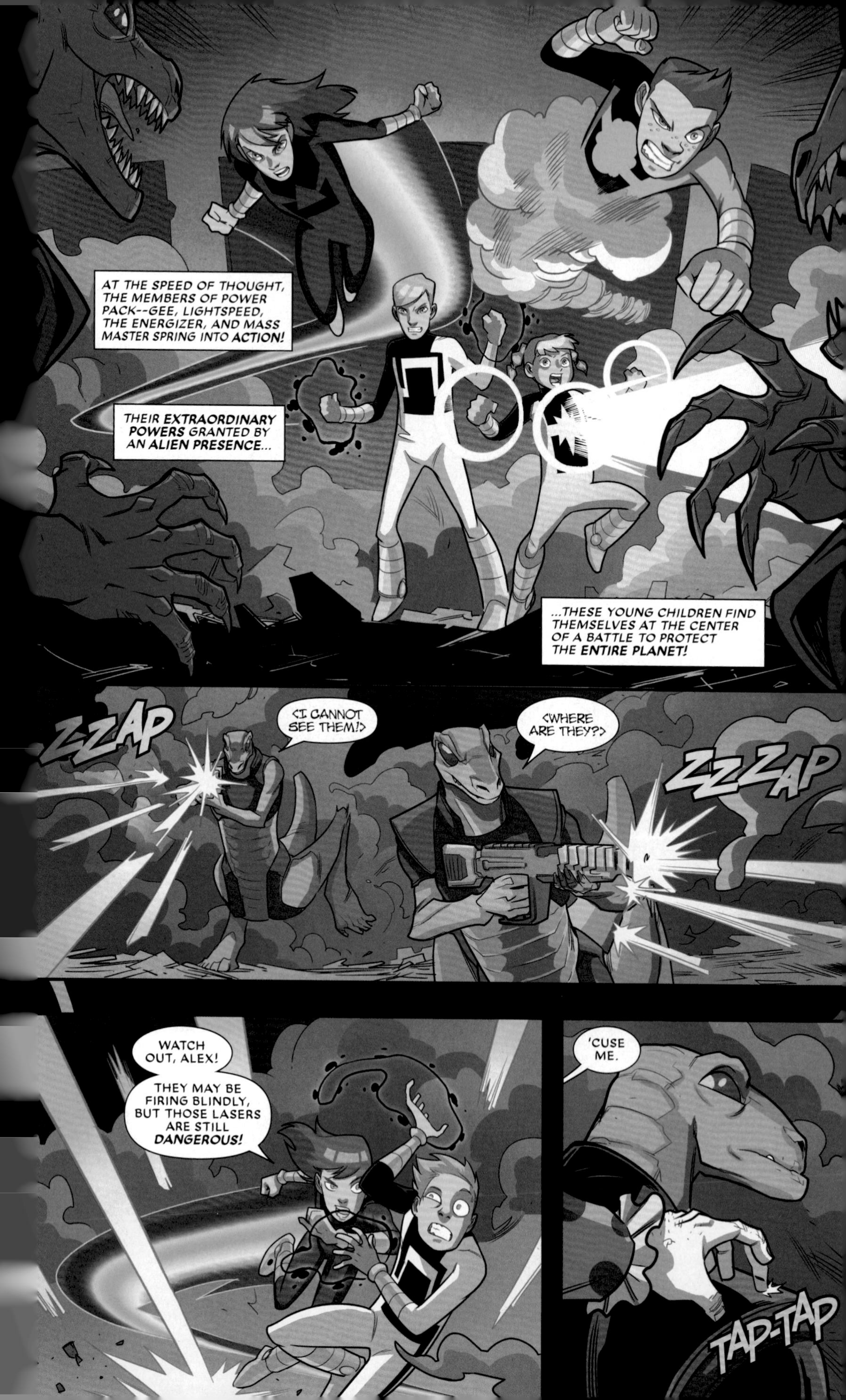
AT THE SPEED OF THOUGHT, THE MEMBERS OF POWER PACK--GEE, LIGHTSPEED, THE ENERGIZER, AND MASS MASTER SPRING INTO ACTION!
THEIR EXTRAORDINARY POWERS GRANTED BY AN ALIEN PRESENCE...
...THESE YOUNG CHILDREN FIND THEMSELVES AT THE CENTER OF A BATTLE TO PROTECT THE ENTIRE PLANET!
ZZAP
<I CANNOT SEE THEM!>
<WHERE ARE THEY?>
ZZZAP
WATCH OUT, ALEX!
THEY MAY BE FIRING BLINDLY, BUT THOSE LASERS ARE STILL DANGEROUS!
'CUSE ME.
TAP-TAP

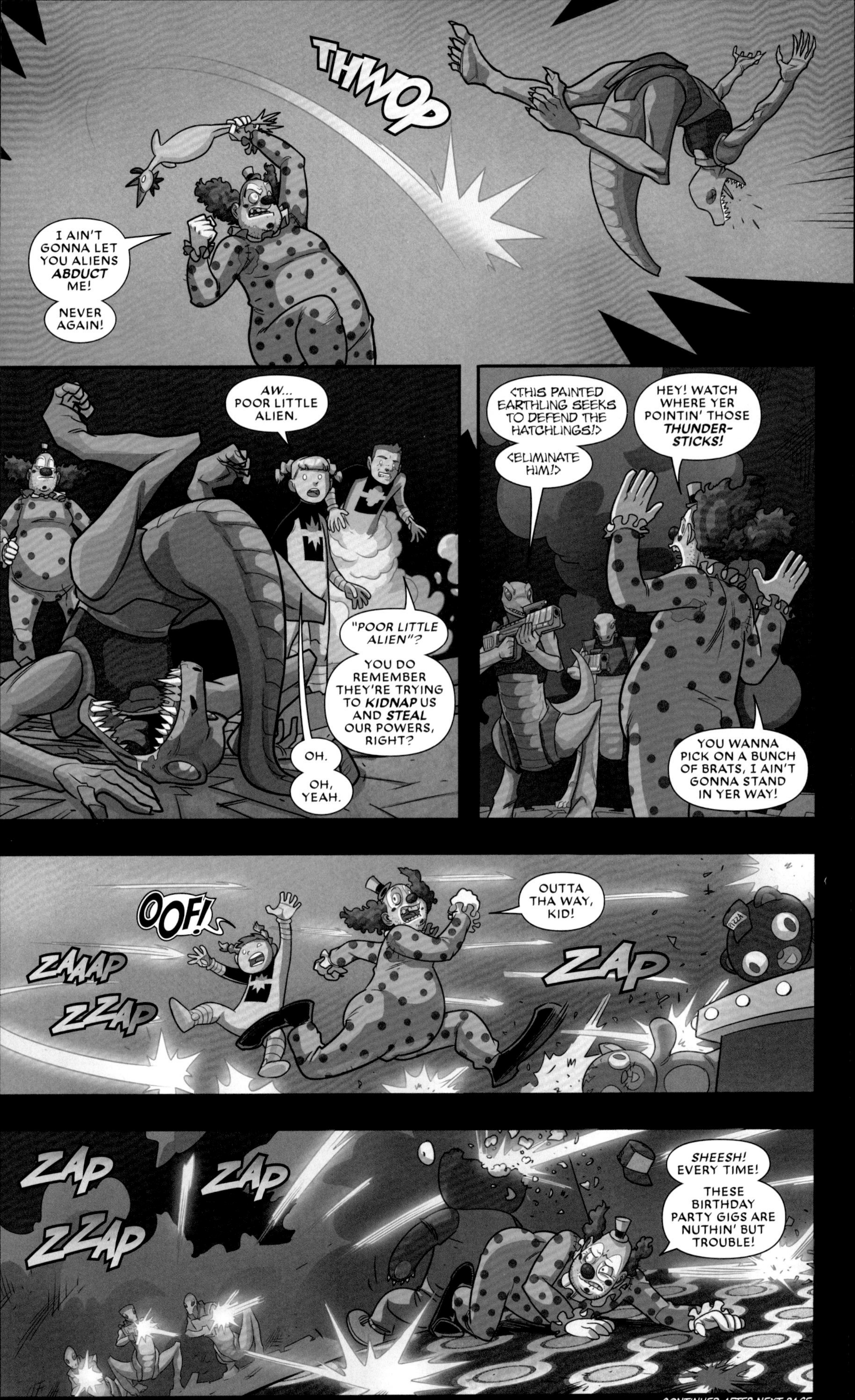
THWOP
I AIN'T GONNA LET YOU ALIENS ABDUCT ME!
NEVER AGAIN!
AW... POOR LITTLE ALIEN.
"POOR LITTLE ALIEN"?
YOU DO REMEMBER THEY'RE TRYING TO KIDNAP US AND STEAL OUR POWERS, RIGHT?
OH.
OH, YEAH.
<THIS PAINTED EARTHLING SEEKS TO DEFEND THE HATCHLINGS!>
<ELIMINATE HIM!>
HEY! WATCH WHERE YER POINTIN' THOSE THUNDER-STICKS!
YOU WANNA PICK ON A BUNCH OF BRATS, I AIN'T GONNA STAND IN YER WAY!
OOF!
ZAAAP
ZZAP
OUTTA THA WAY, KID!
ZAP
PIZZA
ZAP
ZAP
ZZAP
SHEESH! EVERY TIME!
THESE BIRTHDAY PARTY GIGS ARE NUTHIN' BUT TROUBLE!
CONTINUED AFTER NEXT PAGE

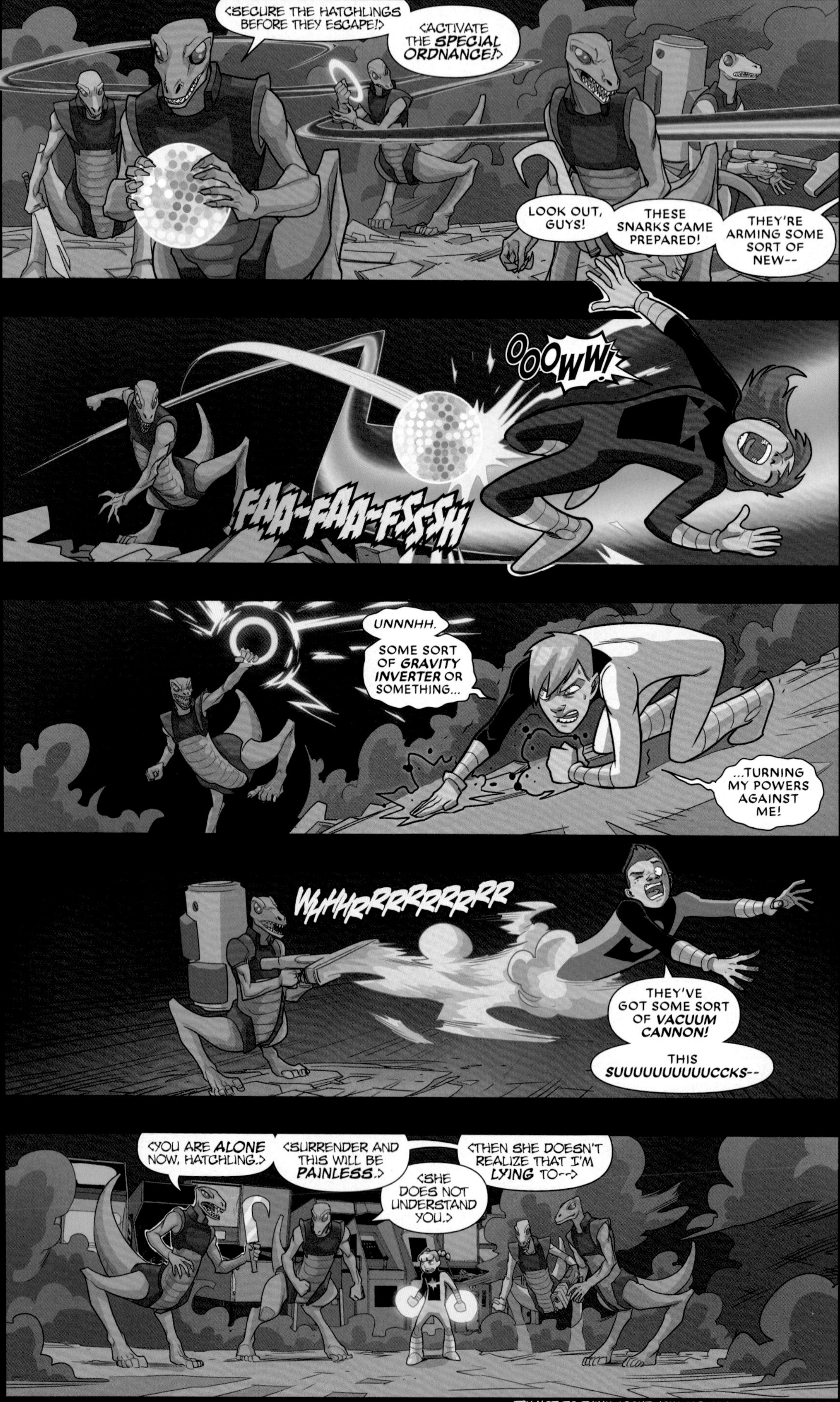
<SECURE THE HATCHLINGS BEFORE THEY ESCAPE!>
<ACTIVATE THE SPECIAL ORDNANCE!>
LOOK OUT, GUYS!
THESE SNARKS CAME PREPARED!
THEY'RE ARMING SOME SORT OF NEW--
OOOWW!
FAA-FAA-FSSSH
UNNNHH.
SOME SORT OF GRAVITY INVERTER OR SOMETHING...
...TURNING MY POWERS AGAINST ME!
WHHHRRRRRRRRR
THEY'VE GOT SOME SORT OF VACUUM CANNON!
THIS SUUUUUUUUUUCCKS--
<YOU ARE ALONE NOW, HATCHLING.>
<SURRENDER AND THIS WILL BE PAINLESS.>
<SHE DOES NOT UNDERSTAND YOU.>
<THEN SHE DOESN'T REALIZE THAT I'M LYING TO-->

TRY NOT TO THINK ABOUT HOW OLD YOU WILL BE IN 31 YEARS.

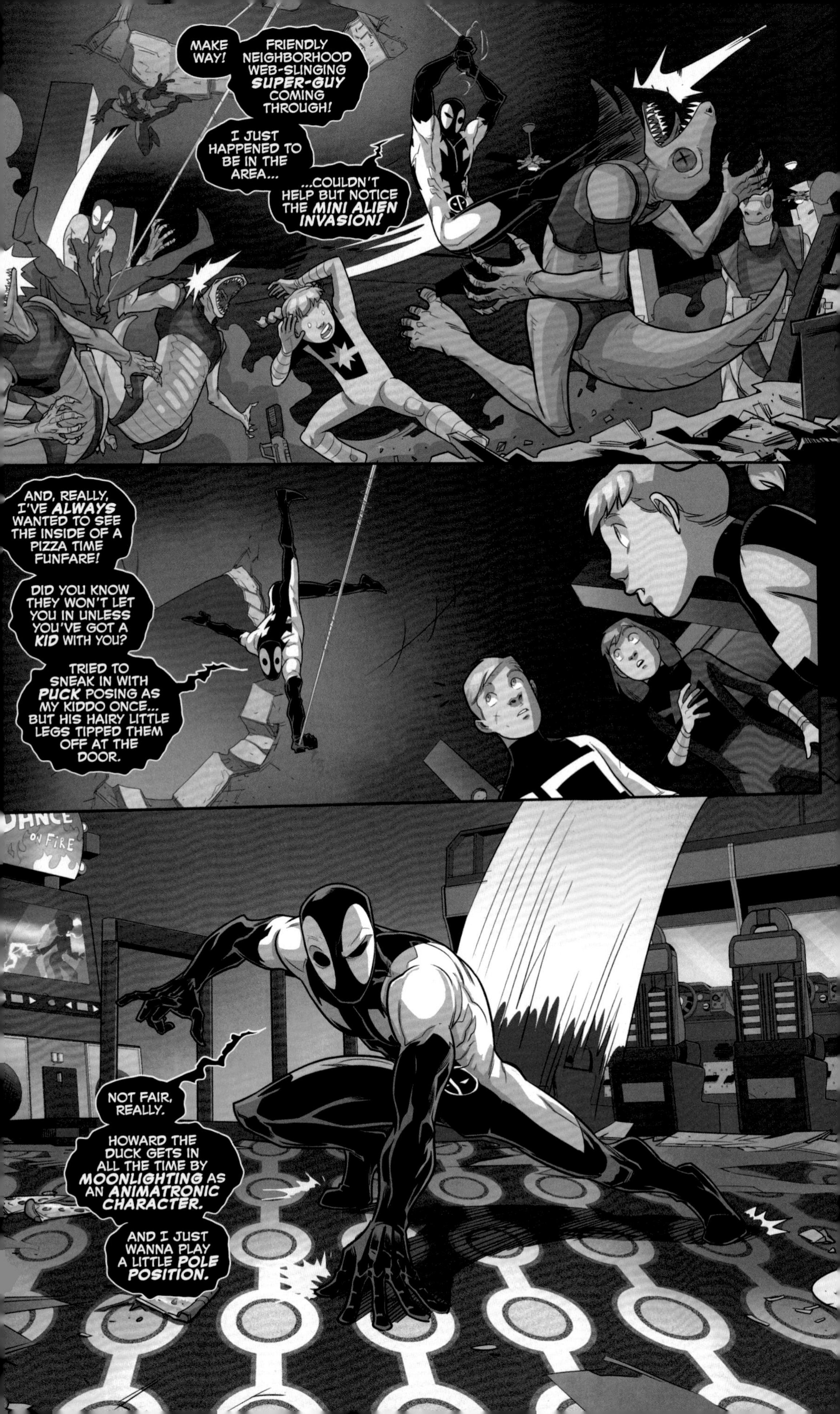

MAKE WAY!
FRIENDLY NEIGHBORHOOD WEB-SLINGING SUPER-GUY COMING THROUGH!
I JUST HAPPENED TO BE IN THE AREA...
...COULDN'T HELP BUT NOTICE THE MINI ALIEN INVASION!
AND, REALLY, I'VE ALWAYS WANTED TO SEE THE INSIDE OF A PIZZA TIME FUNFARE!
DID YOU KNOW THEY WON'T LET YOU IN UNLESS YOU'VE GOT A KID WITH YOU?
TRIED TO SNEAK IN WITH PUCK POSING AS MY KIDDO ONCE... BUT HIS HAIRY LITTLE LEGS TIPPED THEM OFF AT THE DOOR.
DANCE ON FIRE
NOT FAIR, REALLY.
HOWARD THE DUCK GETS IN ALL THE TIME BY MOONLIGHTING AS AN ANIMATRONIC CHARACTER.
AND I JUST WANNA PLAY A LITTLE POLE POSITION.

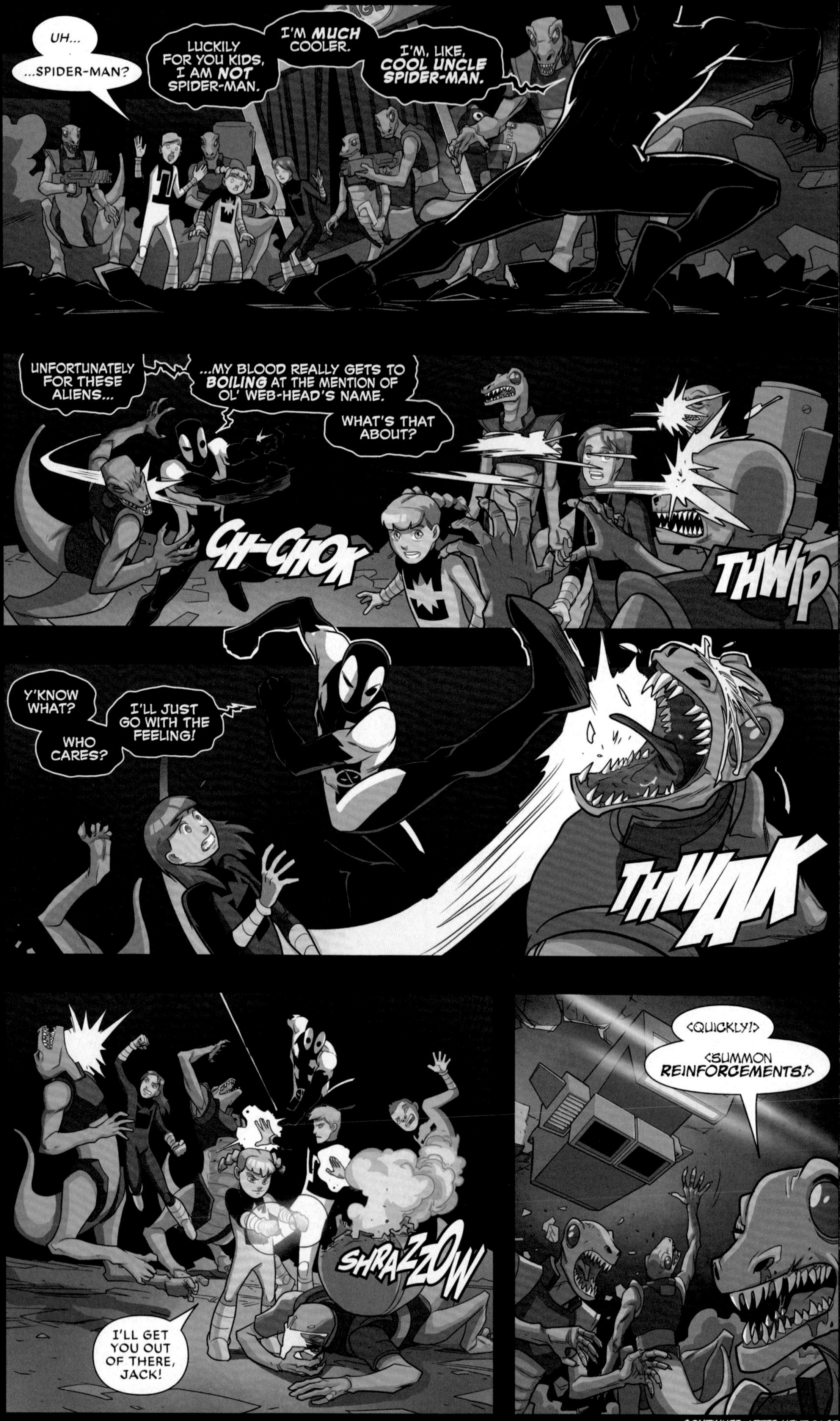
UH...
...SPIDER-MAN?
LUCKILY FOR YOU KIDS, I AM NOT SPIDER-MAN.
I'M MUCH COOLER.
I'M, LIKE, COOL UNCLE SPIDER-MAN.
UNFORTUNATELY FOR THESE ALIENS...
...MY BLOOD REALLY GETS TO BOILING AT THE MENTION OF OL' WEB-HEAD'S NAME.
WHAT'S THAT ABOUT?
CH-CHOK
THWIP
Y'KNOW WHAT?
WHO CARES?
I'LL JUST GO WITH THE FEELING!
THWAK
SHRAZZOW
I'LL GET YOU OUT OF THERE, JACK!
<QUICKLY!>
<SUMMON REINFORCEMENTS!>

CONTINUED AFTER NEXT PAGE

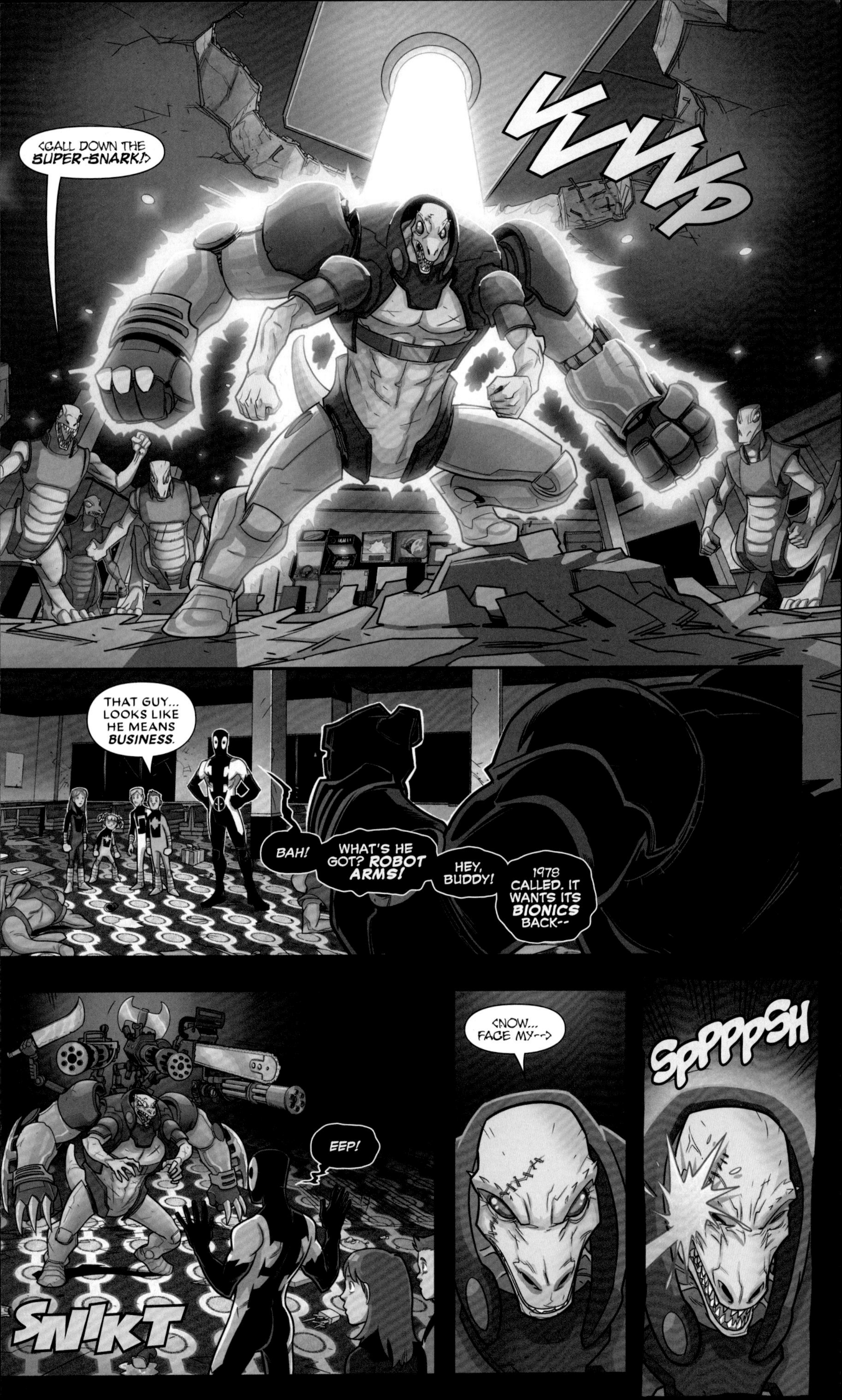

<CALL DOWN THE SUPER-SNARK!>
VVVVVP
THAT GUY... LOOKS LIKE HE MEANS BUSINESS.
BAH!
WHAT'S HE GOT? ROBOT ARMS!
HEY, BUDDY!
1978 CALLED. IT WANTS ITS BIONICS BACK--
SNIKT
EEP!
<NOW... FACE MY-->
SPPPPSH

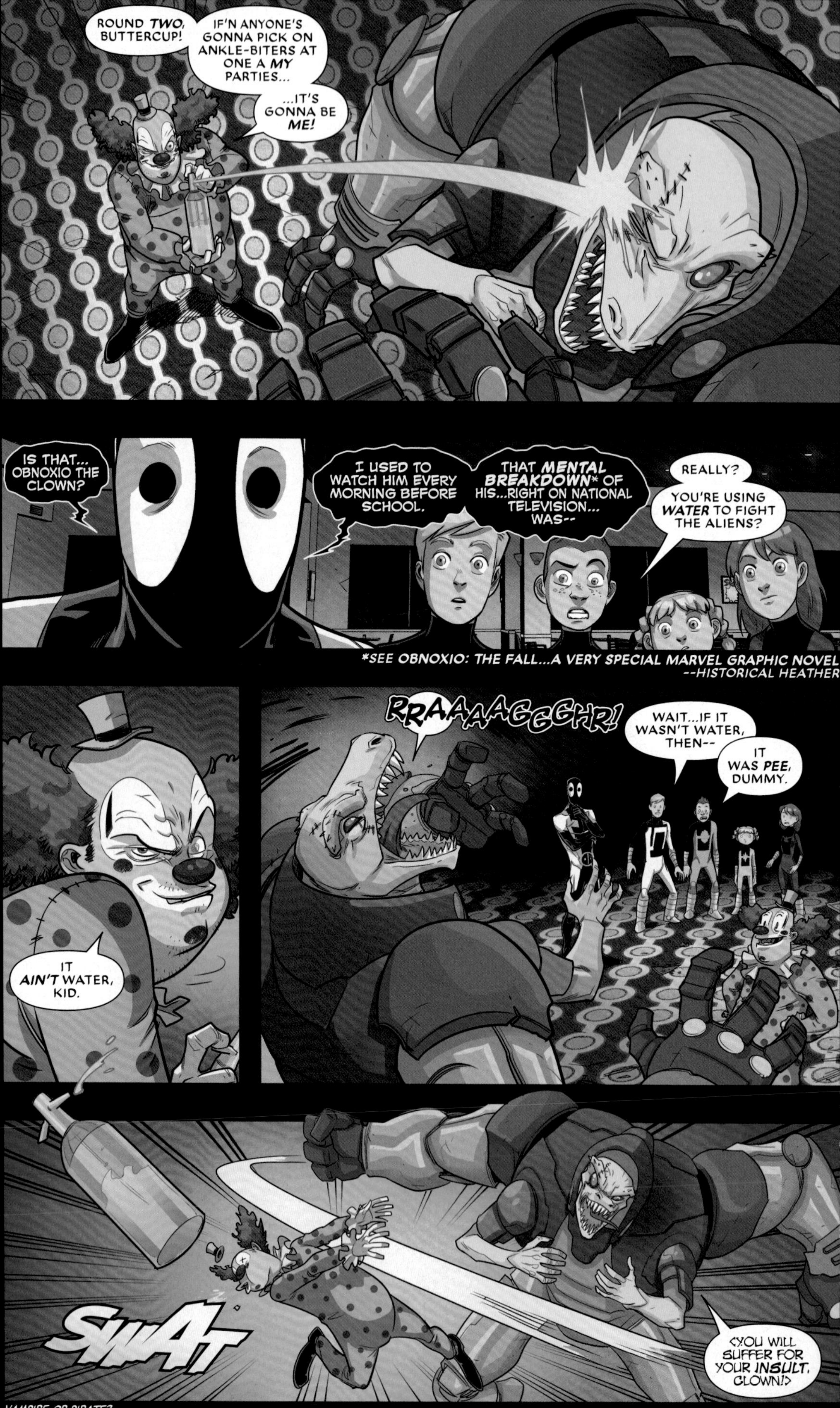

ROUND TWO, BUTTERCUP!
IF'N ANYONE'S GONNA PICK ON ANKLE-BITERS AT ONE A MY PARTIES...
...IT'S GONNA BE ME!
IS THAT... OBNOXIO THE CLOWN?
I USED TO WATCH HIM EVERY MORNING BEFORE SCHOOL.
THAT MENTAL BREAKDOWN* OF HIS...RIGHT ON NATIONAL TELEVISION... WAS--
REALLY?
YOU'RE USING WATER TO FIGHT THE ALIENS?
*SEE OBNOXIO: THE FALL...A VERY SPECIAL MARVEL GRAPHIC NOVEL --HISTORICAL HEATHER
IT AIN'T WATER, KID.
RRAAAAAGGGHR!
WAIT...IF IT WASN'T WATER, THEN--
IT WAS PEE, DUMMY.
SWAT
<YOU WILL SUFFER FOR YOUR INSULT, CLOWN!>

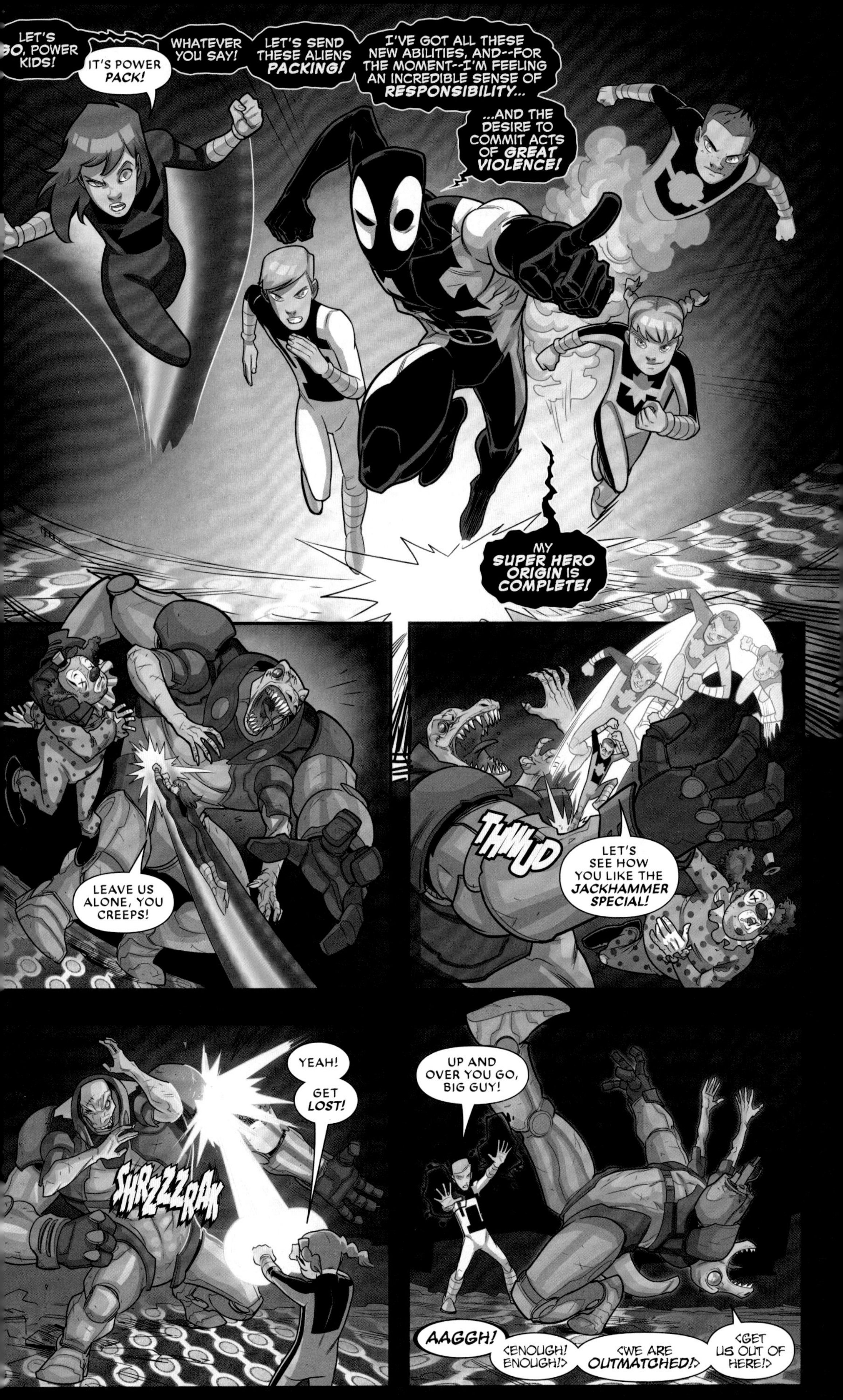
LET'S GO, POWER KIDS!
IT'S POWER PACK!
WHATEVER YOU SAY!
LET'S SEND THESE ALIENS PACKING!
I'VE GOT ALL THESE NEW ABILITIES, AND--FOR THE MOMENT--I'M FEELING AN INCREDIBLE SENSE OF RESPONSIBILITY...
...AND THE DESIRE TO COMMIT ACTS OF GREAT VIOLENCE!
MY SUPER HERO ORIGIN IS COMPLETE!
LEAVE US ALONE, YOU CREEPS!
THWUD
LET'S SEE HOW YOU LIKE THE JACKHAMMER SPECIAL!
YEAH!
GET LOST!
SHRZZZRAK
UP AND OVER YOU GO, BIG GUY!
AAGGH!
<ENOUGH! ENOUGH!>
<WE ARE OUTMATCHED!>
<GET US OUT OF HERE!>

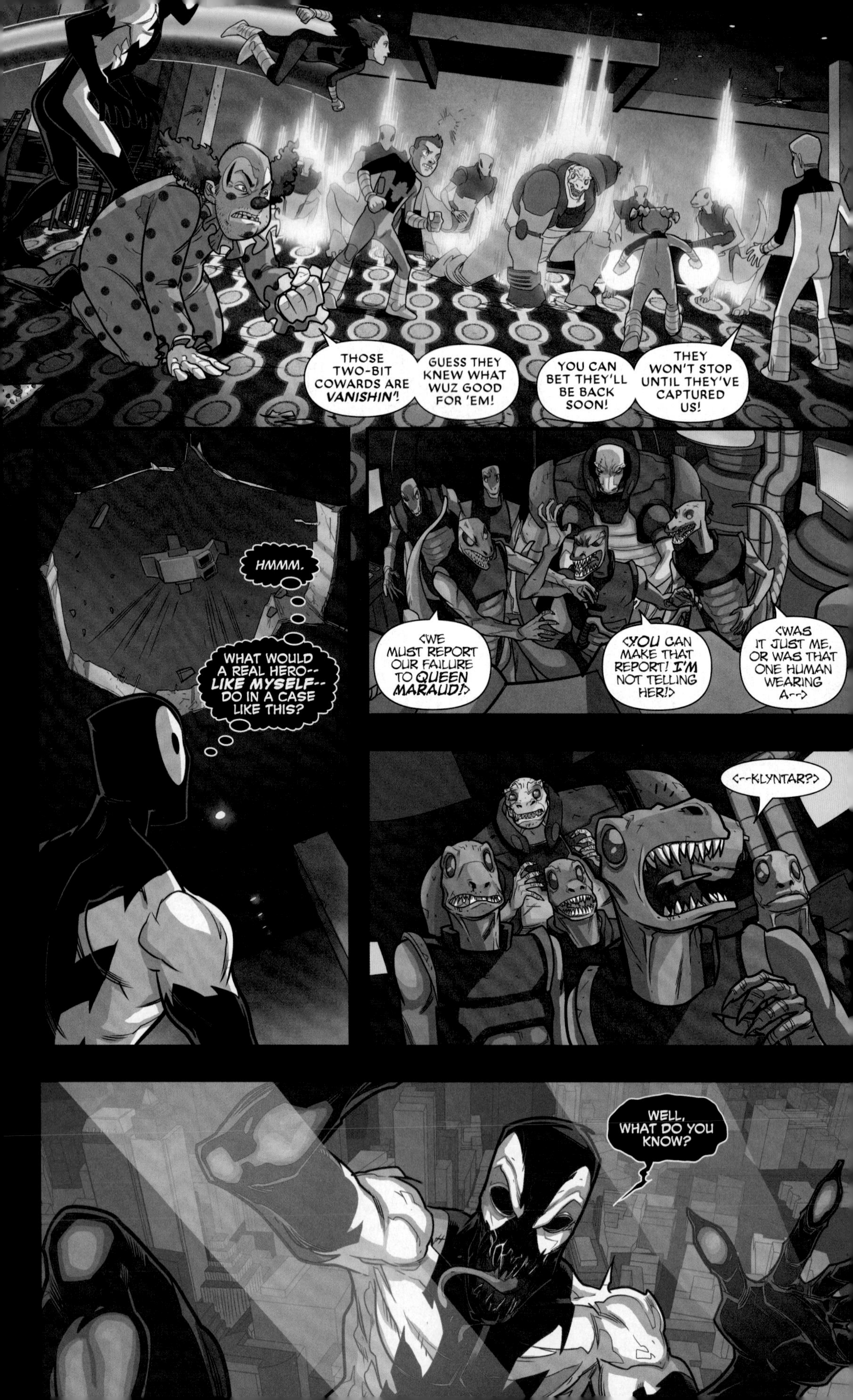
THOSE TWO-BIT COWARDS ARE VANISHIN'!
GUESS THEY KNEW WHAT WUZ GOOD FOR 'EM!
YOU CAN BET THEY'LL BE BACK SOON!
THEY WON'T STOP UNTIL THEY'VE CAPTURED US!
HMMM.
WHAT WOULD A REAL HERO-- LIKE MYSELF-- DO IN A CASE LIKE THIS?
<WE MUST REPORT OUR FAILURE TO QUEEN MARAUD!>
<YOU CAN MAKE THAT REPORT! I'M NOT TELLING HER!>
<WAS IT JUST ME, OR WAS THAT ONE HUMAN WEARING A-->
<--KLYNTAR?>
WELL, WHAT DO YOU KNOW?

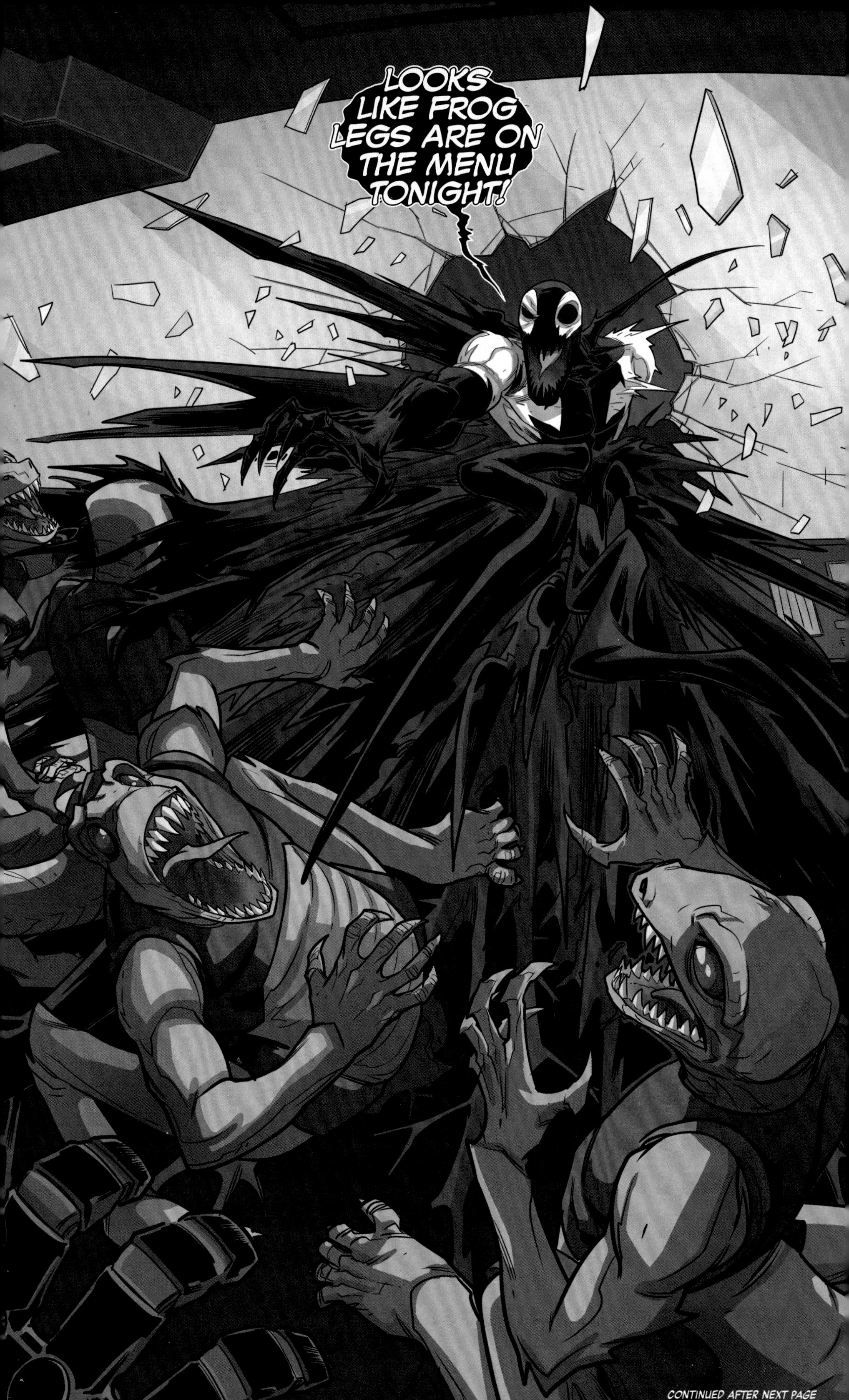
LOOKS LIKE FROG LEGS ARE ON THE MENU TONIGHT!

CONTINUED AFTER NEXT PAGE

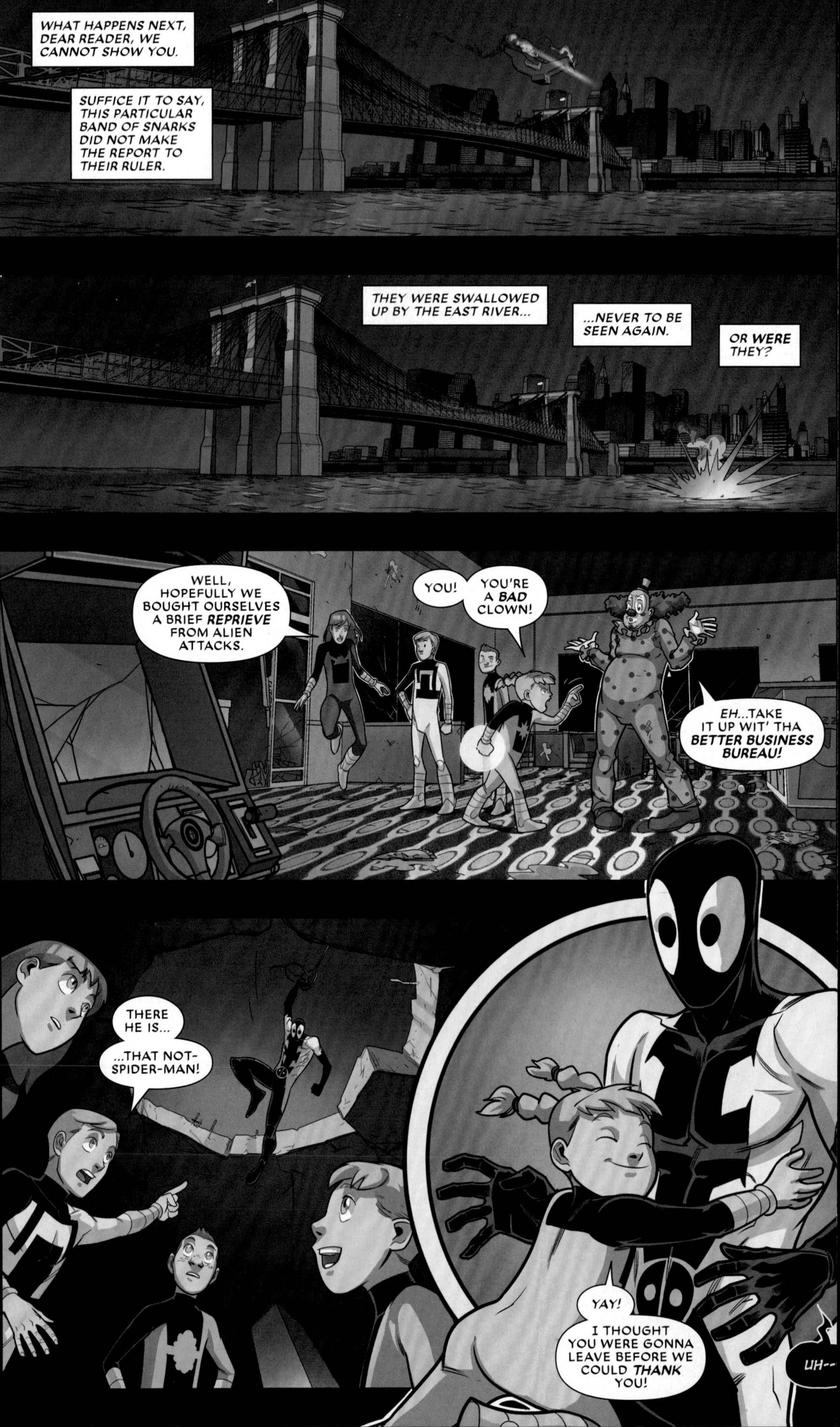
WHAT HAPPENS NEXT, DEAR READER, WE CANNOT SHOW YOU.
SUFFICE IT TO SAY, THIS PARTICULAR BAND OF SNARKS DID NOT MAKE THE REPORT TO THEIR RULER.
THEY WERE SWALLOWED UP BY THE EAST RIVER...
...NEVER TO BE SEEN AGAIN.
OR WERE THEY?
WELL, HOPEFULLY WE BOUGHT OURSELVES A BRIEF REPRIEVE FROM ALIEN ATTACKS.
YOU!
YOU'RE A BAD CLOWN!
EH...TAKE IT UP WIT' THA BETTER BUSINESS BUREAU!
THERE HE IS...
...THAT NOT-SPIDER-MAN!
YAY!
I THOUGHT YOU WERE GONNA LEAVE BEFORE WE COULD THANK YOU!
UH--

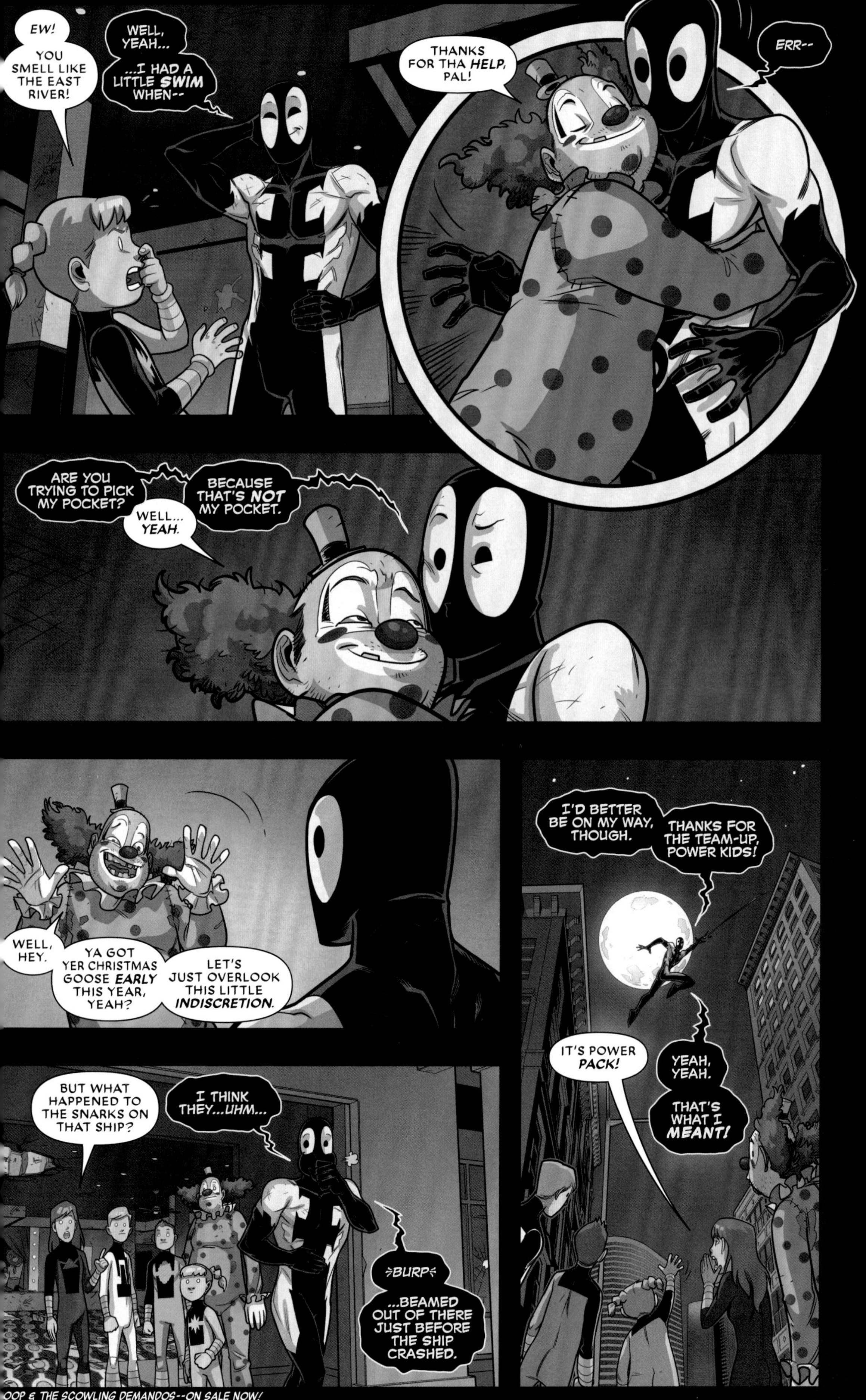
EW!
YOU SMELL LIKE THE EAST RIVER!
WELL, YEAH...
...I HAD A LITTLE SWIM WHEN--
THANKS FOR THA HELP, PAL!
ERR--
ARE YOU TRYING TO PICK MY POCKET?
WELL... YEAH.
BECAUSE THAT'S NOT MY POCKET.
WELL, HEY.
YA GOT YER CHRISTMAS GOOSE EARLY THIS YEAR, YEAH?
LET'S JUST OVERLOOK THIS LITTLE INDISCRETION.
BUT WHAT HAPPENED TO THE SNARKS ON THAT SHIP?
I THINK THEY...UHM...
BURP
...BEAMED OUT OF THERE JUST BEFORE THE SHIP CRASHED.
I'D BETTER BE ON MY WAY, THOUGH.
THANKS FOR THE TEAM-UP, POWER KIDS!
IT'S POWER PACK!
YEAH, YEAH.
THAT'S WHAT I MEANT!

OOP & THE SCOWLING DEMANDOS--ON SALE NOW!

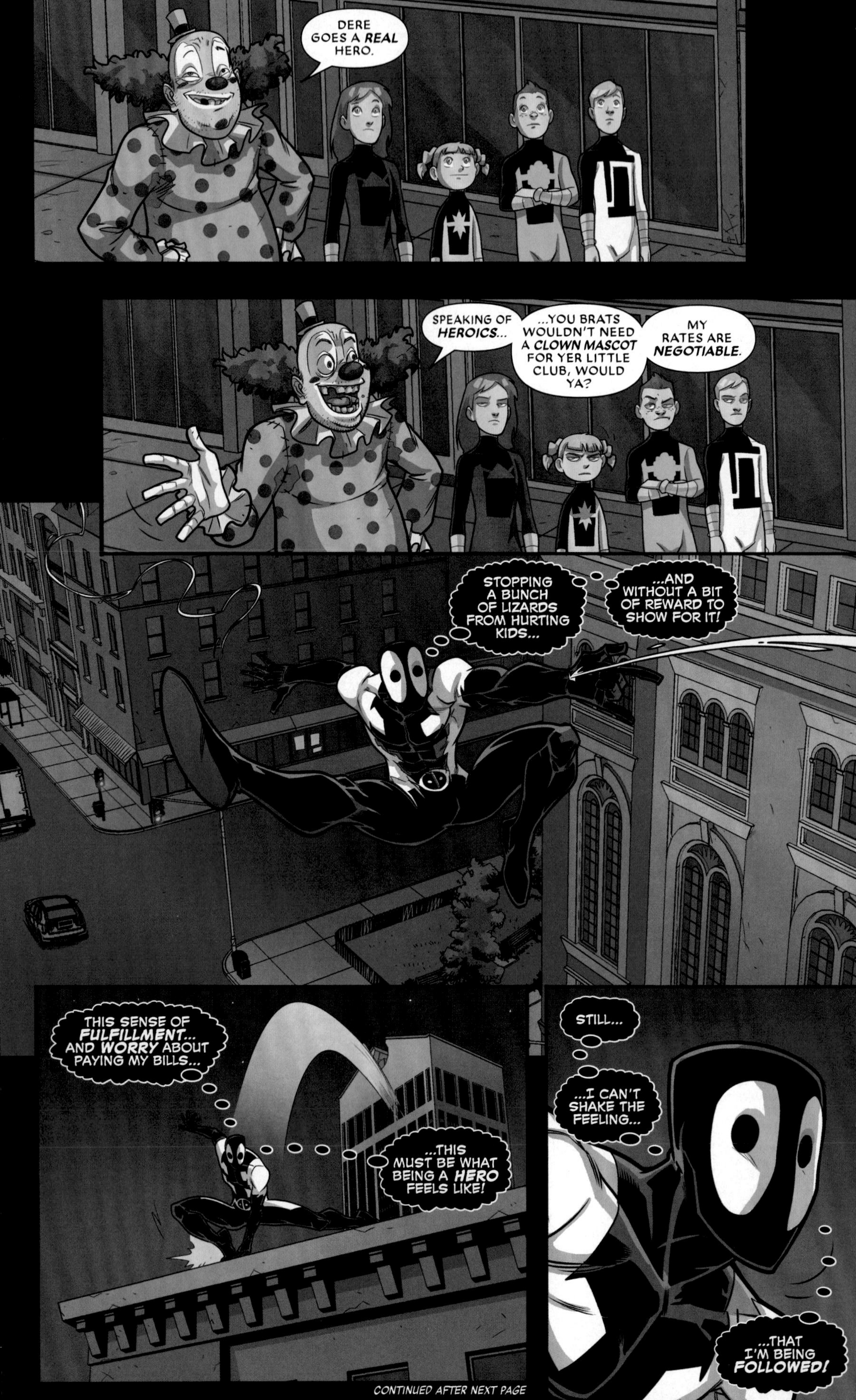
DERE GOES A *REAL* HERO.
SPEAKING OF *HEROICS*...
...YOU BRATS WOULDN'T NEED A *CLOWN MASCOT* FOR YER LITTLE CLUB, WOULD YA?
MY RATES ARE *NEGOTIABLE*.
STOPPING A BUNCH OF LIZARDS FROM HURTING KIDS...
...AND WITHOUT A BIT OF REWARD TO SHOW FOR IT!
THIS SENSE OF *FULFILLMENT*... AND *WORRY* ABOUT PAYING MY BILLS...
...THIS MUST BE WHAT BEING A *HERO* FEELS LIKE!
STILL...
...I CAN'T SHAKE THE FEELING...
...THAT I'M BEING *FOLLOWED!*

CONTINUED AFTER NEXT PAGE

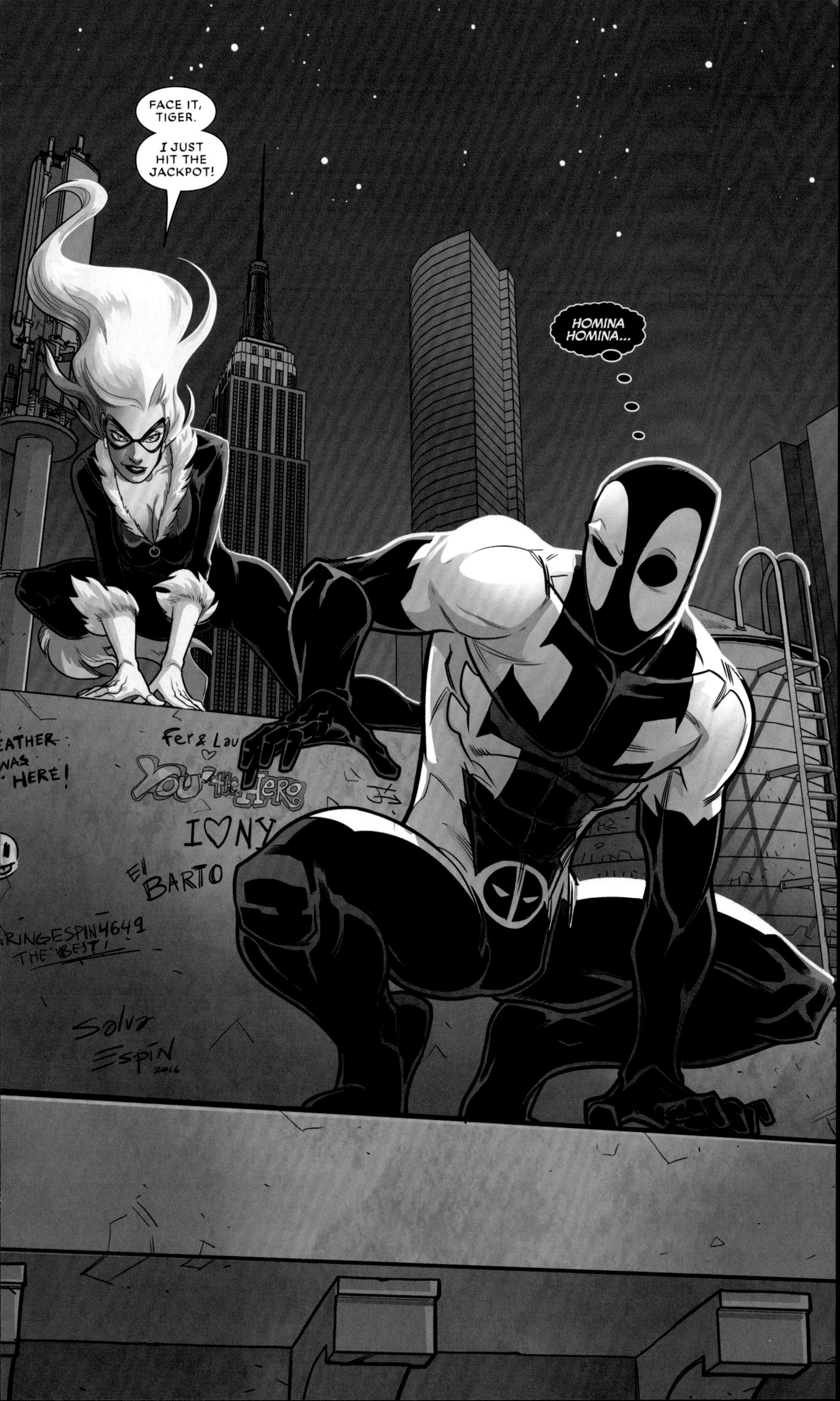
FACE IT, TIGER.
I JUST HIT THE JACKPOT!
HOMINA HOMINA...
El BARTO
Salva Espín 2016

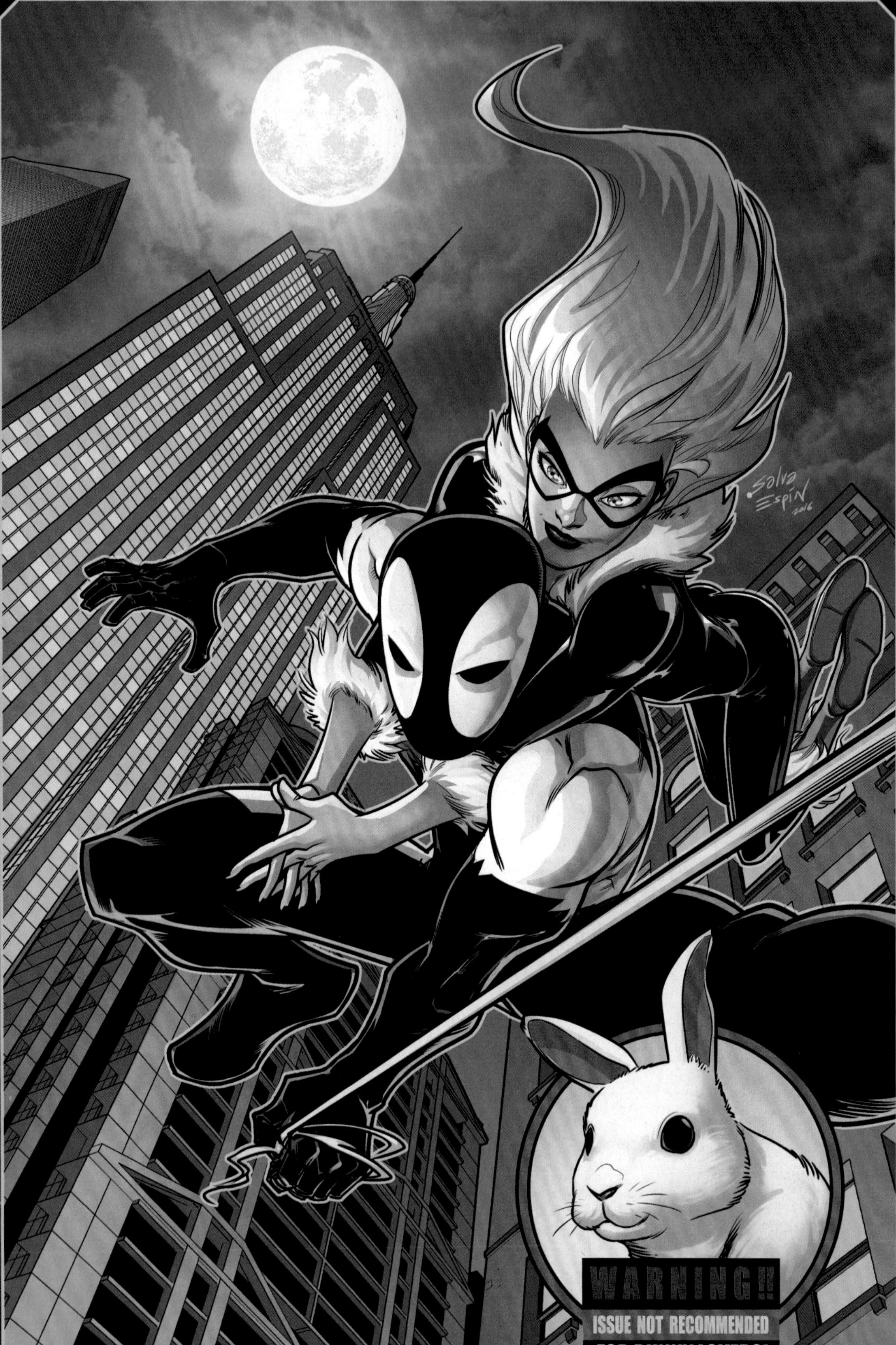

Salva Espin 2016
WARNING!!
ISSUE NOT RECOMMENDED
FOR BUNNY LOVERS!

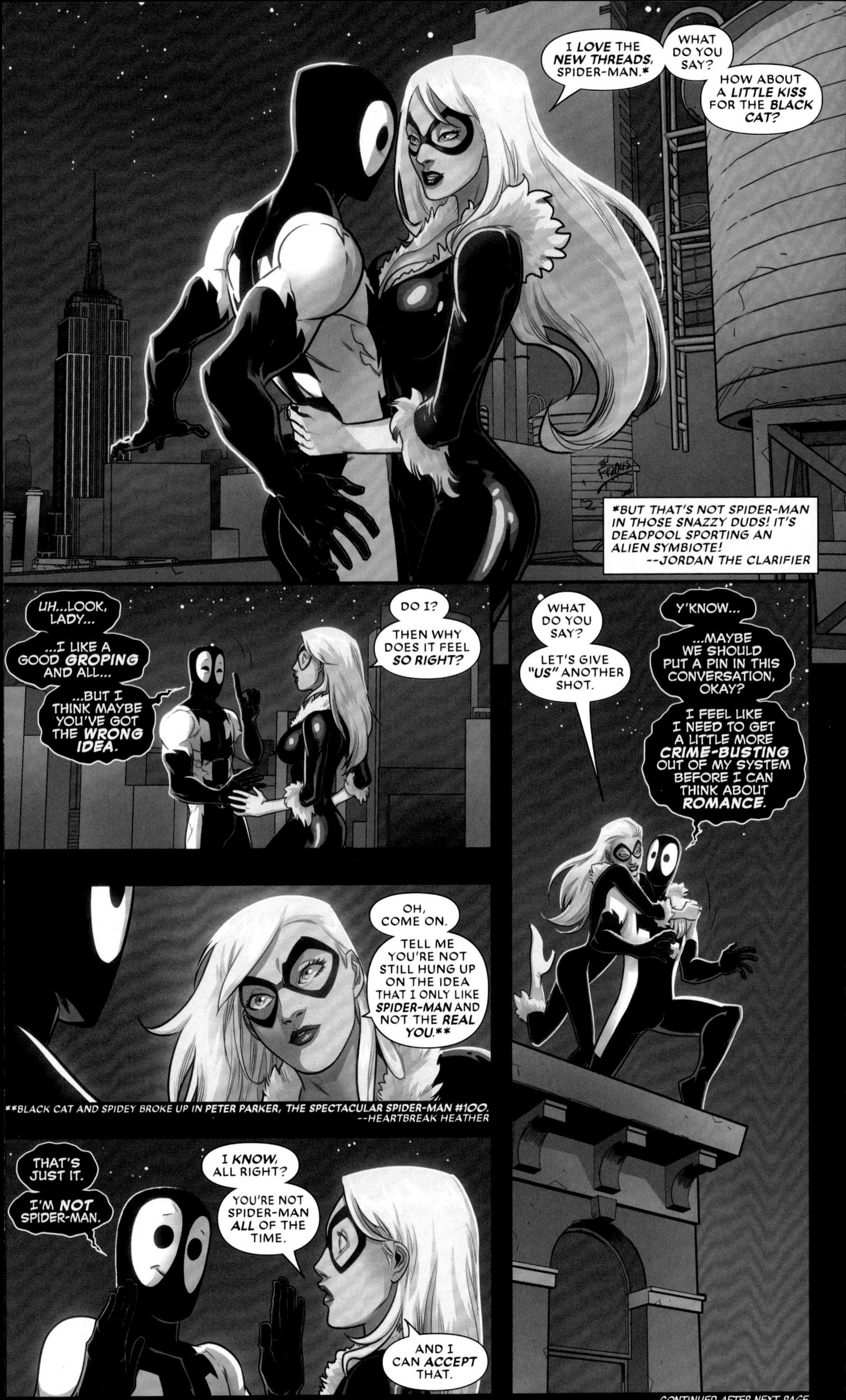

I LOVE THE NEW THREADS, SPIDER-MAN.*
WHAT DO YOU SAY?
HOW ABOUT A LITTLE KISS FOR THE BLACK CAT?
*BUT THAT'S NOT SPIDER-MAN IN THOSE SNAZZY DUDS! IT'S DEADPOOL SPORTING AN ALIEN SYMBIOTE! --JORDAN THE CLARIFIER
UH...LOOK, LADY...
...I LIKE A GOOD GROPING AND ALL...
...BUT I THINK MAYBE YOU'VE GOT THE WRONG IDEA.
DO I?
THEN WHY DOES IT FEEL SO RIGHT?
OH, COME ON.
TELL ME YOU'RE NOT STILL HUNG UP ON THE IDEA THAT I ONLY LIKE SPIDER-MAN AND NOT THE REAL YOU.**
**BLACK CAT AND SPIDEY BROKE UP IN PETER PARKER, THE SPECTACULAR SPIDER-MAN #100. --HEARTBREAK HEATHER
THAT'S JUST IT.
I'M NOT SPIDER-MAN.
I KNOW, ALL RIGHT?
YOU'RE NOT SPIDER-MAN ALL OF THE TIME.
AND I CAN ACCEPT THAT.
WHAT DO YOU SAY?
LET'S GIVE "US" ANOTHER SHOT.
Y'KNOW...
...MAYBE WE SHOULD PUT A PIN IN THIS CONVERSATION, OKAY?
I FEEL LIKE I NEED TO GET A LITTLE MORE CRIME-BUSTING OUT OF MY SYSTEM BEFORE I CAN THINK ABOUT ROMANCE.

CONTINUED AFTER NEXT PAGE

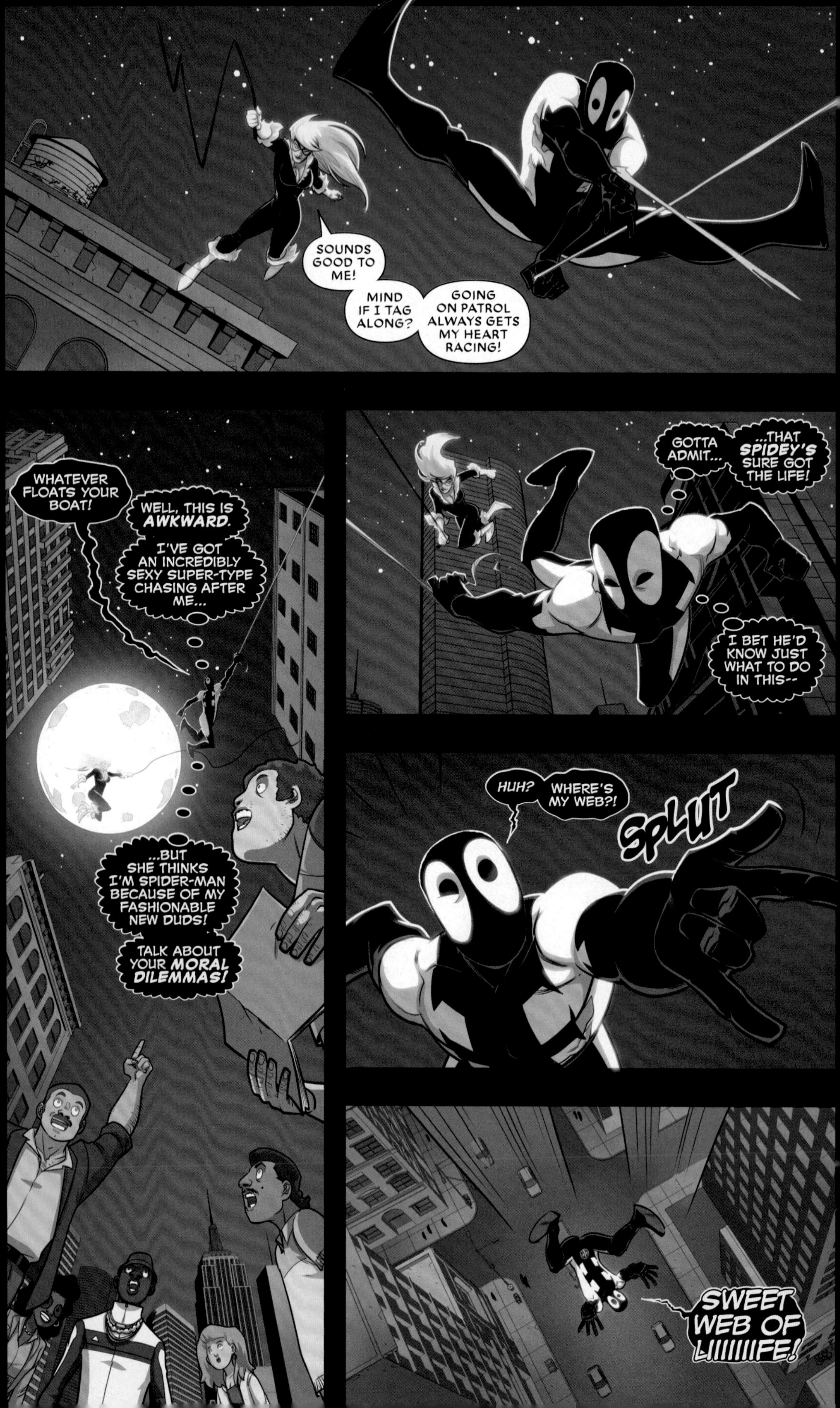

SOUNDS GOOD TO ME!
MIND IF I TAG ALONG?
GOING ON PATROL ALWAYS GETS MY HEART RACING!
WHATEVER FLOATS YOUR BOAT!
WELL, THIS IS AWKWARD.
I'VE GOT AN INCREDIBLY SEXY SUPER-TYPE CHASING AFTER ME...
...BUT SHE THINKS I'M SPIDER-MAN BECAUSE OF MY FASHIONABLE NEW DUDS!
TALK ABOUT YOUR MORAL DILEMMAS!
GOTTA ADMIT...
...THAT SPIDEY'S SURE GOT THE LIFE!
I BET HE'D KNOW JUST WHAT TO DO IN THIS--
HUH?
WHERE'S MY WEB?!
SPLUT
SWEET WEB OF LIIIIIIFE!

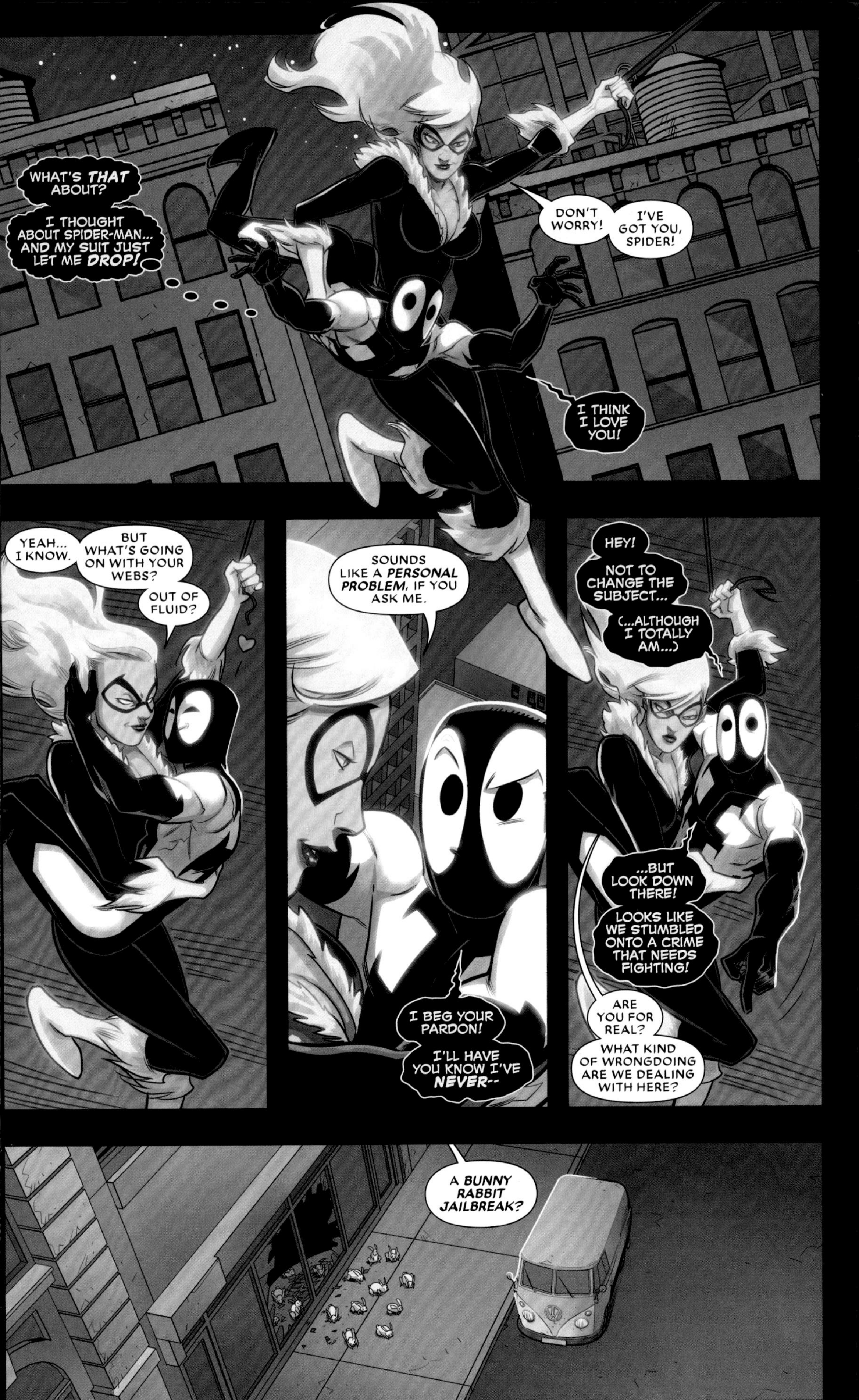
WHAT'S THAT ABOUT?
I THOUGHT ABOUT SPIDER-MAN... AND MY SUIT JUST LET ME DROP!
DON'T WORRY!
I'VE GOT YOU, SPIDER!
I THINK I LOVE YOU!
YEAH... I KNOW.
BUT WHAT'S GOING ON WITH YOUR WEBS?
OUT OF FLUID?
SOUNDS LIKE A PERSONAL PROBLEM, IF YOU ASK ME.
I BEG YOUR PARDON!
I'LL HAVE YOU KNOW I'VE NEVER--
HEY!
NOT TO CHANGE THE SUBJECT...
(...ALTHOUGH I TOTALLY AM...)
...BUT LOOK DOWN THERE!
LOOKS LIKE WE STUMBLED ONTO A CRIME THAT NEEDS FIGHTING!
ARE YOU FOR REAL?
WHAT KIND OF WRONGDOING ARE WE DEALING WITH HERE?
A BUNNY RABBIT JAILBREAK?

THE DOCTOR GOES NUCLEAR IN DR. STRANGE #70!

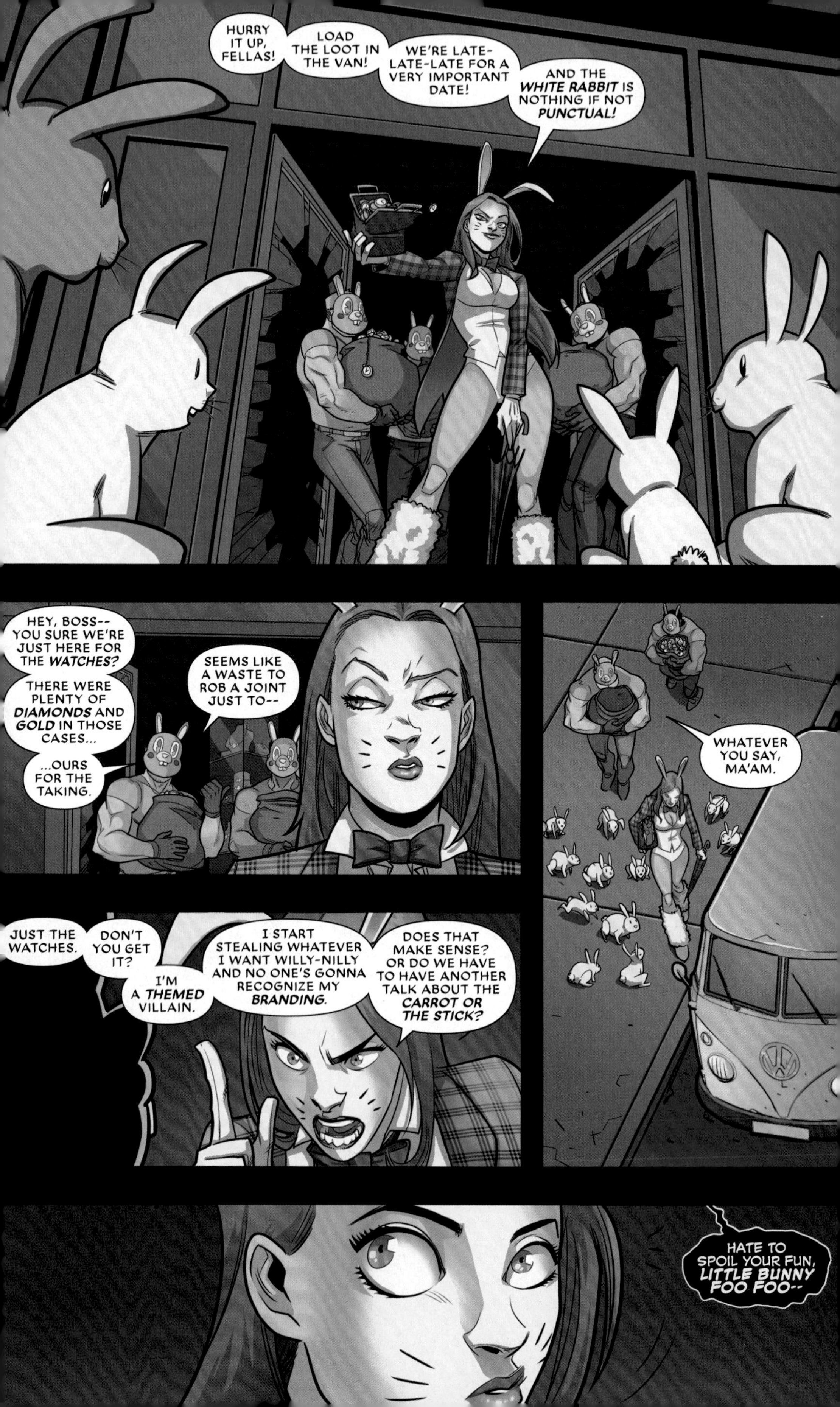
HURRY IT UP, FELLAS!
LOAD THE LOOT IN THE VAN!
WE'RE LATE-LATE-LATE FOR A VERY IMPORTANT DATE!
AND THE WHITE RABBIT IS NOTHING IF NOT PUNCTUAL!
HEY, BOSS-- YOU SURE WE'RE JUST HERE FOR THE WATCHES?
THERE WERE PLENTY OF DIAMONDS AND GOLD IN THOSE CASES...
...OURS FOR THE TAKING.
SEEMS LIKE A WASTE TO ROB A JOINT JUST TO--
JUST THE WATCHES.
DON'T YOU GET IT?
I'M A THEMED VILLAIN.
I START STEALING WHATEVER I WANT WILLY-NILLY AND NO ONE'S GONNA RECOGNIZE MY BRANDING.
DOES THAT MAKE SENSE? OR DO WE HAVE TO HAVE ANOTHER TALK ABOUT THE CARROT OR THE STICK?
WHATEVER YOU SAY, MA'AM.
HATE TO SPOIL YOUR FUN, LITTLE BUNNY FOO FOO--

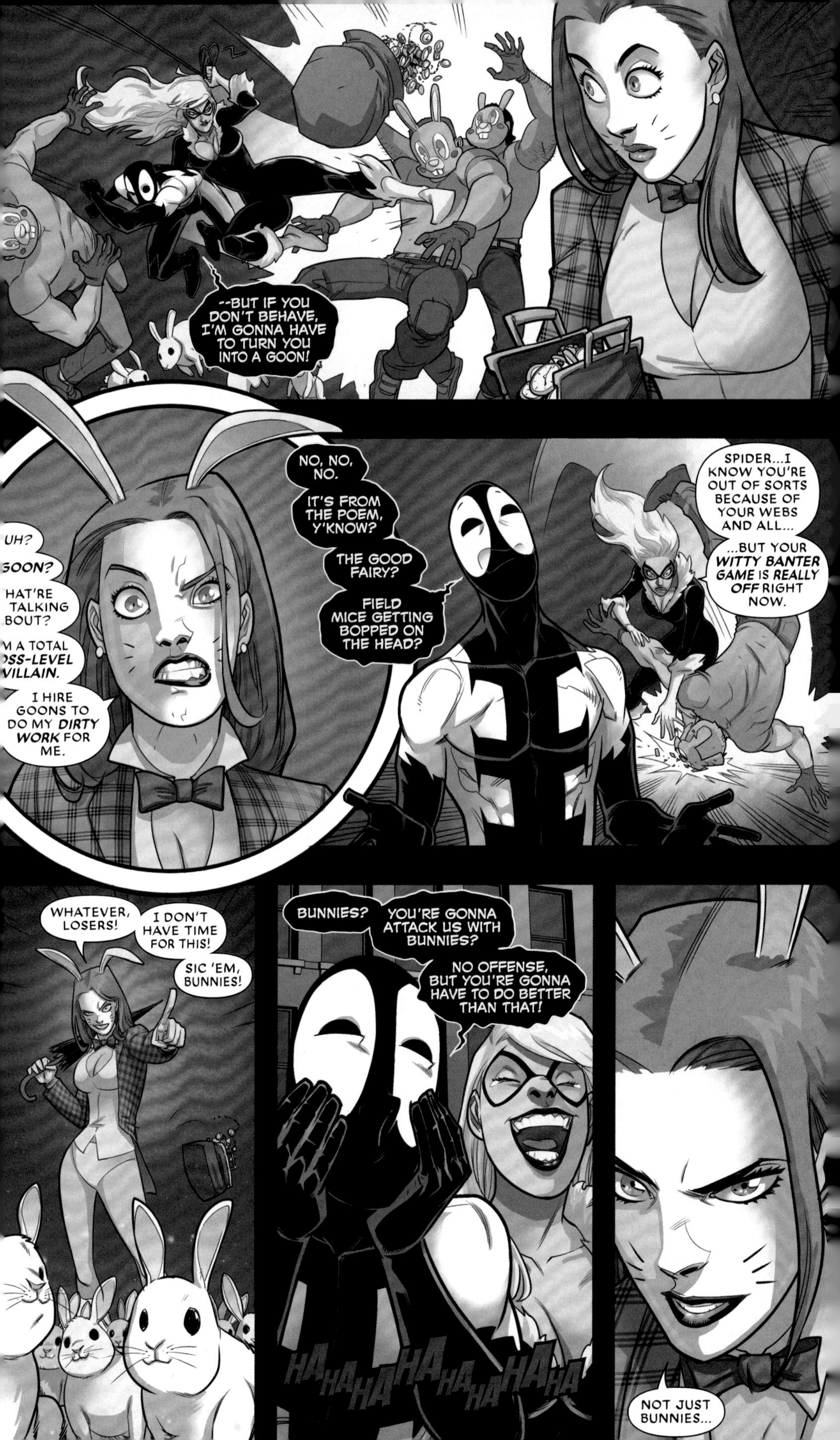

--BUT IF YOU DON'T BEHAVE, I'M GONNA HAVE TO TURN YOU INTO A GOON!
UH?
GOON?
HAT'RE TALKING BOUT?
M A TOTAL OSS-LEVEL VILLAIN.
I HIRE GOONS TO DO MY DIRTY WORK FOR ME.
NO, NO, NO.
IT'S FROM THE POEM, Y'KNOW?
THE GOOD FAIRY?
FIELD MICE GETTING BOPPED ON THE HEAD?
SPIDER...I KNOW YOU'RE OUT OF SORTS BECAUSE OF YOUR WEBS AND ALL...
...BUT YOUR WITTY BANTER GAME IS REALLY OFF RIGHT NOW.
WHATEVER, LOSERS!
I DON'T HAVE TIME FOR THIS!
SIC 'EM, BUNNIES!
BUNNIES?
YOU'RE GONNA ATTACK US WITH BUNNIES?
NO OFFENSE, BUT YOU'RE GONNA HAVE TO DO BETTER THAN THAT!
HA HA HA HA HA HA HA HA HA HA
NOT JUST BUNNIES...

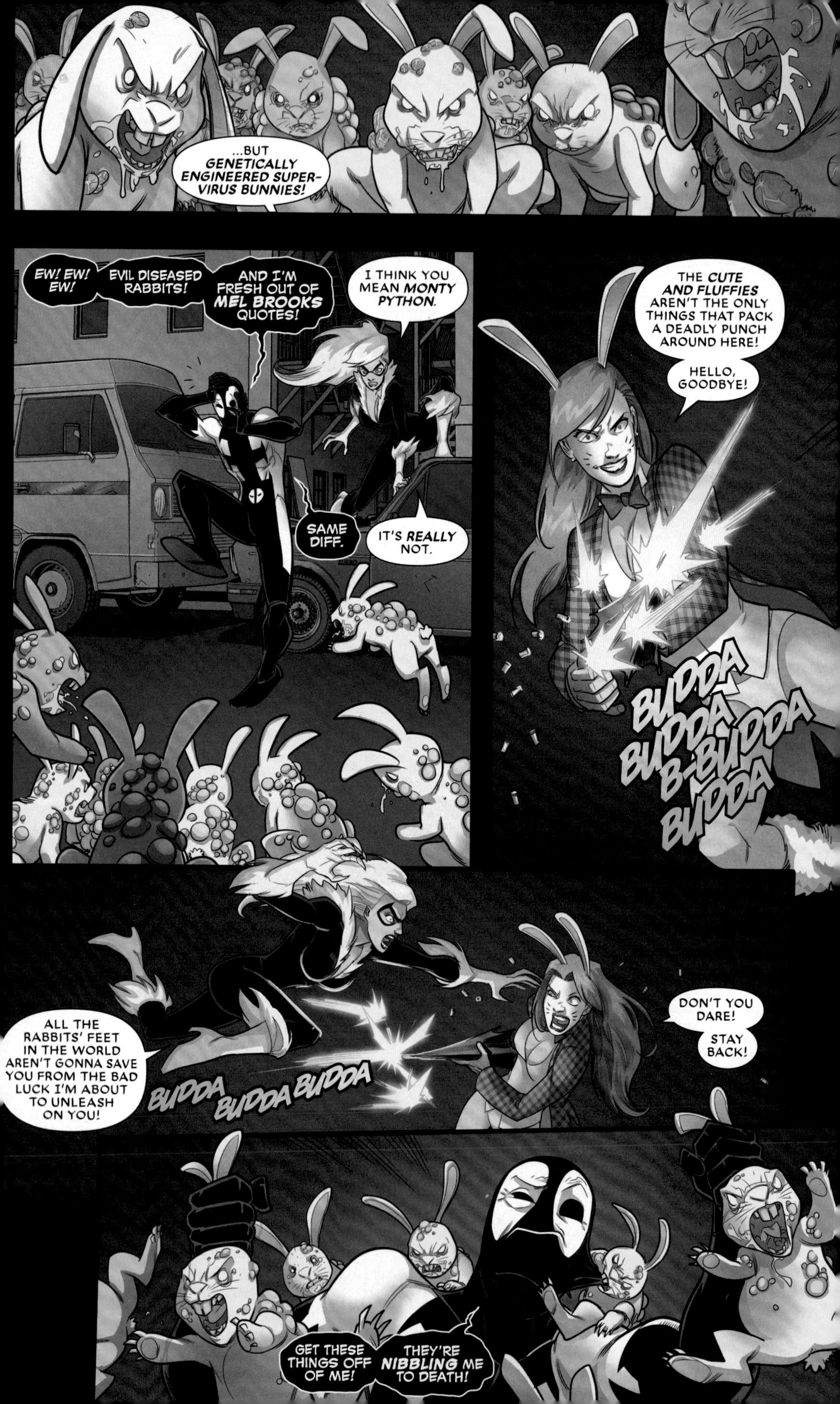
...BUT GENETICALLY ENGINEERED SUPER-VIRUS BUNNIES!
EW! EW! EW!
EVIL DISEASED RABBITS!
AND I'M FRESH OUT OF MEL BROOKS QUOTES!
I THINK YOU MEAN MONTY PYTHON.
SAME DIFF.
IT'S REALLY NOT.
THE CUTE AND FLUFFIES AREN'T THE ONLY THINGS THAT PACK A DEADLY PUNCH AROUND HERE!
HELLO, GOODBYE!
BUDDA BUDDA B-BUDDA BUDDA
ALL THE RABBITS' FEET IN THE WORLD AREN'T GONNA SAVE YOU FROM THE BAD LUCK I'M ABOUT TO UNLEASH ON YOU!
BUDDA BUDDA BUDDA
DON'T YOU DARE!
STAY BACK!
GET THESE THINGS OFF OF ME!
THEY'RE NIBBLING ME TO DEATH!

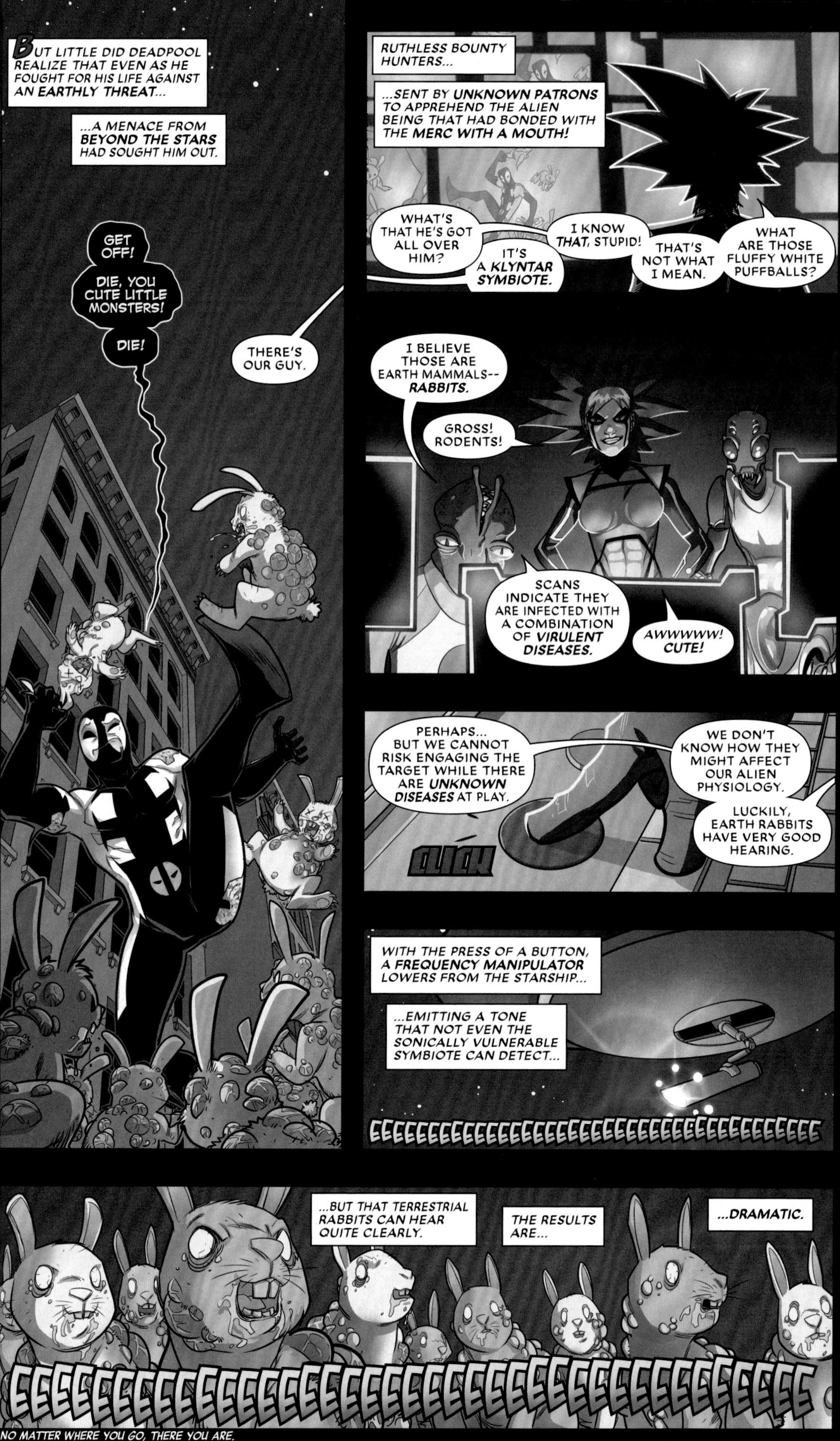
BUT LITTLE DID DEADPOOL REALIZE THAT EVEN AS HE FOUGHT FOR HIS LIFE AGAINST AN EARTHLY THREAT...
...A MENACE FROM BEYOND THE STARS HAD SOUGHT HIM OUT.
GET OFF!
DIE, YOU CUTE LITTLE MONSTERS!
DIE!
THERE'S OUR GUY.
RUTHLESS BOUNTY HUNTERS...
...SENT BY UNKNOWN PATRONS TO APPREHEND THE ALIEN BEING THAT HAD BONDED WITH THE MERC WITH A MOUTH!
WHAT'S THAT HE'S GOT ALL OVER HIM?
IT'S A KLYNTAR SYMBIOTE.
I KNOW THAT, STUPID!
THAT'S NOT WHAT I MEAN.
WHAT ARE THOSE FLUFFY WHITE PUFFBALLS?
I BELIEVE THOSE ARE EARTH MAMMALS-- RABBITS.
GROSS! RODENTS!
SCANS INDICATE THEY ARE INFECTED WITH A COMBINATION OF VIRULENT DISEASES.
AWWWWW! CUTE!
PERHAPS... BUT WE CANNOT RISK ENGAGING THE TARGET WHILE THERE ARE UNKNOWN DISEASES AT PLAY.
WE DON'T KNOW HOW THEY MIGHT AFFECT OUR ALIEN PHYSIOLOGY.
LUCKILY, EARTH RABBITS HAVE VERY GOOD HEARING.
CLICK
WITH THE PRESS OF A BUTTON, A FREQUENCY MANIPULATOR LOWERS FROM THE STARSHIP...
...EMITTING A TONE THAT NOT EVEN THE SONICALLY VULNERABLE SYMBIOTE CAN DETECT...
EEEEEEEEEEEEEEEEEEEEEEEEEEEEEEEEEEEEEEEEEEEEE
...BUT THAT TERRESTRIAL RABBITS CAN HEAR QUITE CLEARLY.
THE RESULTS ARE...
...DRAMATIC.
EEEEEEEEEEEEEEEEEEEEEEEEEEEEEEEEEEEEEEEEEEEE
NO MATTER WHERE YOU GO, THERE YOU ARE.

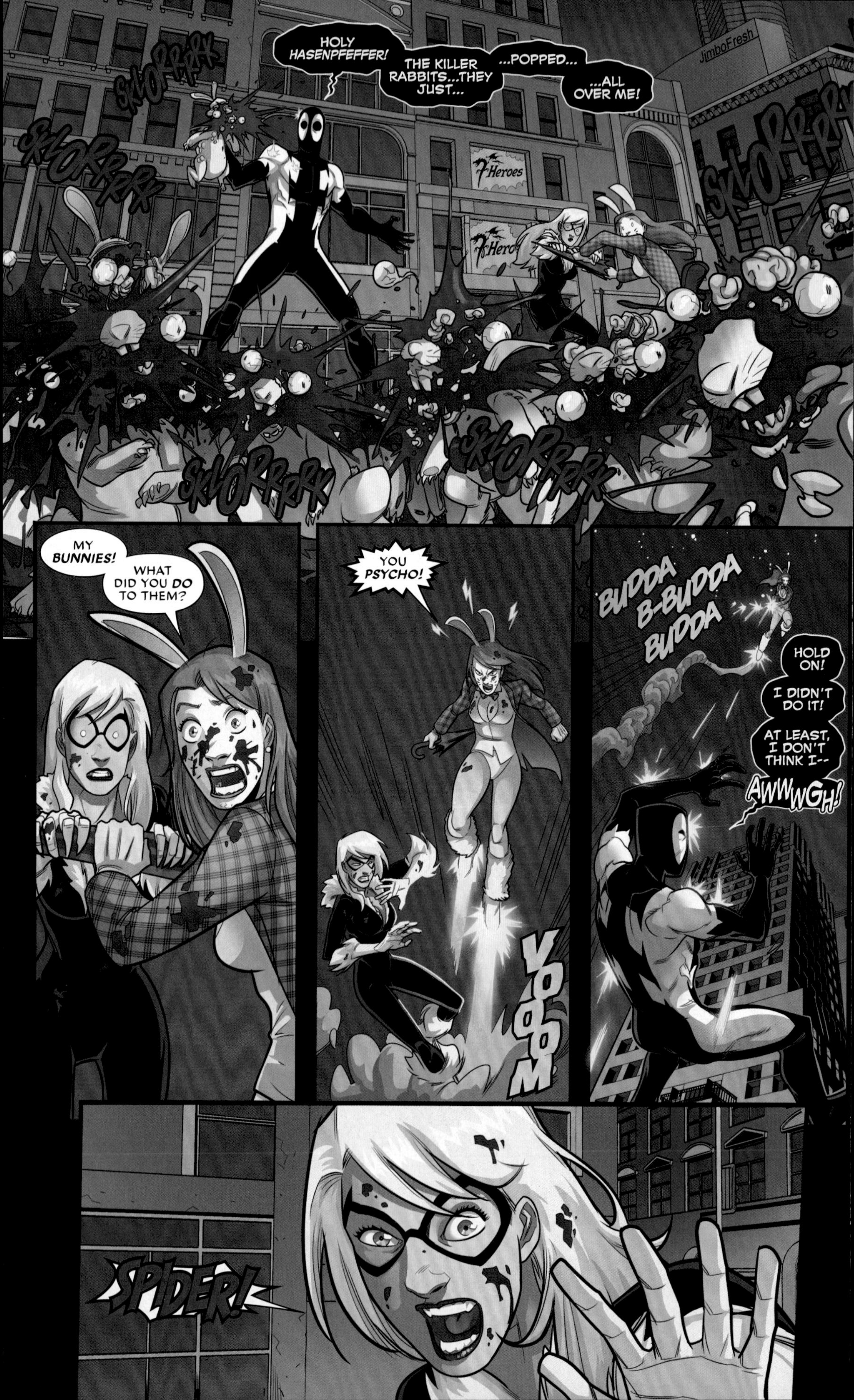
SKLORRRK
SKLORRRRK
HOLY HASENPFEFFER!
THE KILLER RABBITS...THEY JUST...
...POPPED...
...ALL OVER ME!
JimboFresh
Heroes
Heroes
SKLORRRK
SKLORRRRK
SKLORRRRK
MY BUNNIES!
WHAT DID YOU DO TO THEM?
YOU PSYCHO!
VOOOM
BUDDA B-BUDDA BUDDA
HOLD ON!
I DIDN'T DO IT!
AT LEAST, I DON'T THINK I--
AWWWGH!
SPIDER!

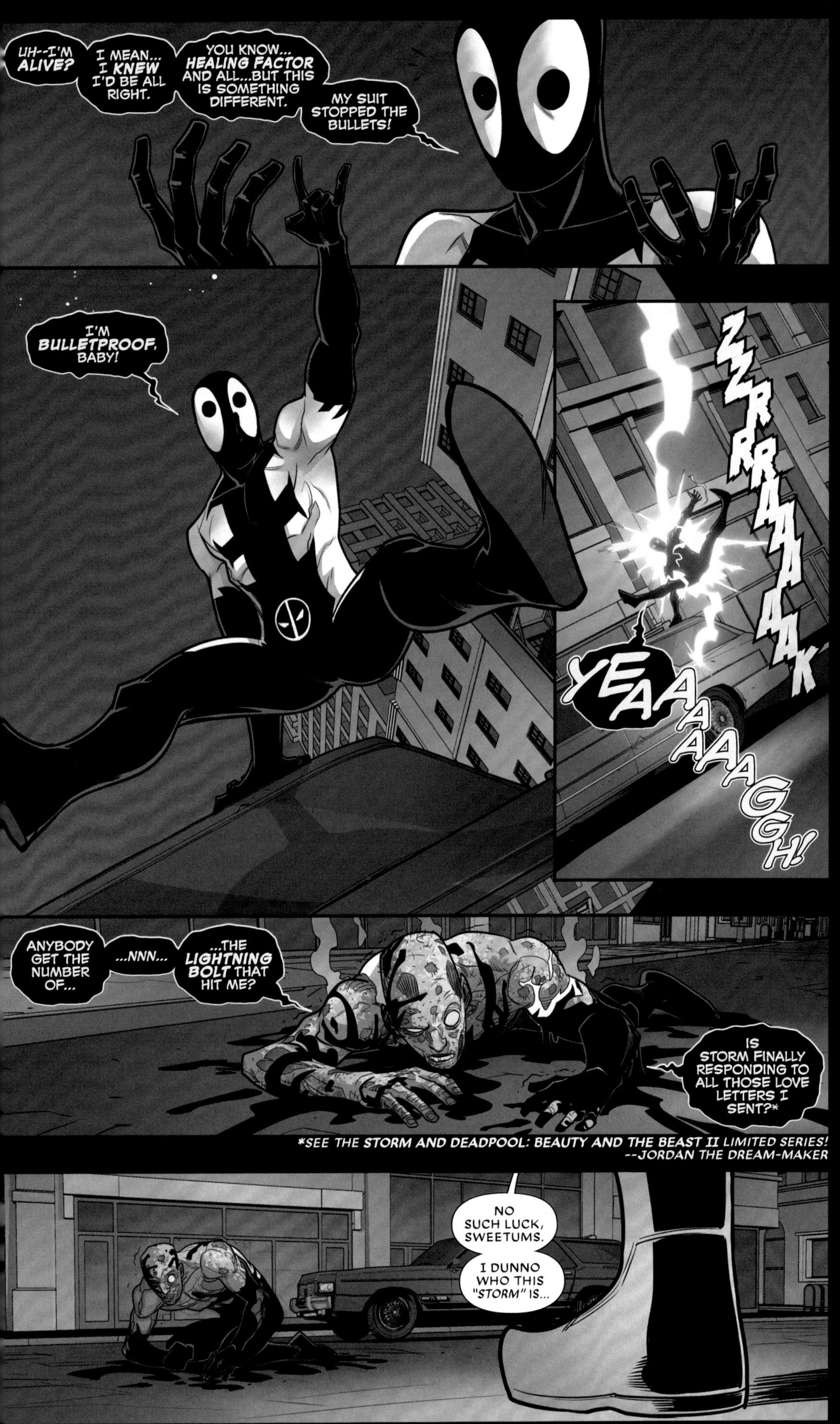

UH--I'M ALIVE?
I MEAN... I KNEW I'D BE ALL RIGHT.
YOU KNOW... HEALING FACTOR AND ALL...BUT THIS IS SOMETHING DIFFERENT.
MY SUIT STOPPED THE BULLETS!
I'M BULLETPROOF, BABY!
ZZRRRAAAAAK
YEAAAAAAAGH!
ANYBODY GET THE NUMBER OF...
...NNN...
...THE LIGHTNING BOLT THAT HIT ME?
IS STORM FINALLY RESPONDING TO ALL THOSE LOVE LETTERS I SENT?*
*SEE THE STORM AND DEADPOOL: BEAUTY AND THE BEAST II LIMITED SERIES! --JORDAN THE DREAM-MAKER
NO SUCH LUCK, SWEETUMS.
I DUNNO WHO THIS "STORM" IS...

AT SOME POINT, THIS STORY WAS CONTINUED FROM...OR WILL BE CONTINUED ON...ANOTHER PAGE.

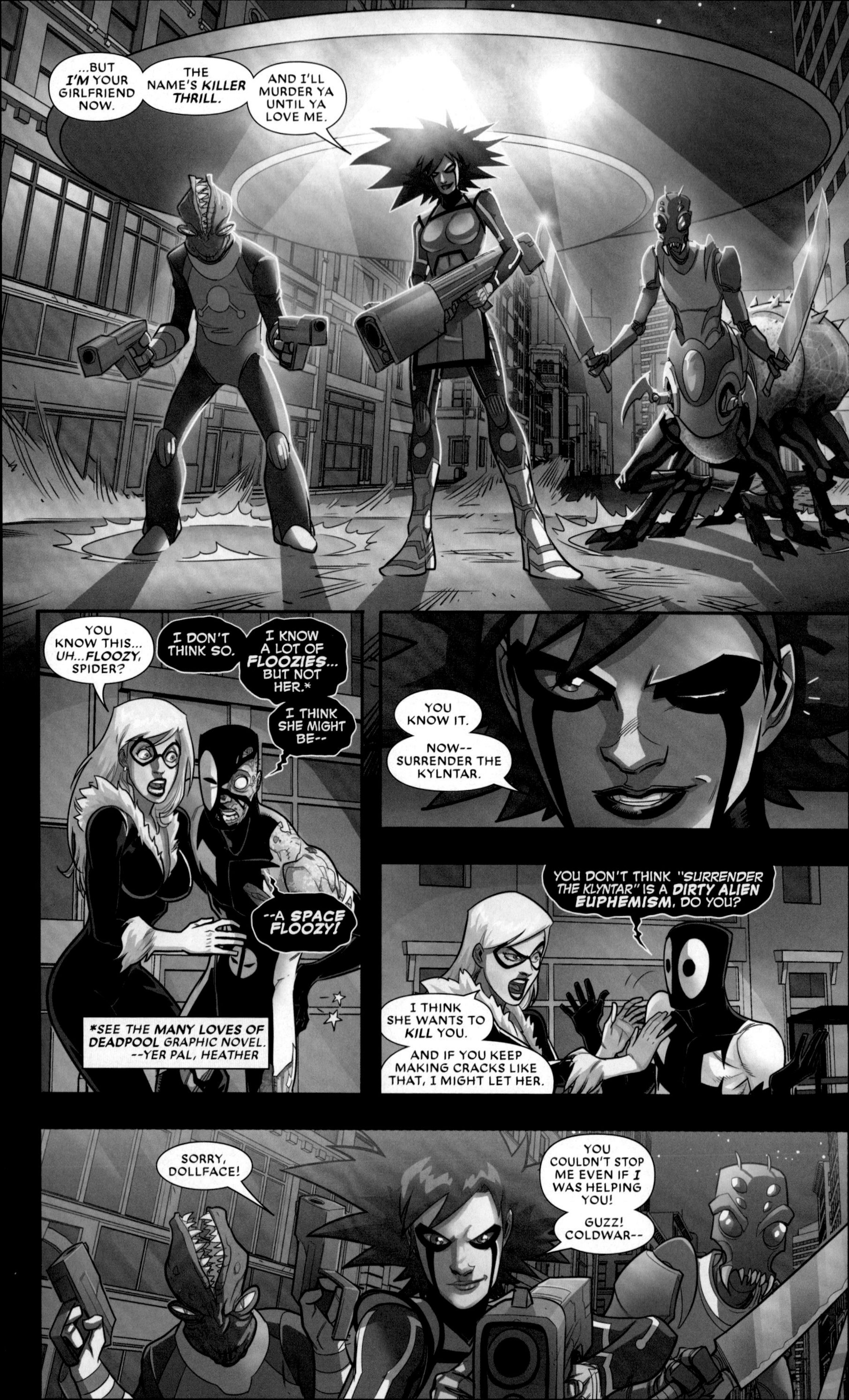
...BUT I'M YOUR GIRLFRIEND NOW.
THE NAME'S KILLER THRILL.
AND I'LL MURDER YA UNTIL YA LOVE ME.
YOU KNOW THIS... UH...FLOOZY, SPIDER?
I DON'T THINK SO.
I KNOW A LOT OF FLOOZIES... BUT NOT HER.*
I THINK SHE MIGHT BE--
--A SPACE FLOOZY!
*SEE THE MANY LOVES OF DEADPOOL GRAPHIC NOVEL. --YER PAL, HEATHER
YOU KNOW IT.
NOW-- SURRENDER THE KYLNTAR.
YOU DON'T THINK "SURRENDER THE KLYNTAR" IS A DIRTY ALIEN EUPHEMISM, DO YOU?
I THINK SHE WANTS TO KILL YOU.
AND IF YOU KEEP MAKING CRACKS LIKE THAT, I MIGHT LET HER.
SORRY, DOLLFACE!
YOU COULDN'T STOP ME EVEN IF I WAS HELPING YOU!
GUZZ! COLDWAR--

CONTINUED AFTER NEXT PAGE

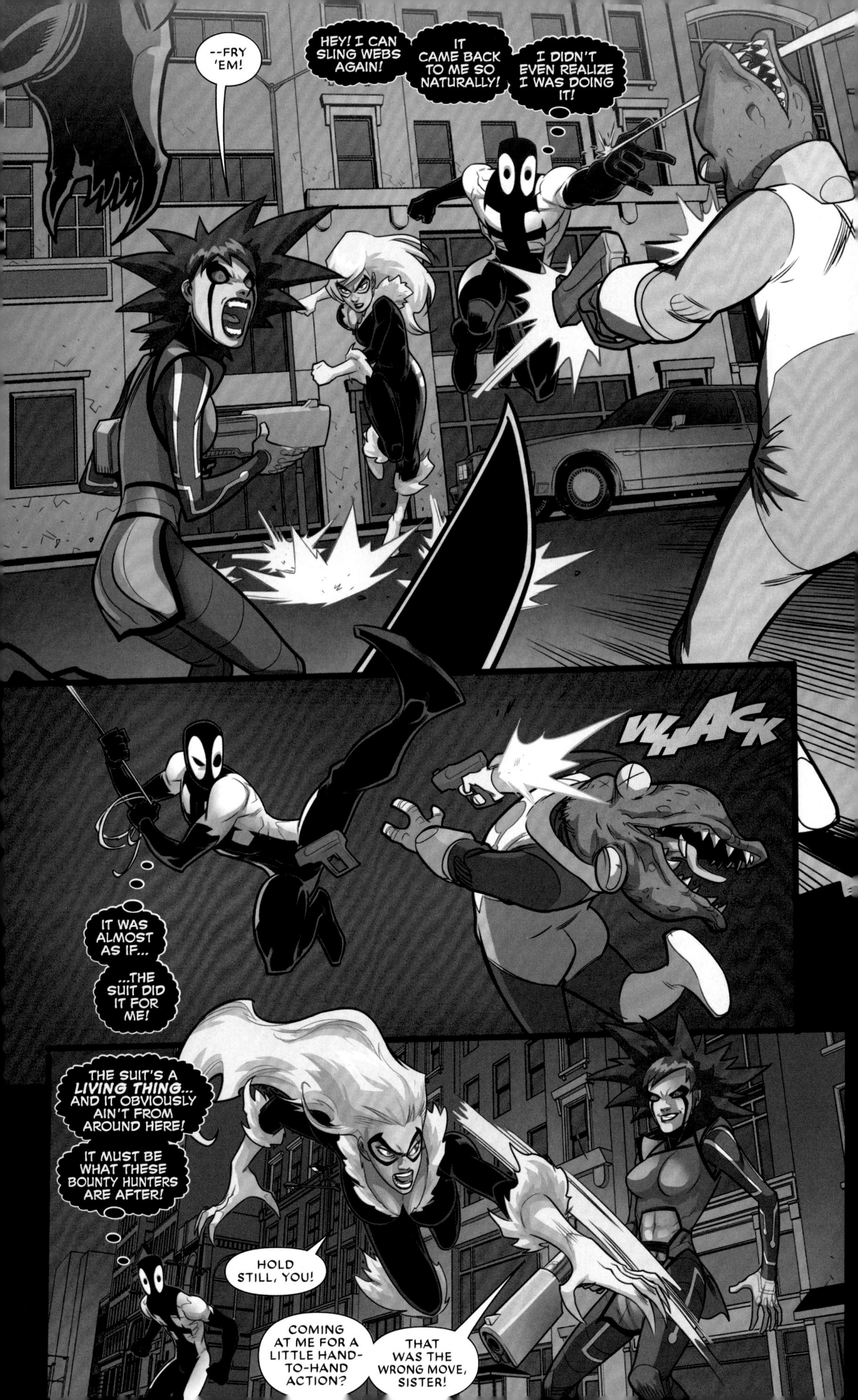
--FRY 'EM!
HEY! I CAN SLING WEBS AGAIN!
IT CAME BACK TO ME SO NATURALLY!
I DIDN'T EVEN REALIZE I WAS DOING IT!
WHACK
IT WAS ALMOST AS IF...
...THE SUIT DID IT FOR ME!
THE SUIT'S A LIVING THING... AND IT OBVIOUSLY AIN'T FROM AROUND HERE!
IT MUST BE WHAT THESE BOUNTY HUNTERS ARE AFTER!
HOLD STILL, YOU!
COMING AT ME FOR A LITTLE HAND-TO-HAND ACTION?
THAT WAS THE WRONG MOVE, SISTER!

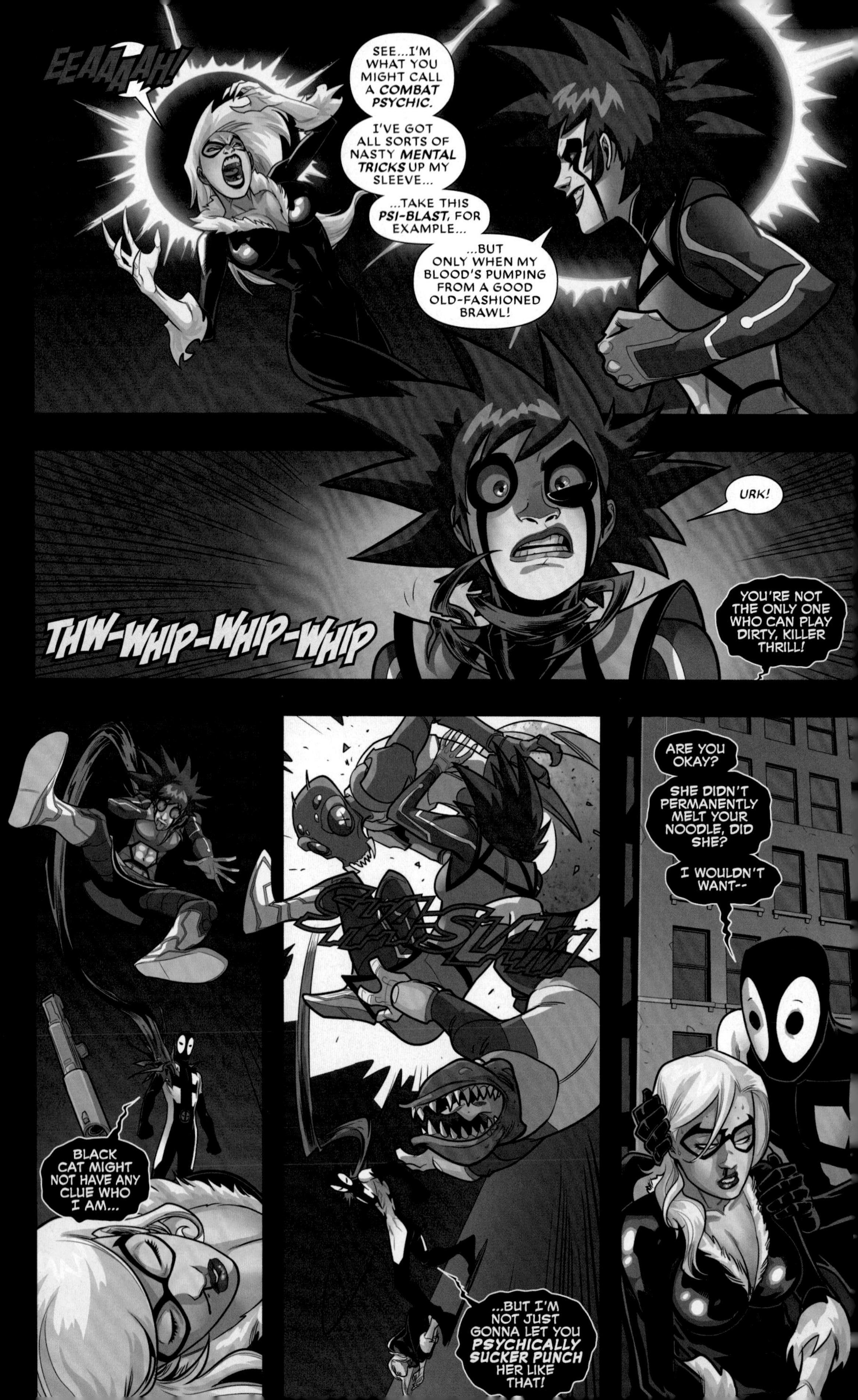

EEAAAAH!
SEE...I'M WHAT YOU MIGHT CALL A *COMBAT PSYCHIC.*
I'VE GOT ALL SORTS OF NASTY *MENTAL TRICKS* UP MY SLEEVE...
...TAKE THIS *PSI-BLAST*, FOR EXAMPLE...
...BUT ONLY WHEN MY BLOOD'S PUMPING FROM A GOOD OLD-FASHIONED BRAWL!
URK!
THW-WHIP-WHIP-WHIP
YOU'RE NOT THE ONLY ONE WHO CAN PLAY DIRTY, KILLER THRILL!
BLACK CAT MIGHT NOT HAVE ANY CLUE WHO I AM...
...BUT I'M NOT JUST GONNA LET YOU *PSYCHICALLY SUCKER PUNCH* HER LIKE THAT!
ARE YOU OKAY?
SHE DIDN'T PERMANENTLY MELT YOUR NOODLE, DID SHE?
I WOULDN'T WANT--

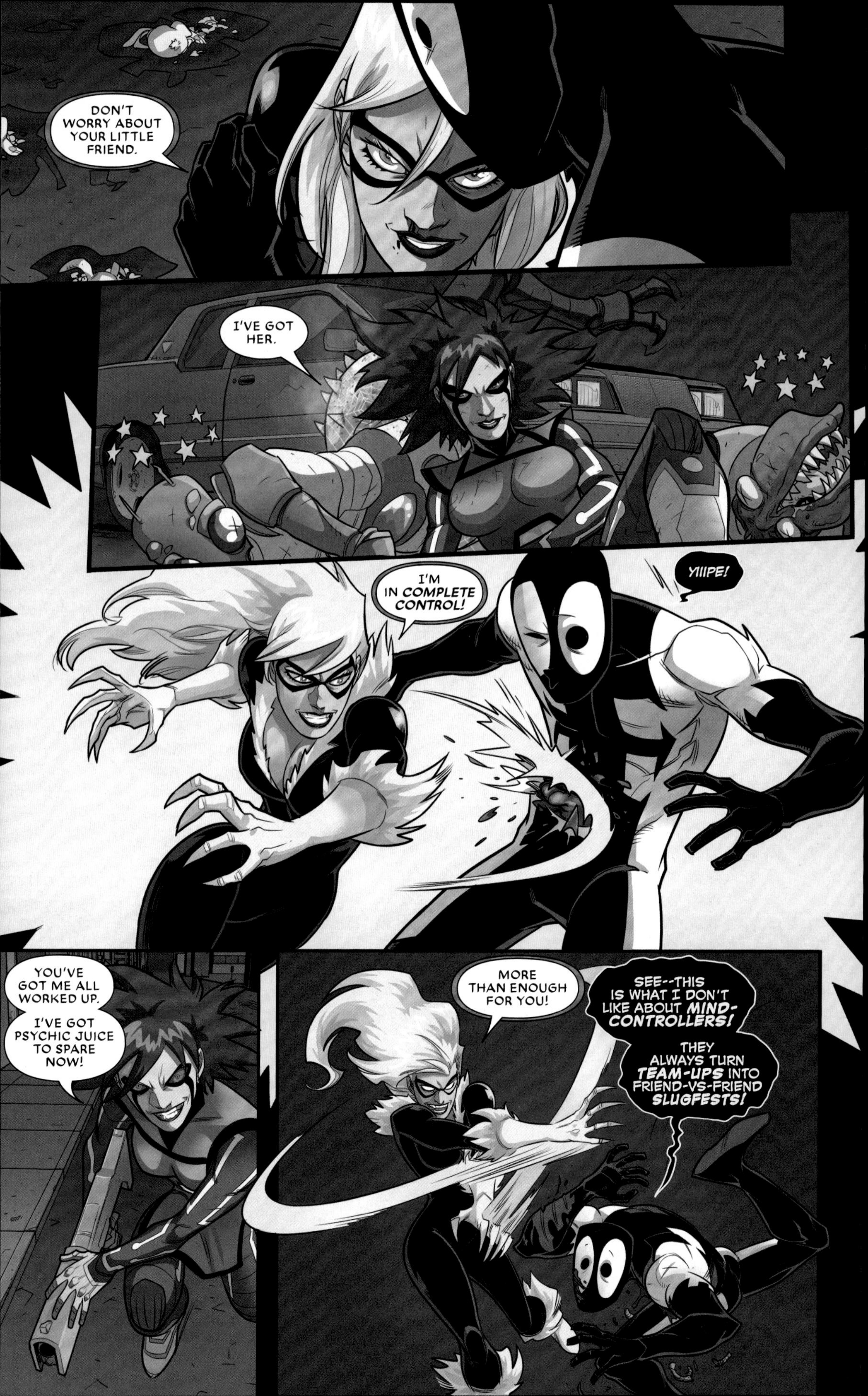
DON'T WORRY ABOUT YOUR LITTLE FRIEND.
I'VE GOT HER.
I'M IN COMPLETE CONTROL!
YIIIPE!
YOU'VE GOT ME ALL WORKED UP.
I'VE GOT PSYCHIC JUICE TO SPARE NOW!
MORE THAN ENOUGH FOR YOU!
SEE--THIS IS WHAT I DON'T LIKE ABOUT MIND-CONTROLLERS!
THEY ALWAYS TURN TEAM-UPS INTO FRIEND-VS-FRIEND SLUGFESTS!

CONTINUED AFTER NEXT PAGE

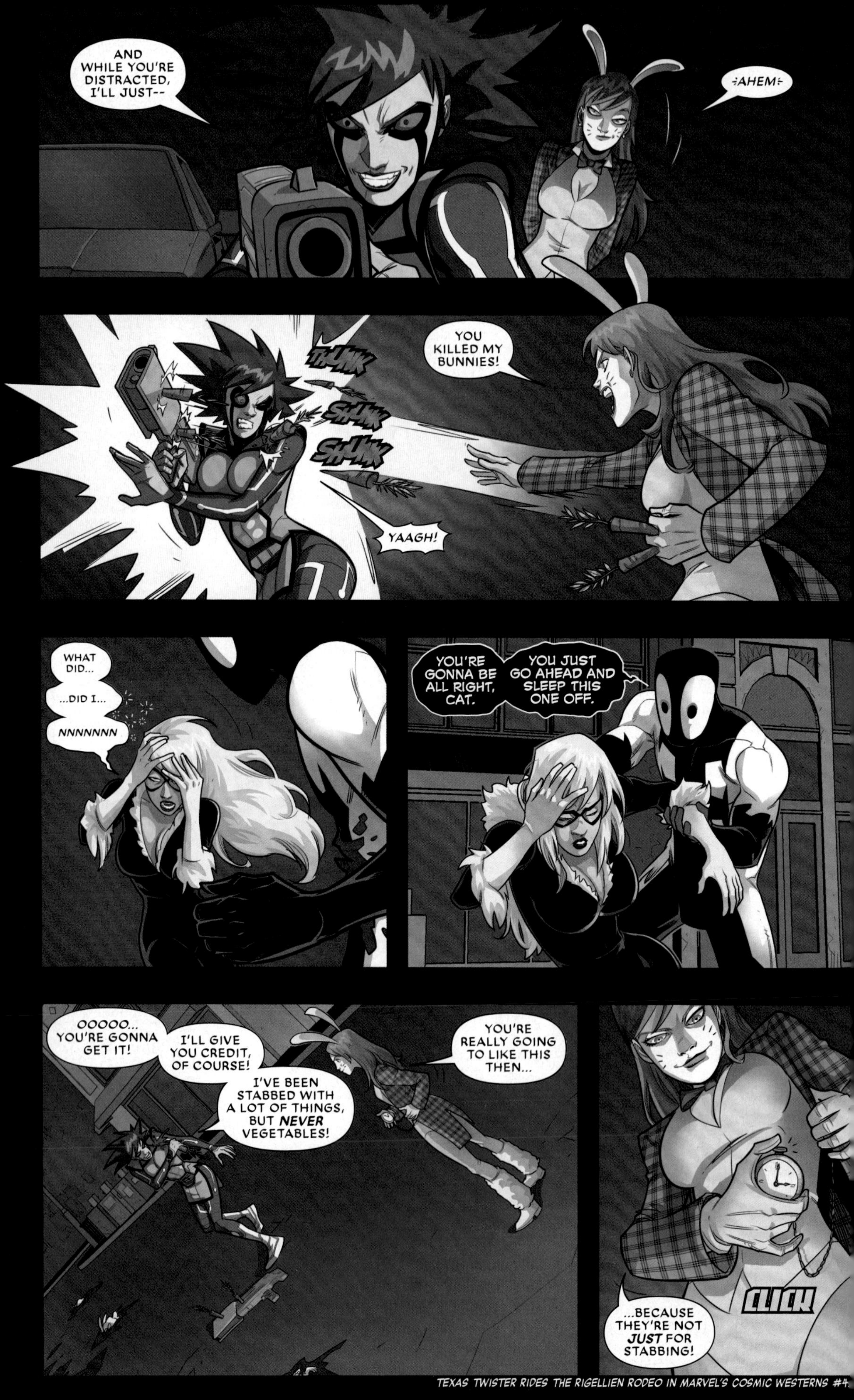
AND WHILE YOU'RE DISTRACTED, I'LL JUST--
AHEM
YOU KILLED MY BUNNIES!
THUNK
SHUNK
SHUNK
YAAGH!
WHAT DID...
...DID I...
NNNNNNN
YOU'RE GONNA BE ALL RIGHT, CAT.
YOU JUST GO AHEAD AND SLEEP THIS ONE OFF.
OOOOO... YOU'RE GONNA GET IT!
I'LL GIVE YOU CREDIT, OF COURSE!
I'VE BEEN STABBED WITH A LOT OF THINGS, BUT NEVER VEGETABLES!
YOU'RE REALLY GOING TO LIKE THIS THEN...
CLICK
...BECAUSE THEY'RE NOT JUST FOR STABBING!

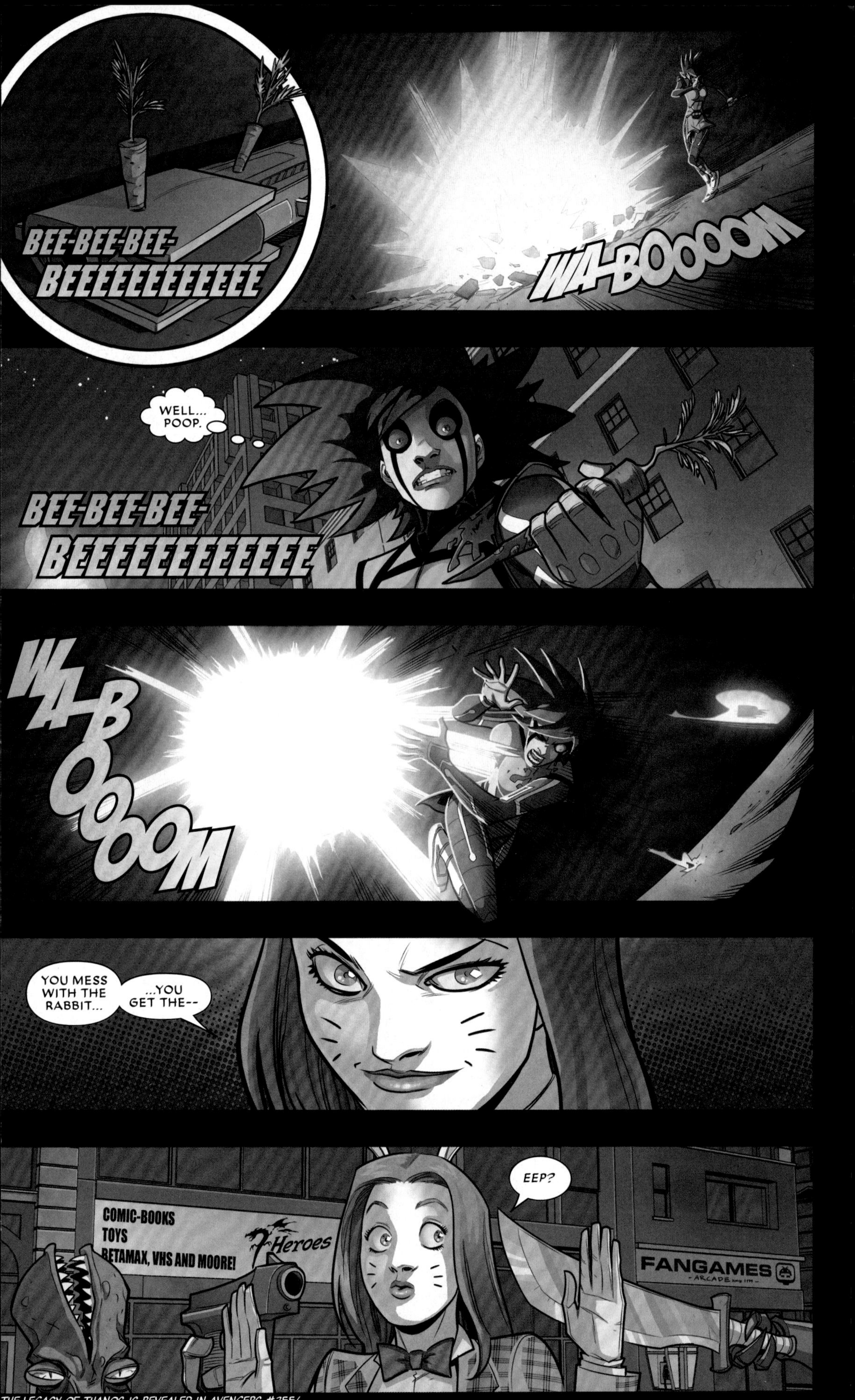
BEE-BEE-BEE-
BEEEEEEEEEEEE
WA-BOOOOM
WELL... POOP.
BEE-BEE-BEE-
BEEEEEEEEEEEE
WA-BOOOOM
YOU MESS WITH THE RABBIT...
...YOU GET THE--
EEP?
COMIC-BOOKS
TOYS
BETAMAX, VHS AND MOORE!
Heroes
FANGAMES
ARCADE

THE LEGACY OF THANOS IS REVEALED IN AVENGERS #255!

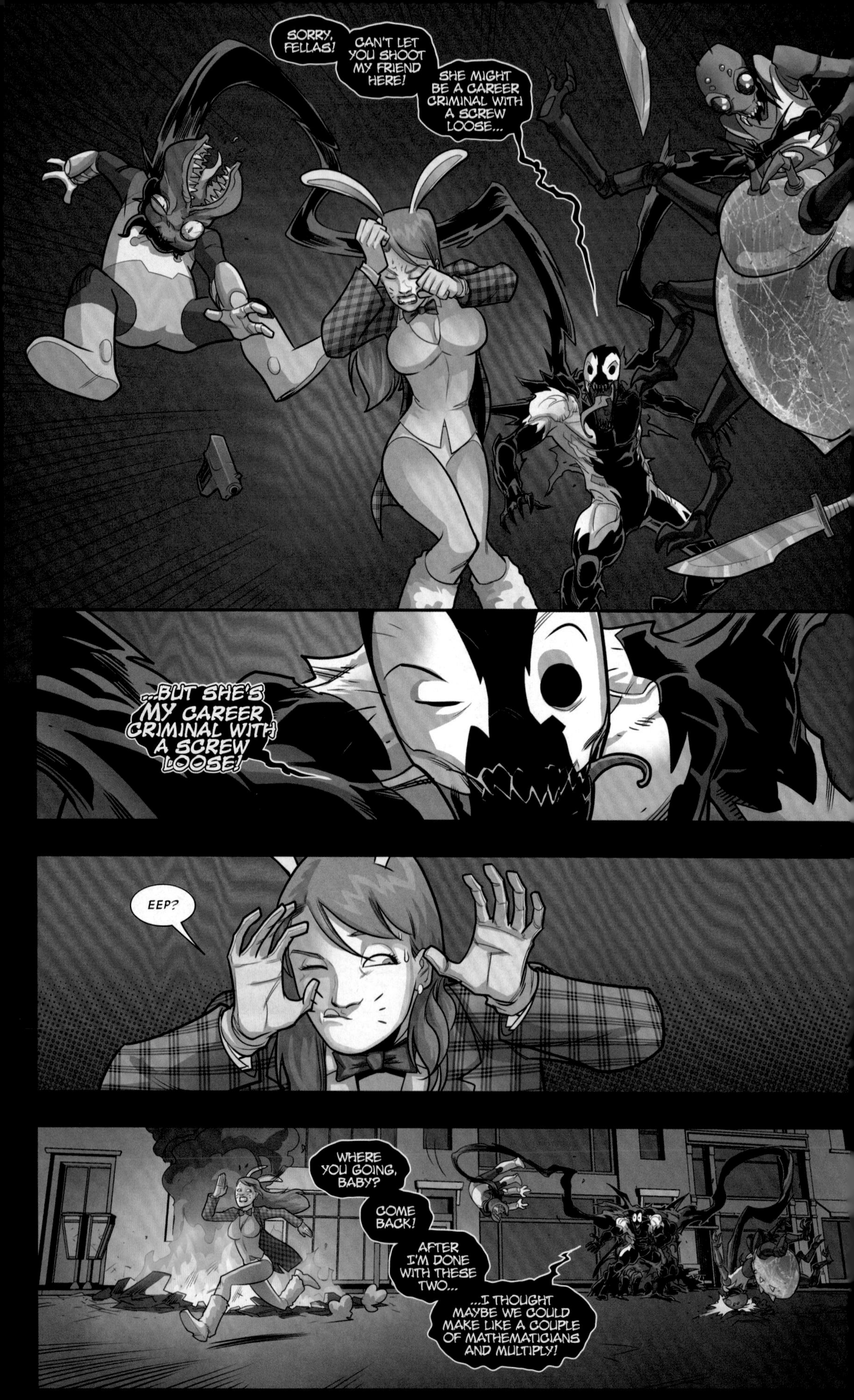
SORRY, FELLAS!
CAN'T LET YOU SHOOT MY FRIEND HERE!
SHE MIGHT BE A CAREER CRIMINAL WITH A SCREW LOOSE...
...BUT SHE'S MY CAREER CRIMINAL WITH A SCREW LOOSE!
EEP?
WHERE YOU GOING, BABY?
COME BACK!
AFTER I'M DONE WITH THESE TWO...
...I THOUGHT MAYBE WE COULD MAKE LIKE A COUPLE OF MATHEMATICIANS AND MULTIPLY!

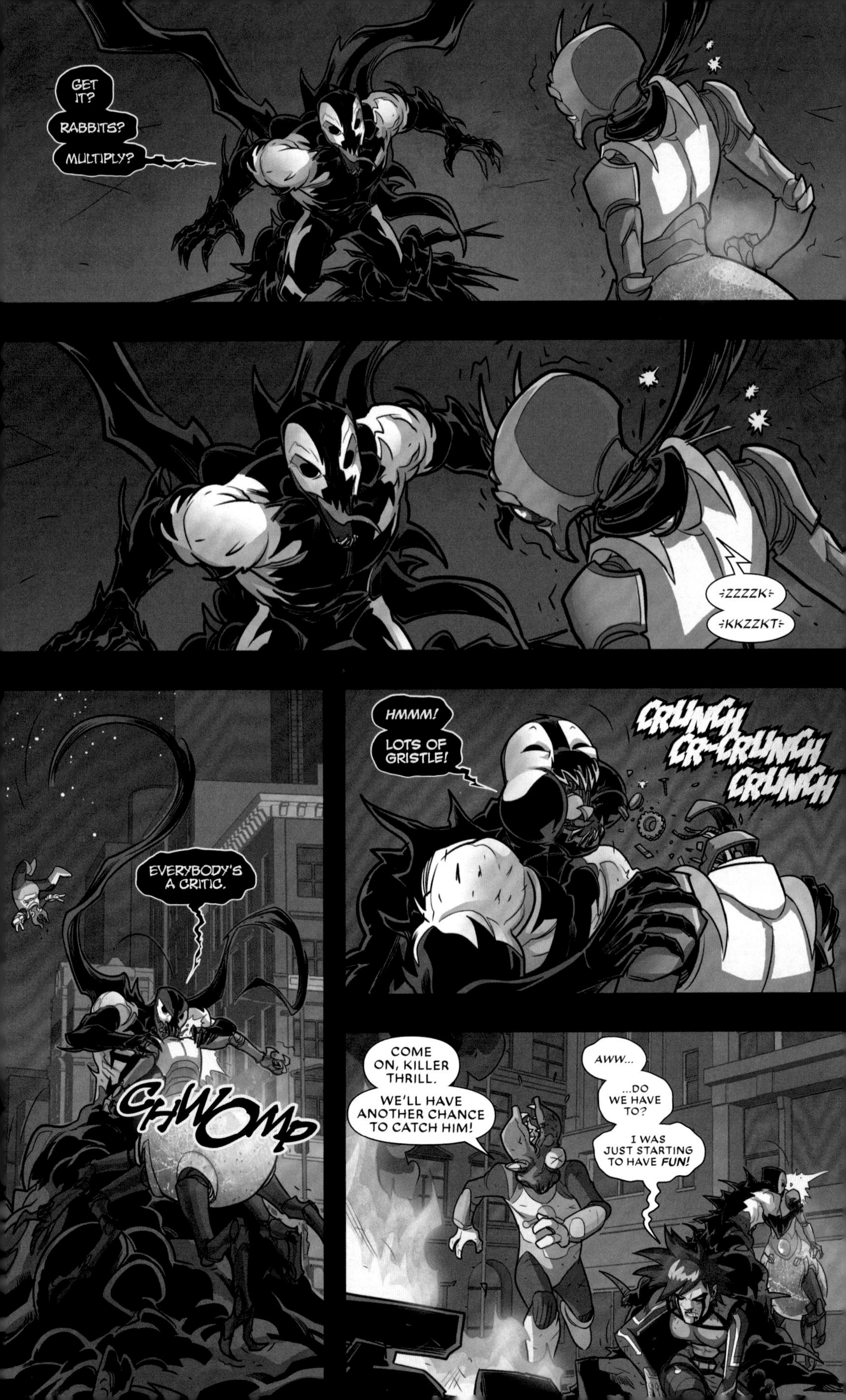
GET IT?
RABBITS?
MULTIPLY?
ZZZZK
KKZZZKT
EVERYBODY'S A CRITIC.
CHWOMP
HMMM!
LOTS OF GRISTLE!
CRUNCH CR-CRUNCH CRUNCH
COME ON, KILLER THRILL.
WE'LL HAVE ANOTHER CHANCE TO CATCH HIM!
AWW...
...DO WE HAVE TO?
I WAS JUST STARTING TO HAVE *FUN!*

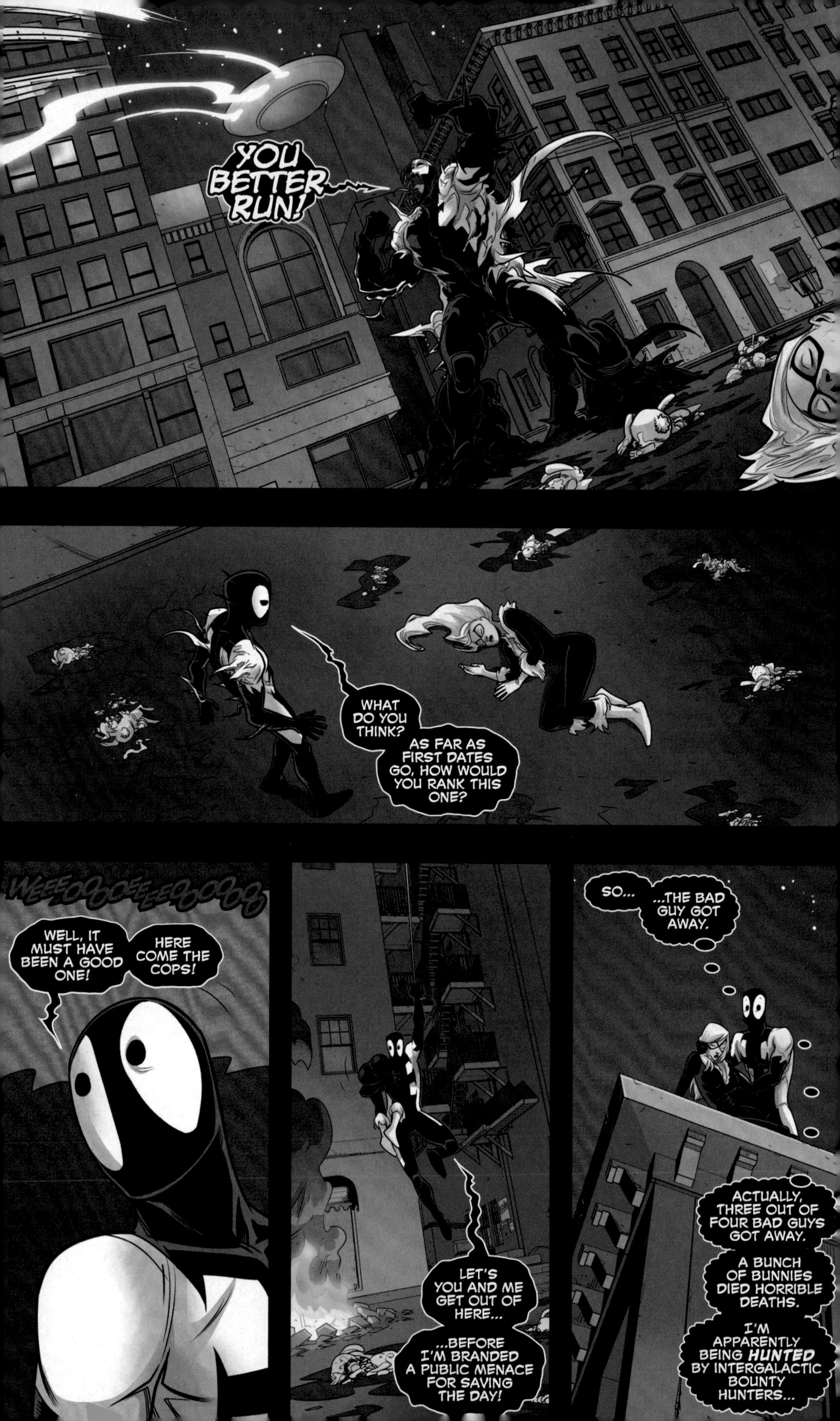
YOU BETTER RUN!
WHAT DO YOU THINK?
AS FAR AS FIRST DATES GO, HOW WOULD YOU RANK THIS ONE?
WEEEOOOOEEEEOOOOOO
WELL, IT MUST HAVE BEEN A GOOD ONE!
HERE COME THE COPS!
LET'S YOU AND ME GET OUT OF HERE...
...BEFORE I'M BRANDED A PUBLIC MENACE FOR SAVING THE DAY!
SO...
...THE BAD GUY GOT AWAY.
ACTUALLY, THREE OUT OF FOUR BAD GUYS GOT AWAY.
A BUNCH OF BUNNIES DIED HORRIBLE DEATHS.
I'M APPARENTLY BEING HUNTED BY INTERGALACTIC BOUNTY HUNTERS...

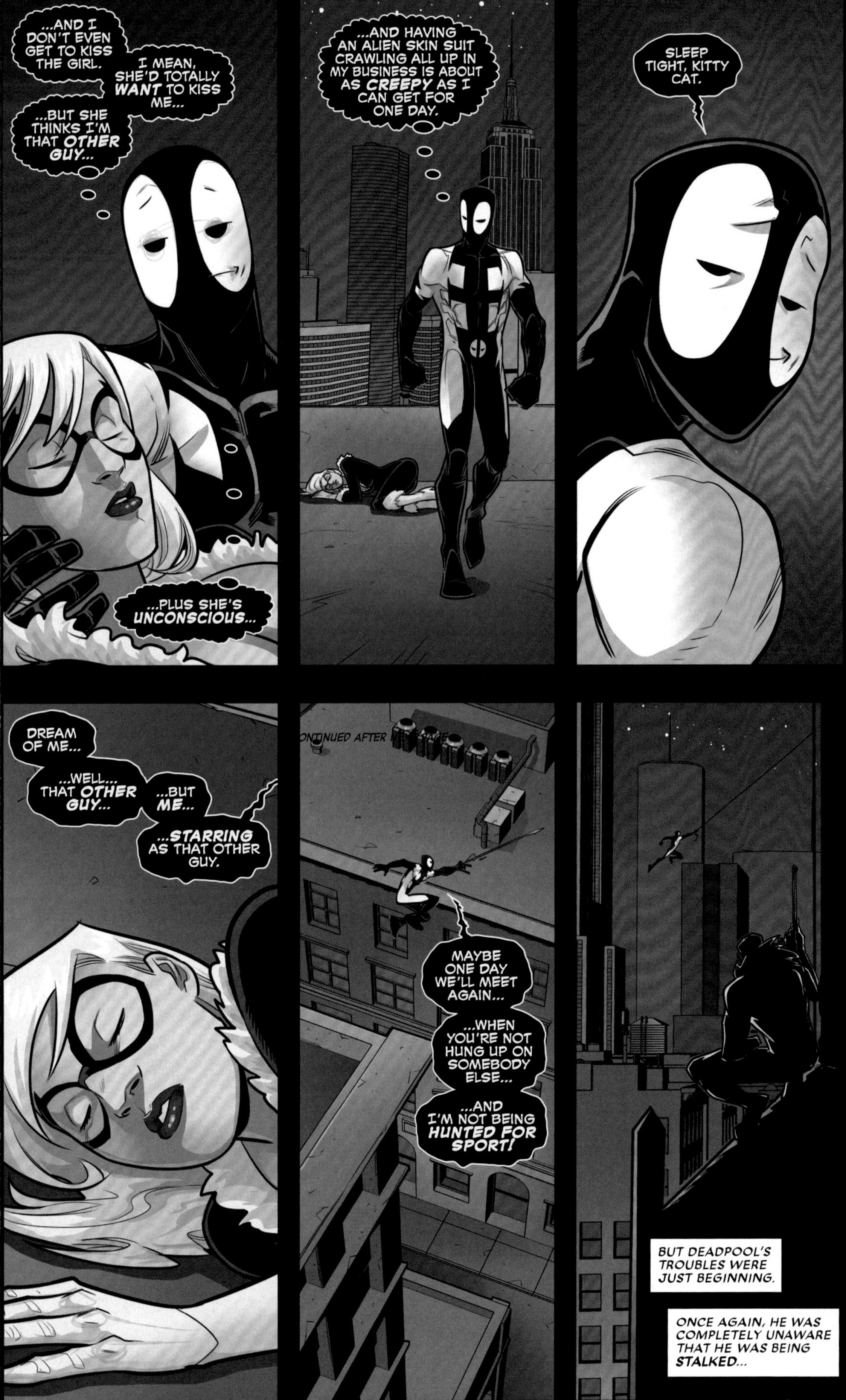
...AND I DON'T EVEN GET TO KISS THE GIRL.
I MEAN, SHE'D TOTALLY WANT TO KISS ME...
...BUT SHE THINKS I'M THAT OTHER GUY...
...PLUS SHE'S UNCONSCIOUS...
...AND HAVING AN ALIEN SKIN SUIT CRAWLING ALL UP IN MY BUSINESS IS ABOUT AS CREEPY AS I CAN GET FOR ONE DAY.
SLEEP TIGHT, KITTY CAT.
DREAM OF ME...
...WELL... THAT OTHER GUY...
...BUT ME...
...STARRING AS THAT OTHER GUY.
MAYBE ONE DAY WE'LL MEET AGAIN...
...WHEN YOU'RE NOT HUNG UP ON SOMEBODY ELSE...
...AND I'M NOT BEING HUNTED FOR SPORT!
BUT DEADPOOL'S TROUBLES WERE JUST BEGINNING.
ONCE AGAIN, HE WAS COMPLETELY UNAWARE THAT HE WAS BEING STALKED...

CONTINUED AFTER NEXT PAGE

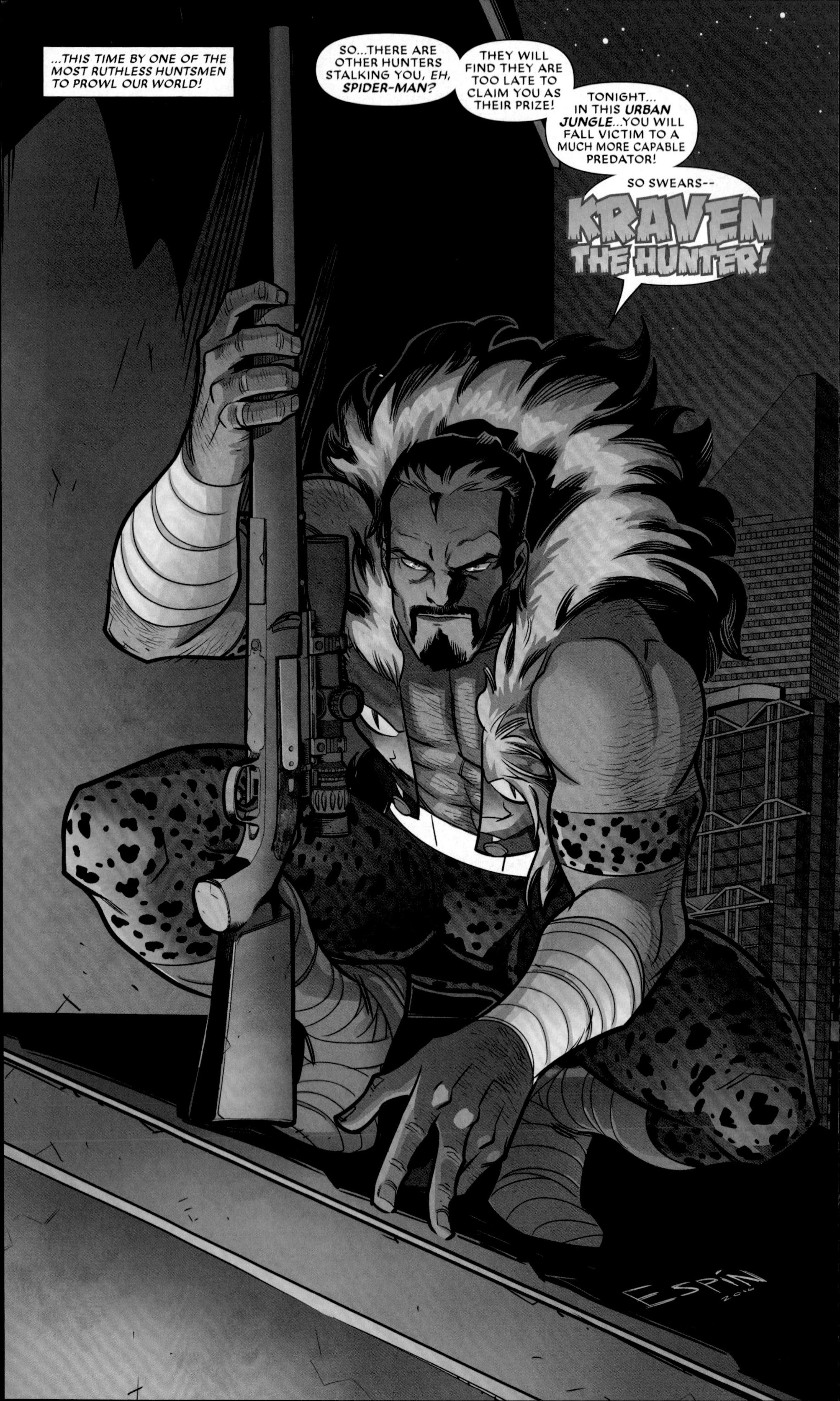
...THIS TIME BY ONE OF THE MOST RUTHLESS HUNTSMEN TO PROWL OUR WORLD!
SO...THERE ARE OTHER HUNTERS STALKING YOU, EH, SPIDER-MAN?
THEY WILL FIND THEY ARE TOO LATE TO CLAIM YOU AS THEIR PRIZE!
TONIGHT... IN THIS URBAN JUNGLE...YOU WILL FALL VICTIM TO A MUCH MORE CAPABLE PREDATOR!
SO SWEARS-- KRAVEN THE HUNTER!
ESPÍN 2016

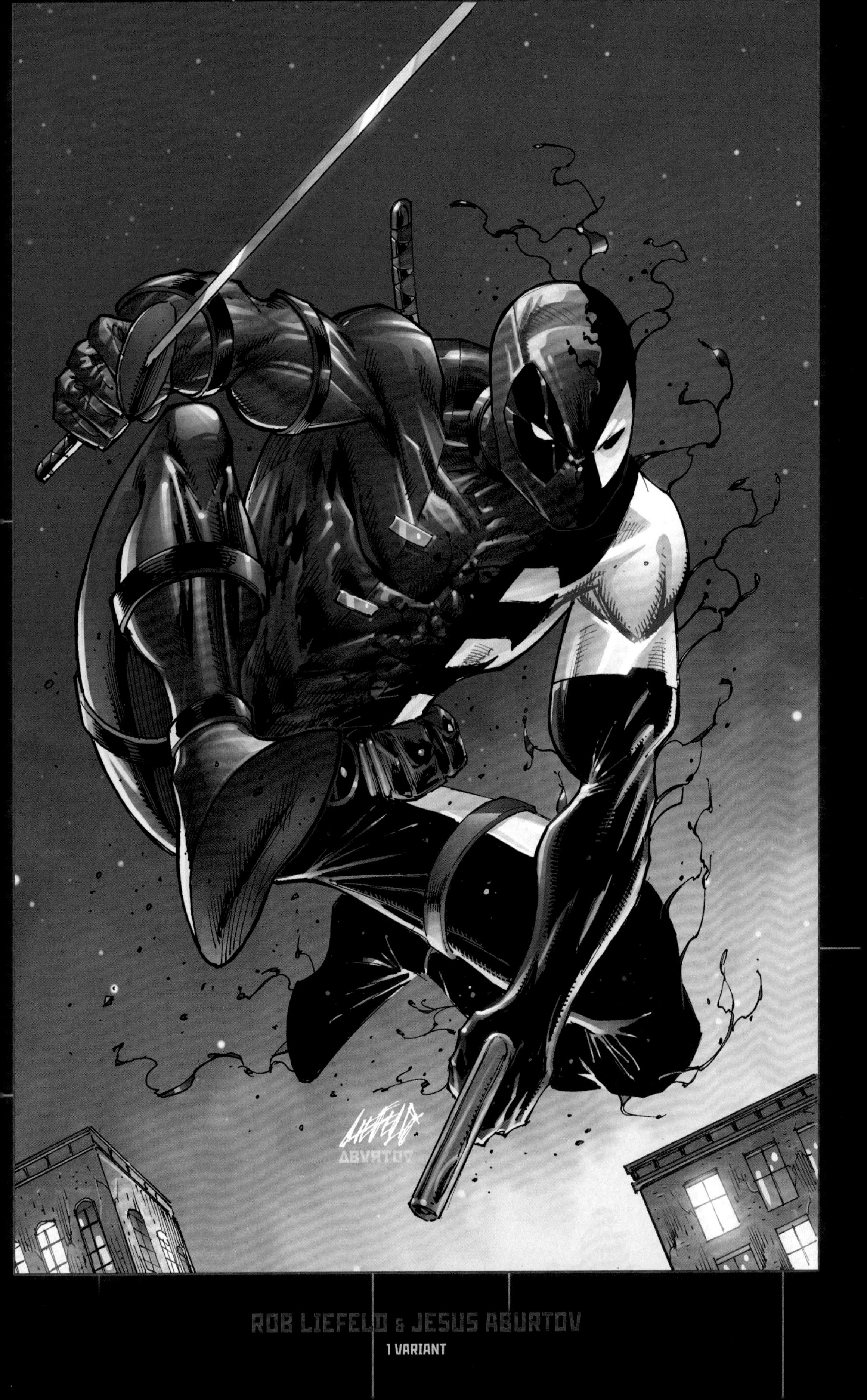
LIEFELD
ABURTOV

ROB LIEFELD & JESUS ABURTOV
1 VARIANT

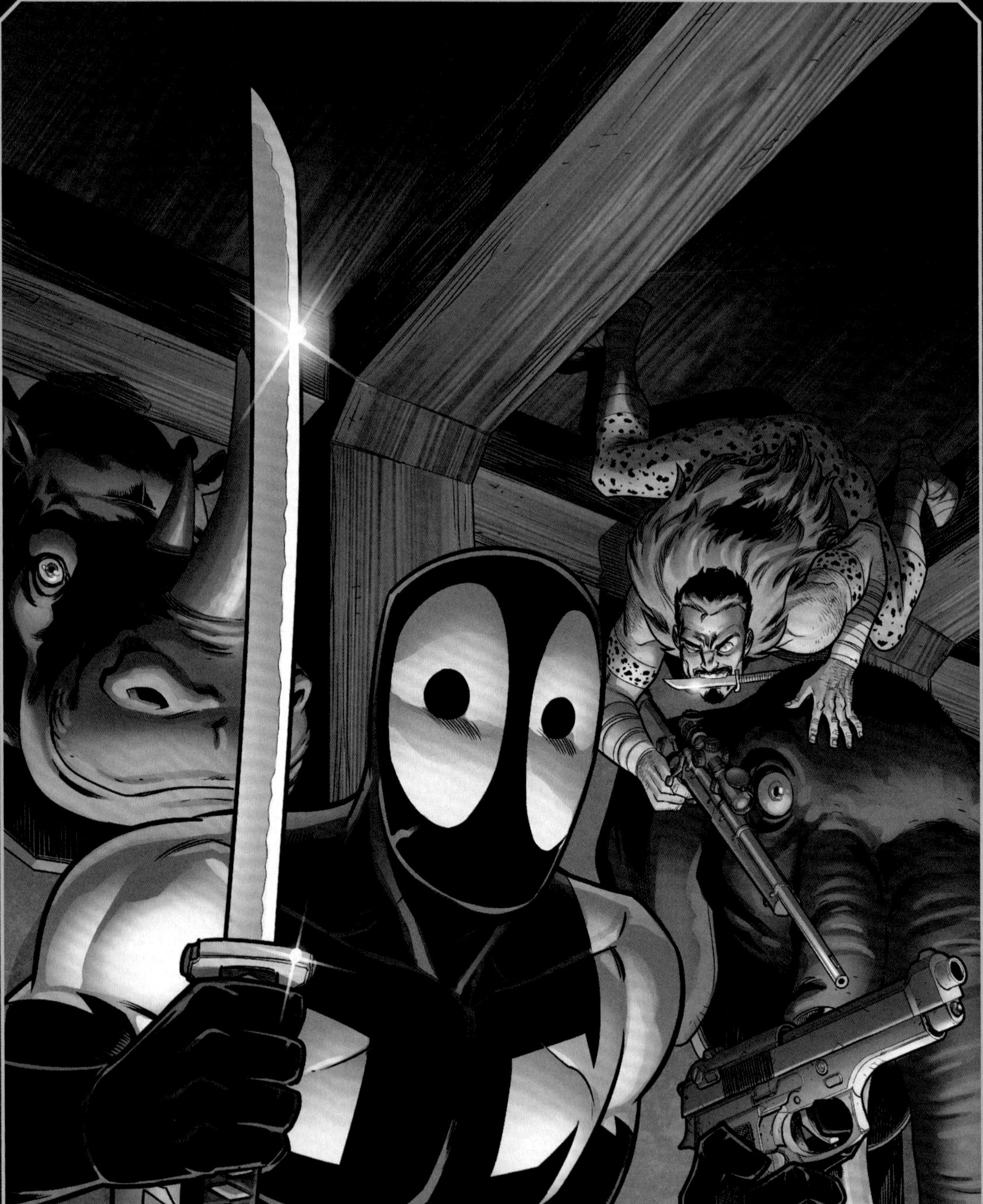
With apologies to Mike Zeck!
Salva Espín 2016

4

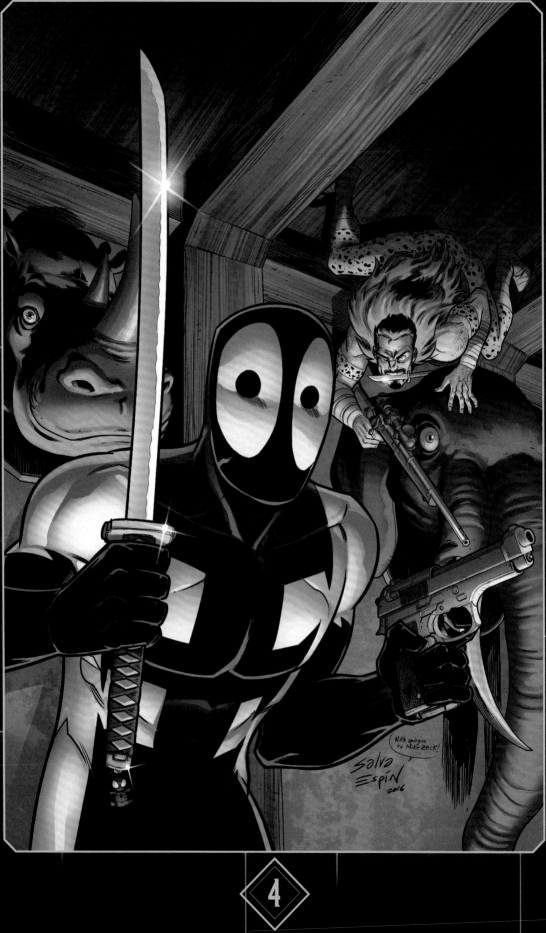

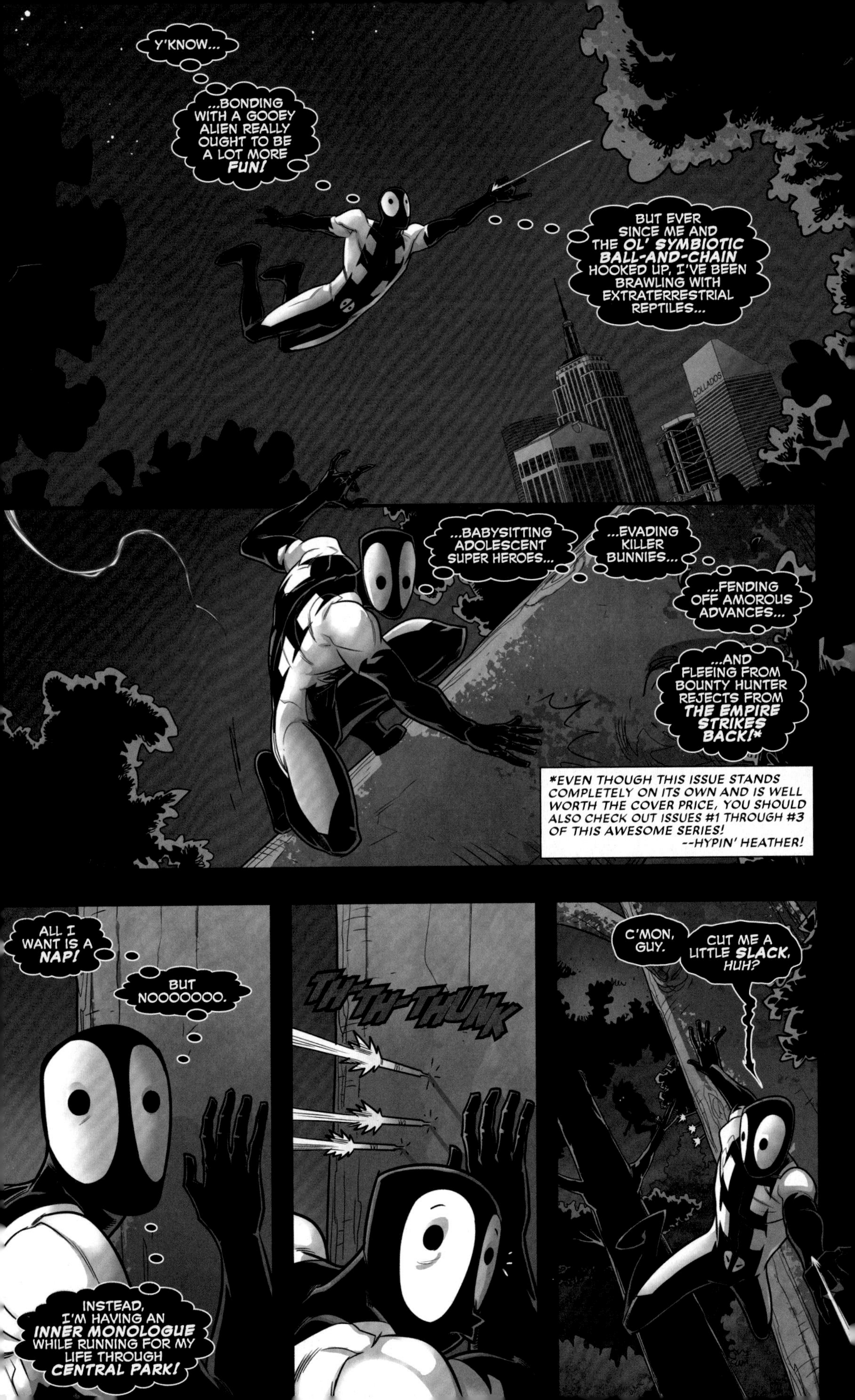
Y'KNOW...
...BONDING WITH A GOOEY ALIEN REALLY OUGHT TO BE A LOT MORE FUN!
BUT EVER SINCE ME AND THE OL' SYMBIOTIC BALL-AND-CHAIN HOOKED UP, I'VE BEEN BRAWLING WITH EXTRATERRESTRIAL REPTILES...
COLLADOS
...BABYSITTING ADOLESCENT SUPER HEROES...
...EVADING KILLER BUNNIES...
...FENDING OFF AMOROUS ADVANCES...
...AND FLEEING FROM BOUNTY HUNTER REJECTS FROM THE EMPIRE STRIKES BACK!*
*EVEN THOUGH THIS ISSUE STANDS COMPLETELY ON ITS OWN AND IS WELL WORTH THE COVER PRICE, YOU SHOULD ALSO CHECK OUT ISSUES #1 THROUGH #3 OF THIS AWESOME SERIES! --HYPIN' HEATHER!
ALL I WANT IS A NAP!
BUT NOOOOOOO.
INSTEAD, I'M HAVING AN INNER MONOLOGUE WHILE RUNNING FOR MY LIFE THROUGH CENTRAL PARK!
TH-TH-THUNK
C'MON, GUY.
CUT ME A LITTLE SLACK, HUH?

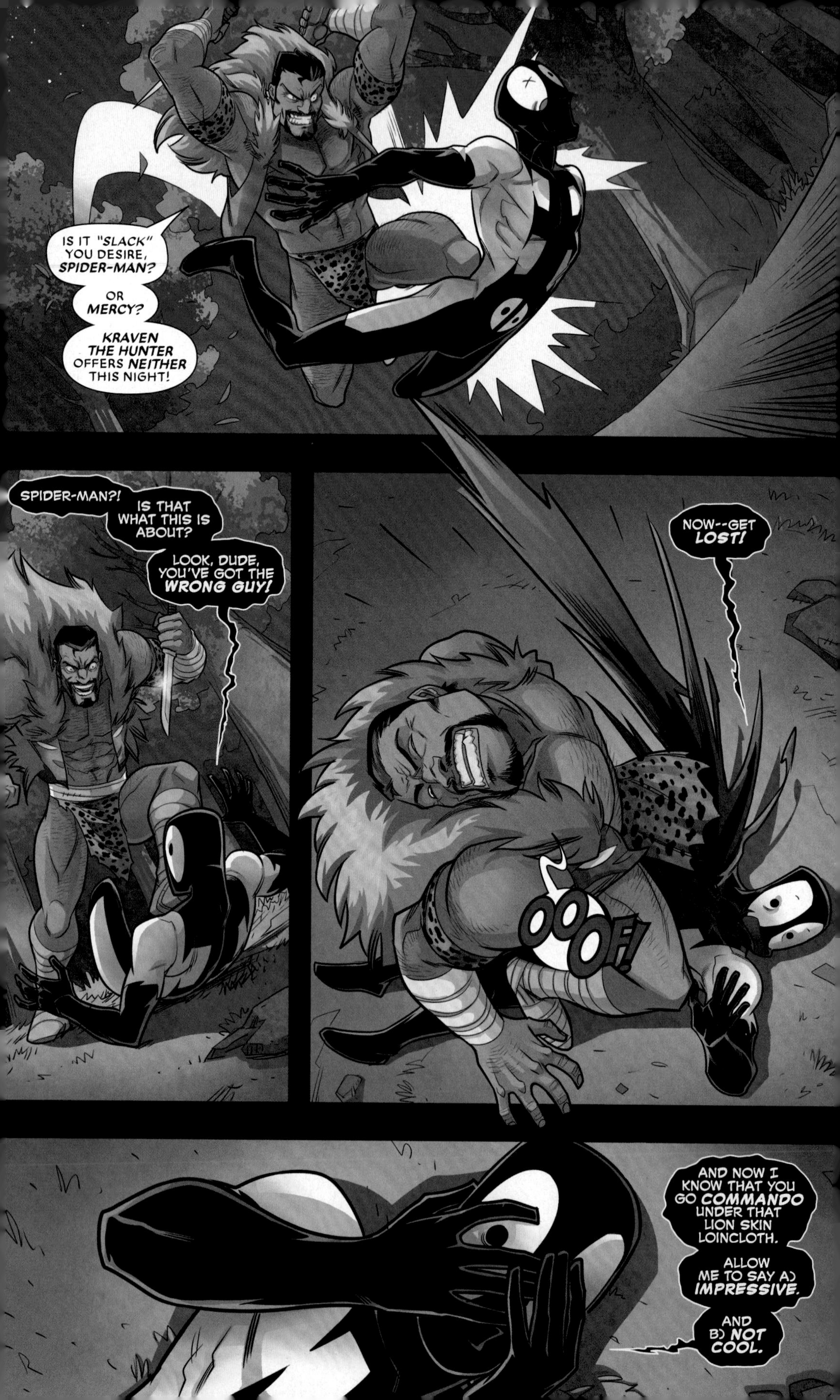
IS IT "SLACK" YOU DESIRE, SPIDER-MAN?
OR MERCY?
KRAVEN THE HUNTER OFFERS NEITHER THIS NIGHT!
SPIDER-MAN?!
IS THAT WHAT THIS IS ABOUT?
LOOK, DUDE, YOU'VE GOT THE WRONG GUY!
NOW--GET LOST!
OOOF!
AND NOW I KNOW THAT YOU GO COMMANDO UNDER THAT LION SKIN LOINCLOTH.
ALLOW ME TO SAY A) IMPRESSIVE.
AND B) NOT COOL.

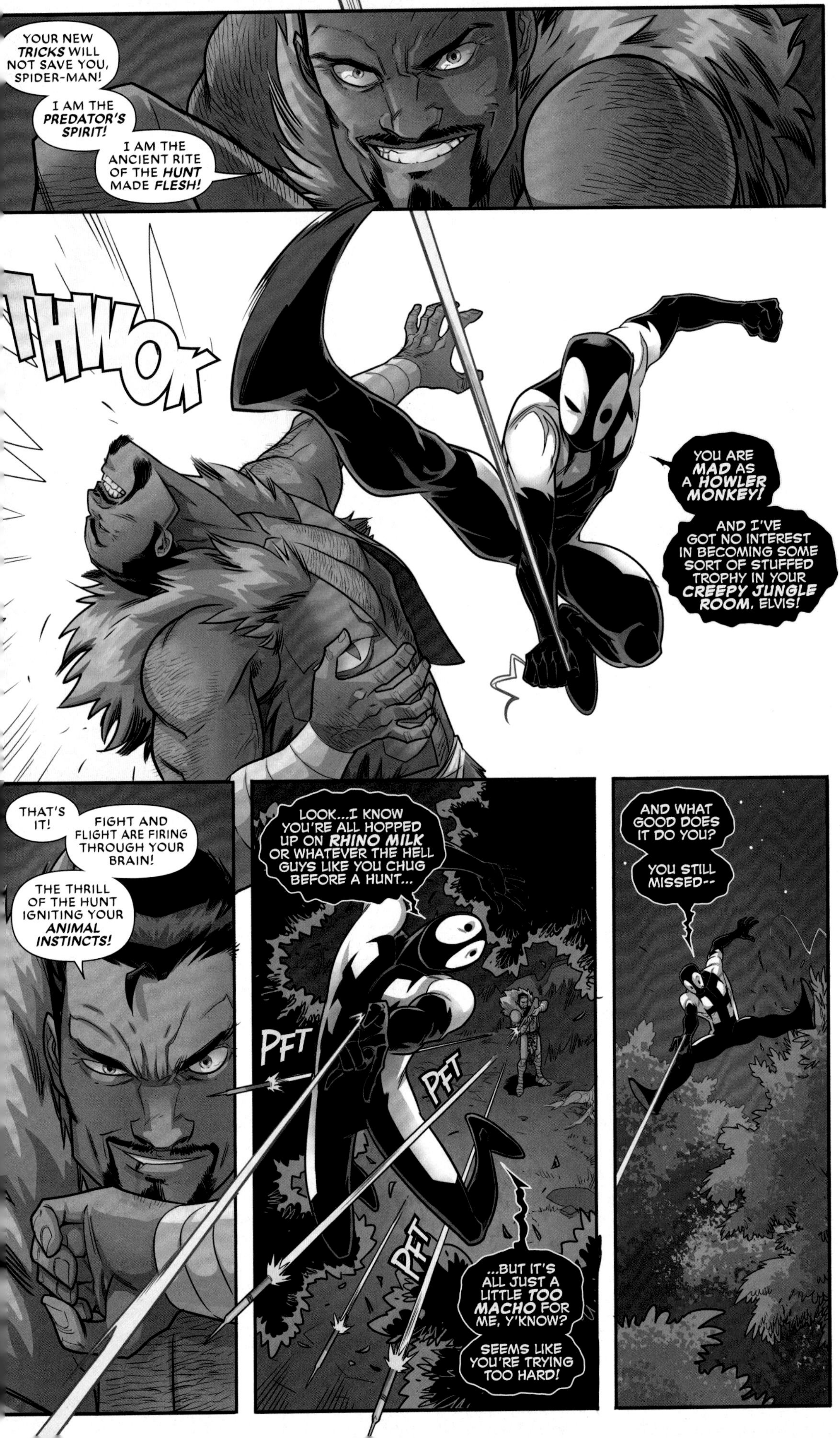
YOUR NEW TRICKS WILL NOT SAVE YOU, SPIDER-MAN!
I AM THE PREDATOR'S SPIRIT!
I AM THE ANCIENT RITE OF THE HUNT MADE FLESH!
THWOK
YOU ARE MAD AS A HOWLER MONKEY!
AND I'VE GOT NO INTEREST IN BECOMING SOME SORT OF STUFFED TROPHY IN YOUR CREEPY JUNGLE ROOM, ELVIS!
THAT'S IT!
FIGHT AND FLIGHT ARE FIRING THROUGH YOUR BRAIN!
THE THRILL OF THE HUNT IGNITING YOUR ANIMAL INSTINCTS!
LOOK...I KNOW YOU'RE ALL HOPPED UP ON RHINO MILK OR WHATEVER THE HELL GUYS LIKE YOU CHUG BEFORE A HUNT...
PFT
PFT
PFT
...BUT IT'S ALL JUST A LITTLE TOO MACHO FOR ME, Y'KNOW?
SEEMS LIKE YOU'RE TRYING TOO HARD!
AND WHAT GOOD DOES IT DO YOU?
YOU STILL MISSED--

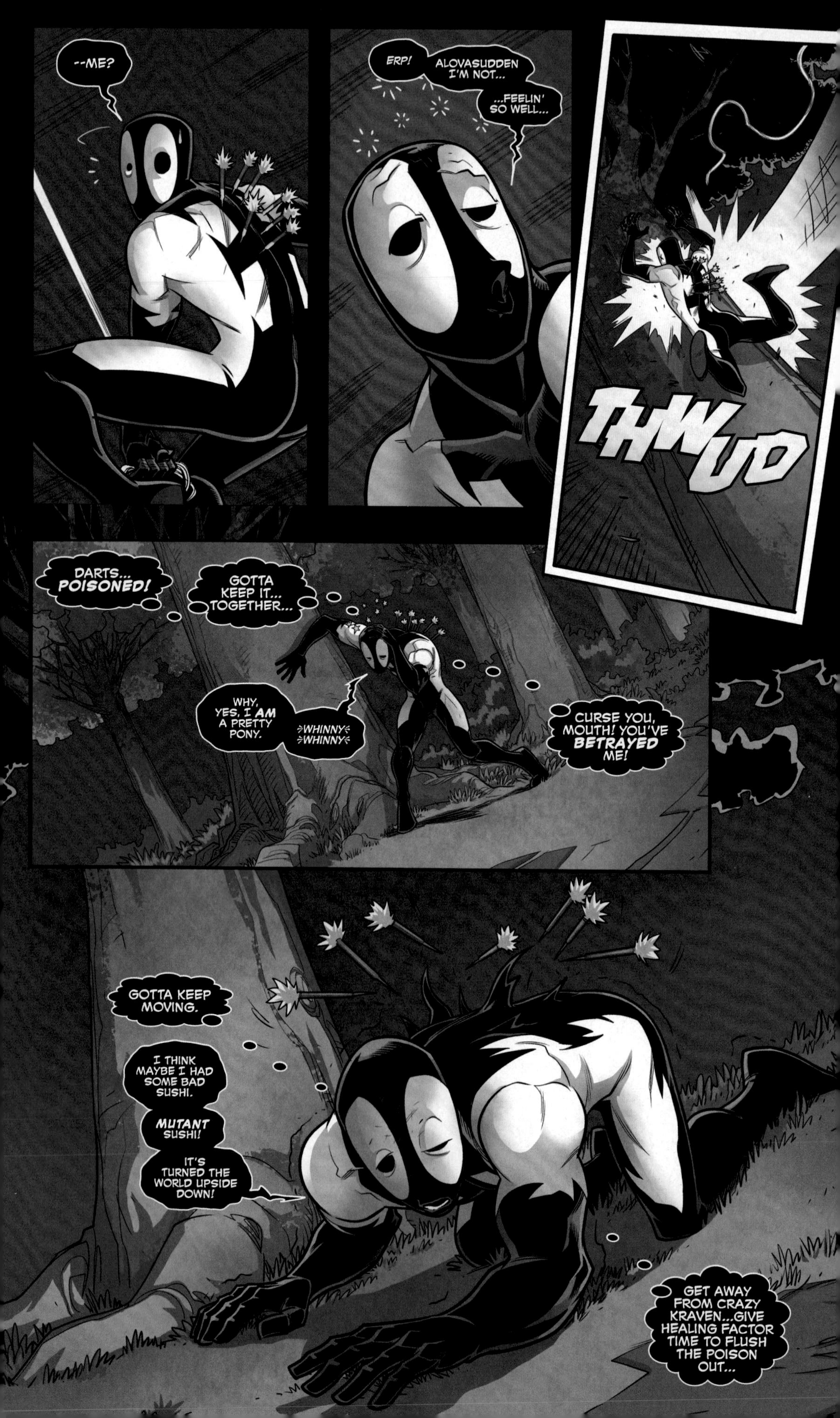
--ME?
ERP!
ALOVASUDDEN I'M NOT...
...FEELIN' SO WELL...
THWUD
DARTS... POISONED!
GOTTA KEEP IT... TOGETHER...
WHY, YES, I AM A PRETTY PONY.
WHINNY WHINNY
CURSE YOU, MOUTH! YOU'VE BETRAYED ME!
GOTTA KEEP MOVING.
I THINK MAYBE I HAD SOME BAD SUSHI.
MUTANT SUSHI!
IT'S TURNED THE WORLD UPSIDE DOWN!
GET AWAY FROM CRAZY KRAVEN...GIVE HEALING FACTOR TIME TO FLUSH THE POISON OUT...

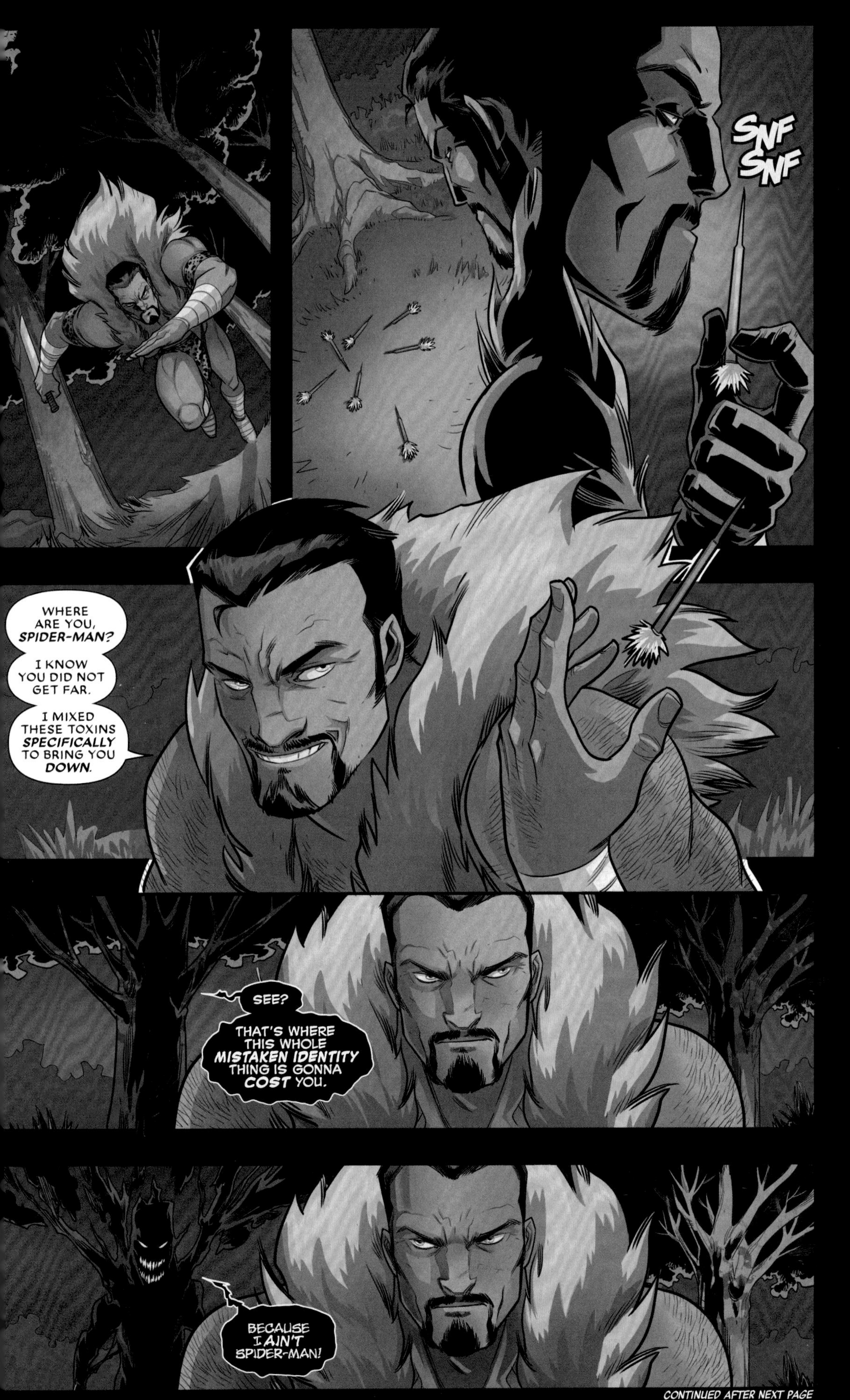
SNF SNF
WHERE ARE YOU, SPIDER-MAN?
I KNOW YOU DID NOT GET FAR.
I MIXED THESE TOXINS SPECIFICALLY TO BRING YOU DOWN.
SEE?
THAT'S WHERE THIS WHOLE MISTAKEN IDENTITY THING IS GONNA COST YOU.
BECAUSE I AIN'T SPIDER-MAN!

CONTINUED AFTER NEXT PAGE

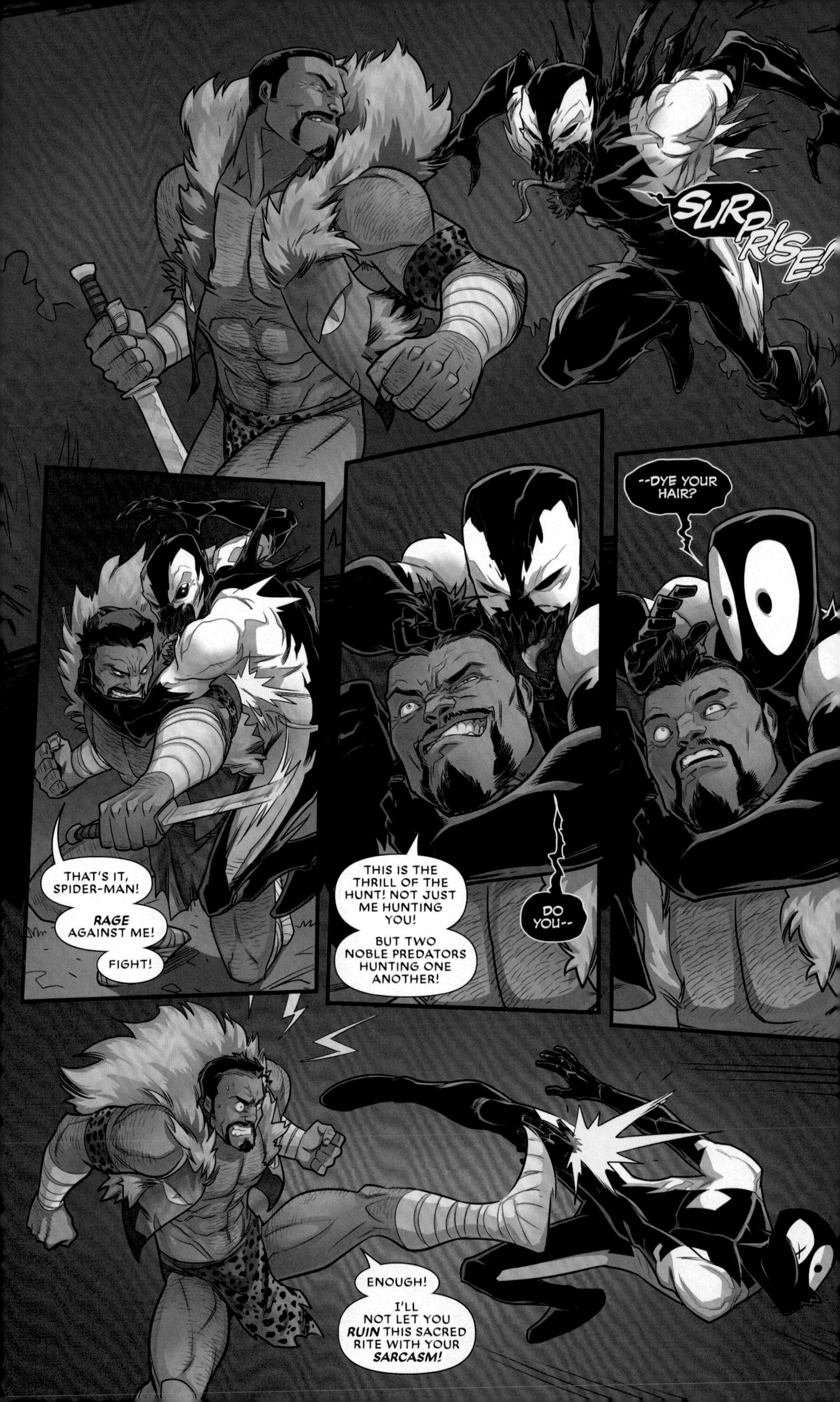
SURPRISE!
THAT'S IT, SPIDER-MAN!
RAGE AGAINST ME!
FIGHT!
THIS IS THE THRILL OF THE HUNT! NOT JUST ME HUNTING YOU!
BUT TWO NOBLE PREDATORS HUNTING ONE ANOTHER!
DO YOU--
--DYE YOUR HAIR?
ENOUGH!
I'LL NOT LET YOU RUIN THIS SACRED RITE WITH YOUR SARCASM!

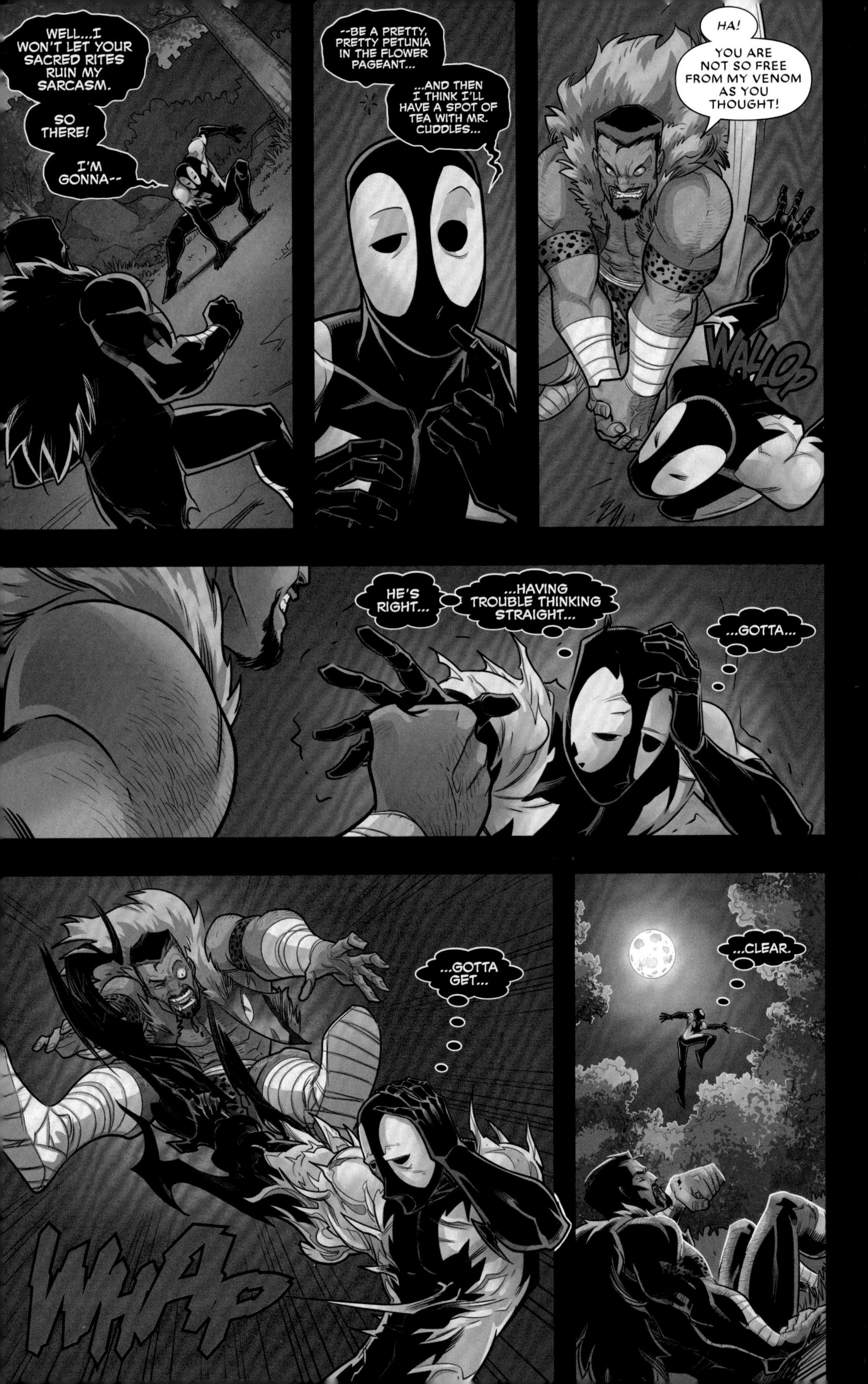
WELL...I WON'T LET YOUR SACRED RITES RUIN MY SARCASM.
SO THERE!
I'M GONNA--
--BE A PRETTY, PRETTY PETUNIA IN THE FLOWER PAGEANT...
...AND THEN I THINK I'LL HAVE A SPOT OF TEA WITH MR. CUDDLES...
HA!
YOU ARE NOT SO FREE FROM MY VENOM AS YOU THOUGHT!
WALLOP
HE'S RIGHT...
...HAVING TROUBLE THINKING STRAIGHT...
...GOTTA...
...GOTTA GET...
WHAP
...CLEAR.

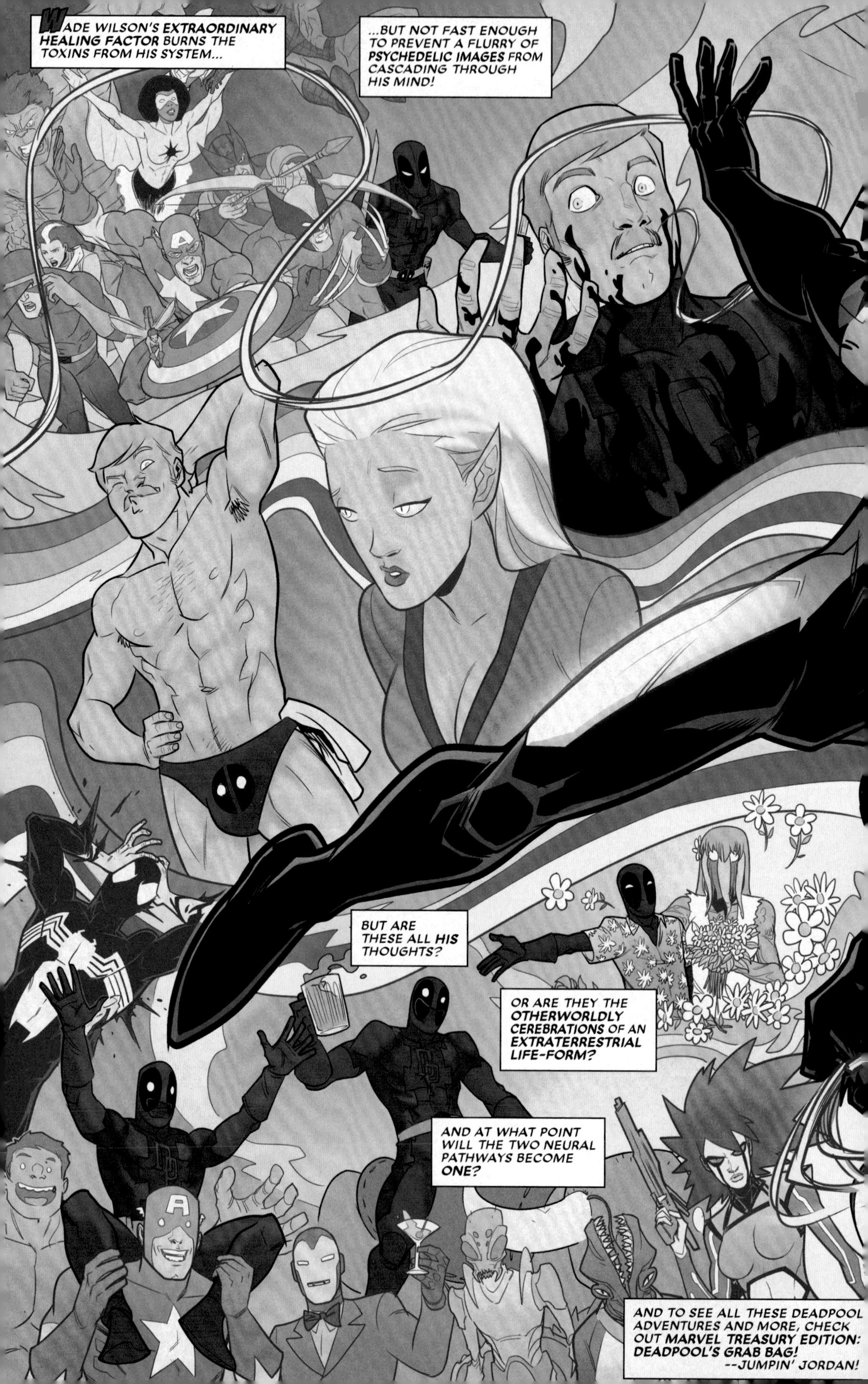
WADE WILSON'S EXTRAORDINARY HEALING FACTOR BURNS THE TOXINS FROM HIS SYSTEM...
...BUT NOT FAST ENOUGH TO PREVENT A FLURRY OF PSYCHEDELIC IMAGES FROM CASCADING THROUGH HIS MIND!
BUT ARE THESE ALL HIS THOUGHTS?
OR ARE THEY THE OTHERWORLDLY CEREBRATIONS OF AN EXTRATERRESTRIAL LIFE-FORM?
AND AT WHAT POINT WILL THE TWO NEURAL PATHWAYS BECOME ONE?
AND TO SEE ALL THESE DEADPOOL ADVENTURES AND MORE, CHECK OUT MARVEL TREASURY EDITION: DEADPOOL'S GRAB BAG!
--JUMPIN' JORDAN!

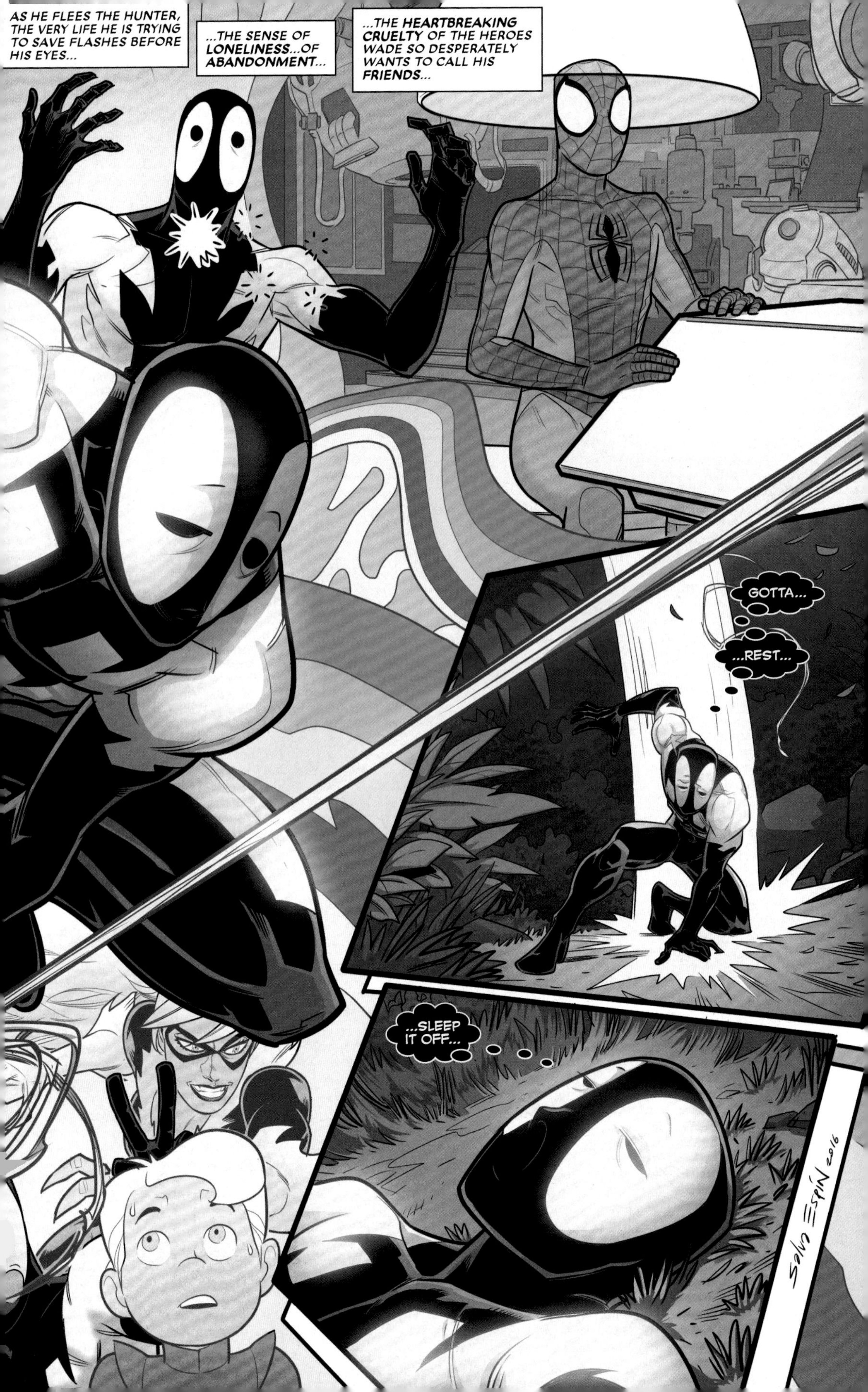
AS HE FLEES THE HUNTER, THE VERY LIFE HE IS TRYING TO SAVE FLASHES BEFORE HIS EYES...
...THE SENSE OF LONELINESS...OF ABANDONMENT...
...THE HEARTBREAKING CRUELTY OF THE HEROES WADE SO DESPERATELY WANTS TO CALL HIS FRIENDS...
GOTTA...
...REST...
...SLEEP IT OFF...
SALVA ESPÍN 2016

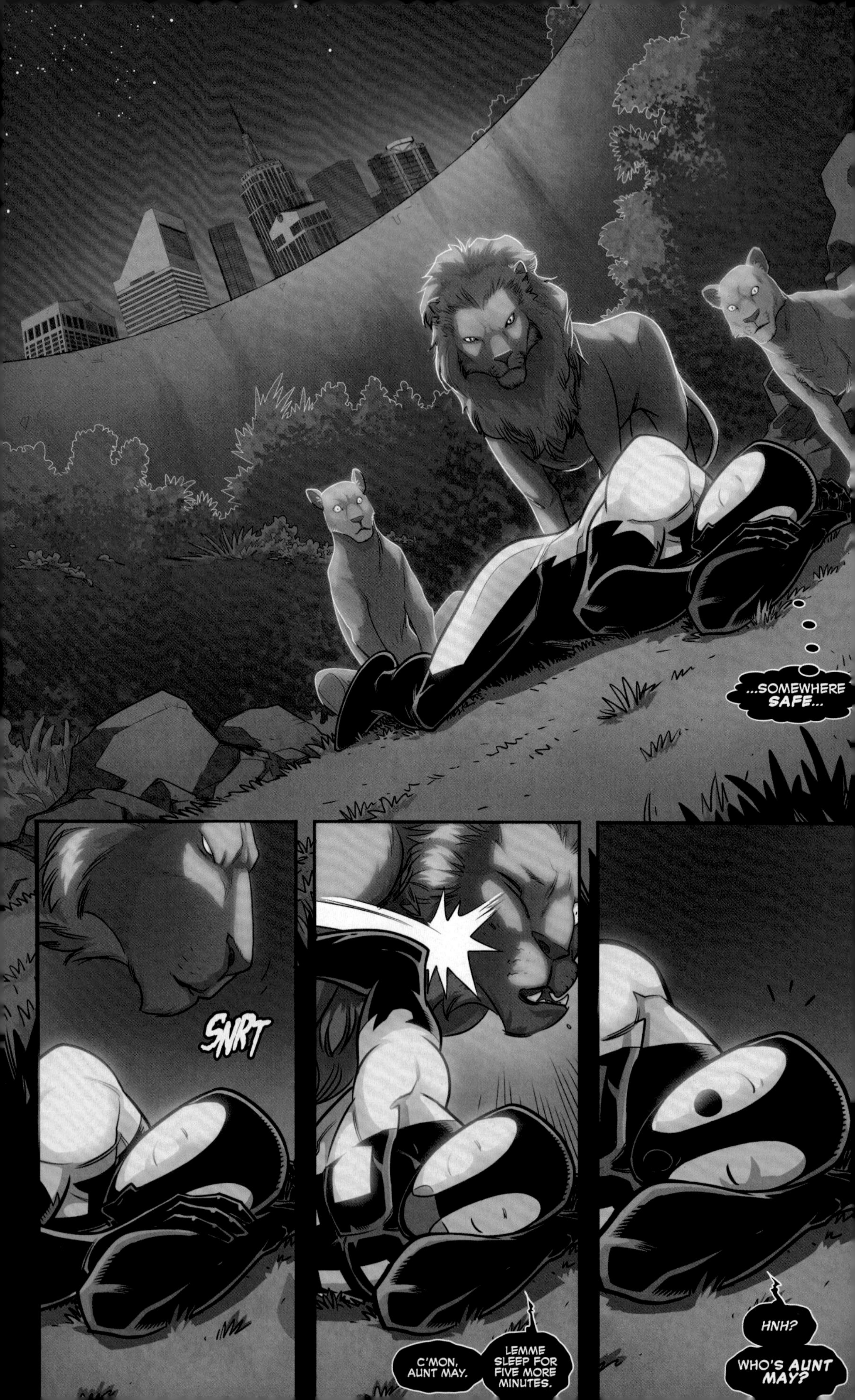
...SOMEWHERE SAFE...
SNRT
C'MON, AUNT MAY.
LEMME SLEEP FOR FIVE MORE MINUTES.
HNH?
WHO'S AUNT MAY?

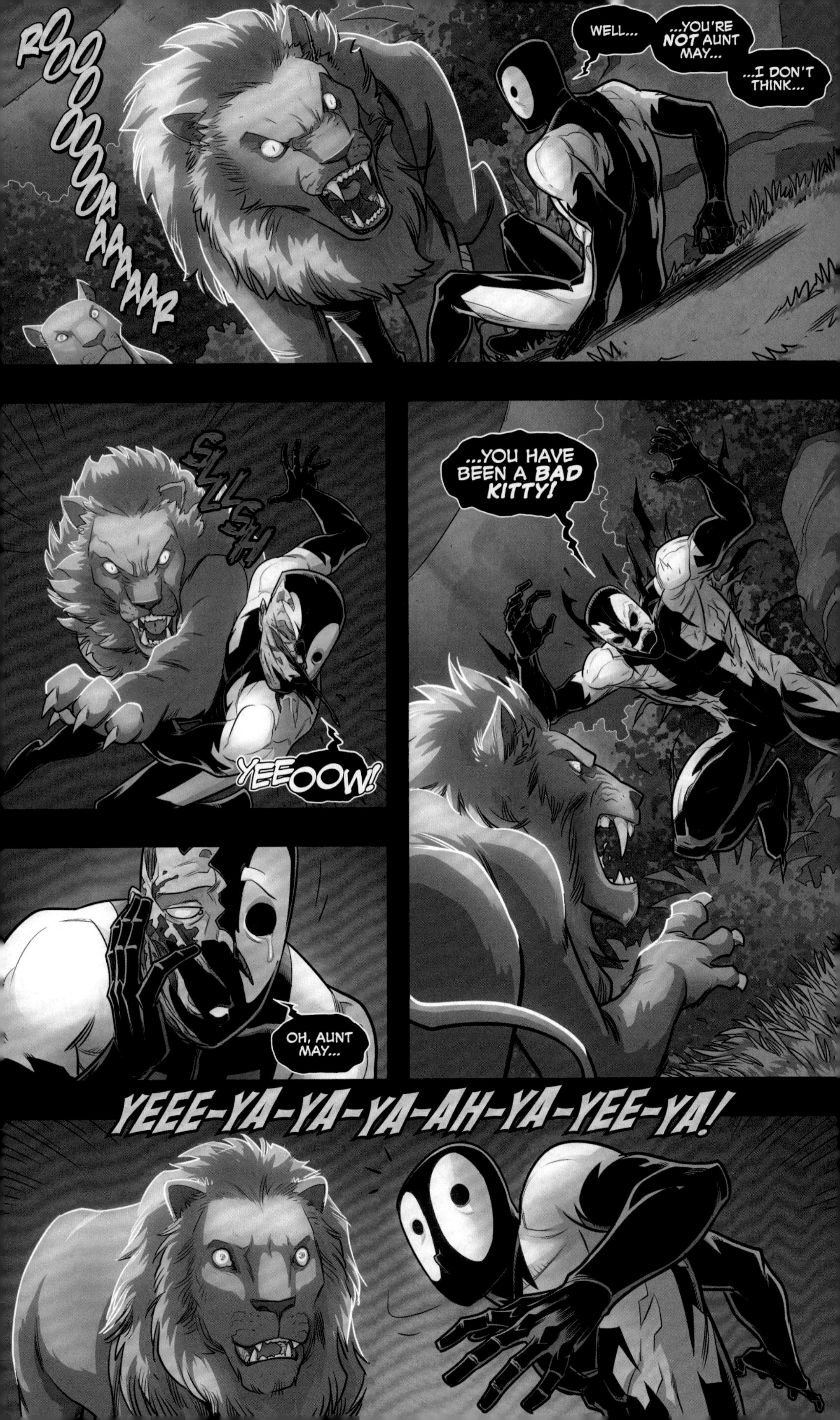
ROOOOOOOOAAAAAAAR
WELL...
...YOU'RE NOT AUNT MAY...
...I DON'T THINK...
SHLUSH
YEEOOW!
...YOU HAVE BEEN A BAD KITTY!
OH, AUNT MAY...
YEEE-YA-YA-YA-AH-YA-YEE-YA!

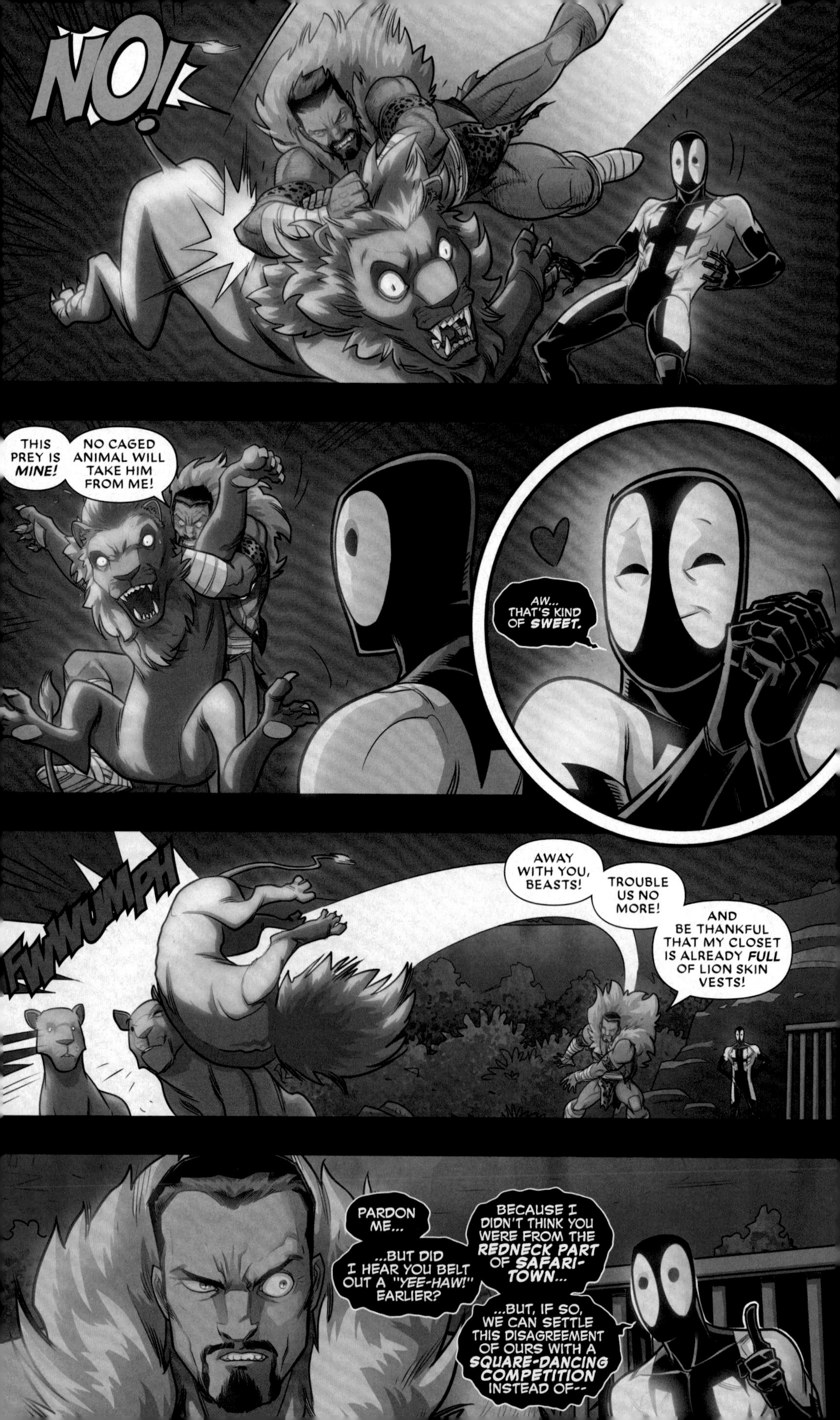
NO!
THIS PREY IS MINE!
NO CAGED ANIMAL WILL TAKE HIM FROM ME!
AW... THAT'S KIND OF SWEET.
FWUMPH
AWAY WITH YOU, BEASTS!
TROUBLE US NO MORE!
AND BE THANKFUL THAT MY CLOSET IS ALREADY FULL OF LION SKIN VESTS!
PARDON ME...
...BUT DID I HEAR YOU BELT OUT A "YEE-HAW!" EARLIER?
BECAUSE I DIDN'T THINK YOU WERE FROM THE REDNECK PART OF SAFARI-TOWN...
...BUT, IF SO, WE CAN SETTLE THIS DISAGREEMENT OF OURS WITH A SQUARE-DANCING COMPETITION INSTEAD OF--

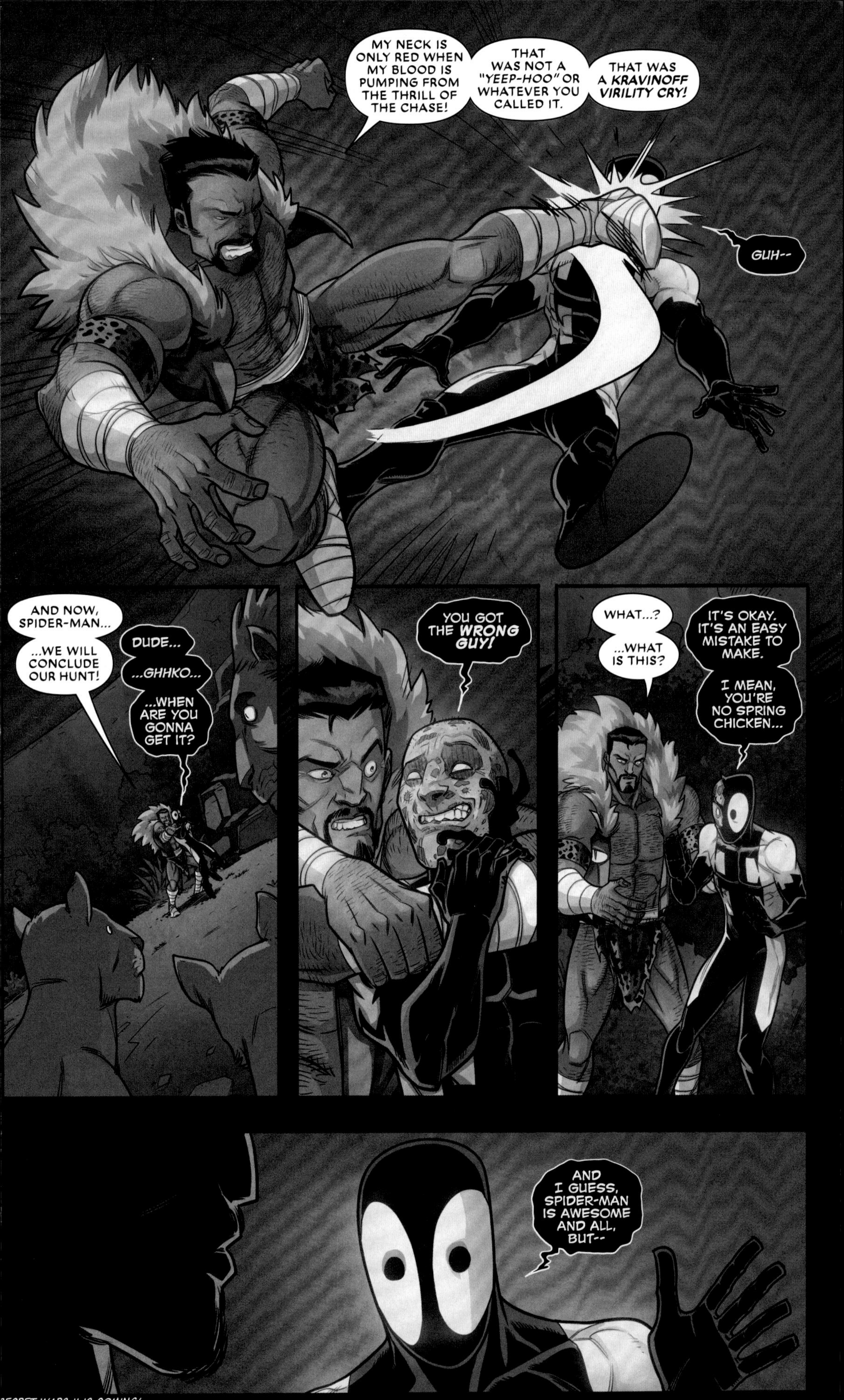

MY NECK IS ONLY RED WHEN MY BLOOD IS PUMPING FROM THE THRILL OF THE CHASE!
THAT WAS NOT A "YEEP-HOO" OR WHATEVER YOU CALLED IT.
THAT WAS A KRAVINOFF VIRILITY CRY!
GUH--
AND NOW, SPIDER-MAN...
...WE WILL CONCLUDE OUR HUNT!
DUDE...
...GHHKO...
...WHEN ARE YOU GONNA GET IT?
YOU GOT THE WRONG GUY!
WHAT...?
...WHAT IS THIS?
IT'S OKAY. IT'S AN EASY MISTAKE TO MAKE.
I MEAN, YOU'RE NO SPRING CHICKEN...
AND I GUESS, SPIDER-MAN IS AWESOME AND ALL, BUT--

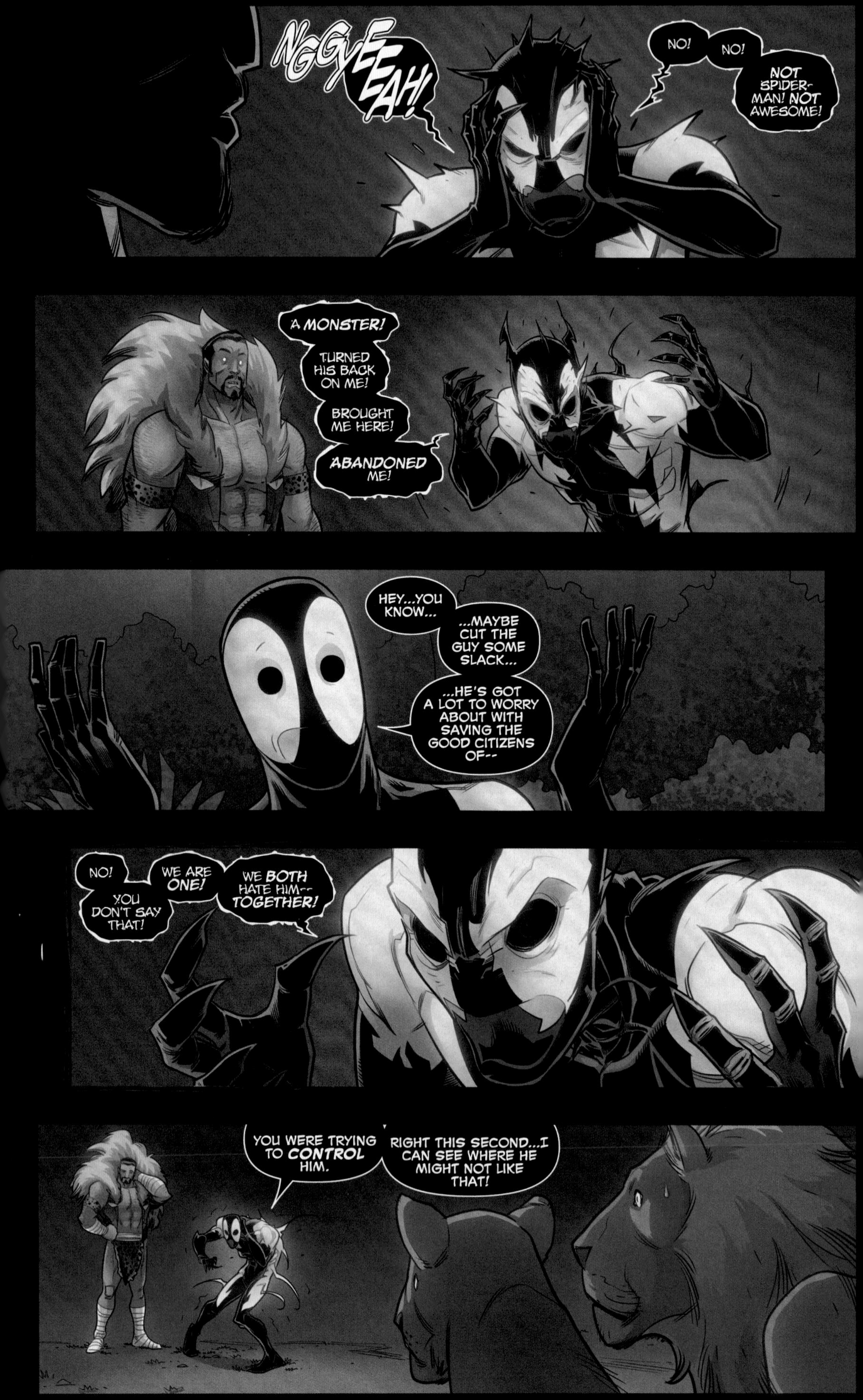
NGGYEEAH!
NO!
NO!
NOT SPIDER-MAN! NOT AWESOME!
A MONSTER!
TURNED HIS BACK ON ME!
BROUGHT ME HERE!
ABANDONED ME!
HEY...YOU KNOW...
...MAYBE CUT THE GUY SOME SLACK...
...HE'S GOT A LOT TO WORRY ABOUT WITH SAVING THE GOOD CITIZENS OF--
NO!
YOU DON'T SAY THAT!
WE ARE ONE!
WE BOTH HATE HIM-- TOGETHER!
YOU WERE TRYING TO CONTROL HIM.
RIGHT THIS SECOND...I CAN SEE WHERE HE MIGHT NOT LIKE THAT!

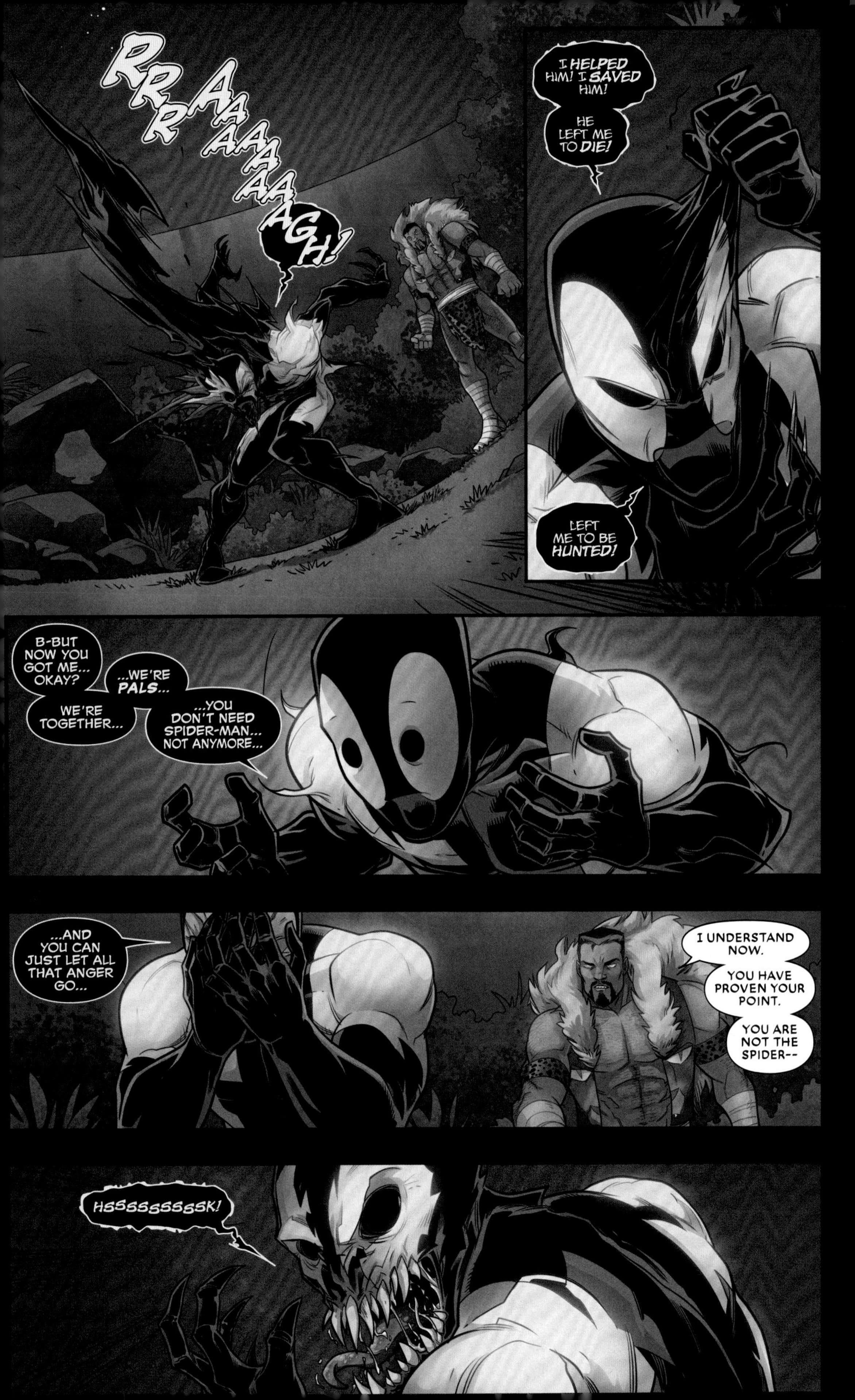
RRRAAAAAAAAGH!
I HELPED HIM! I SAVED HIM!
HE LEFT ME TO DIE!
LEFT ME TO BE HUNTED!
B-BUT NOW YOU GOT ME... OKAY?
...WE'RE PALS...
WE'RE TOGETHER...
...YOU DON'T NEED SPIDER-MAN... NOT ANYMORE...
...AND YOU CAN JUST LET ALL THAT ANGER GO...
I UNDERSTAND NOW.
YOU HAVE PROVEN YOUR POINT.
YOU ARE NOT THE SPIDER--
HSSSSSSSSSK!

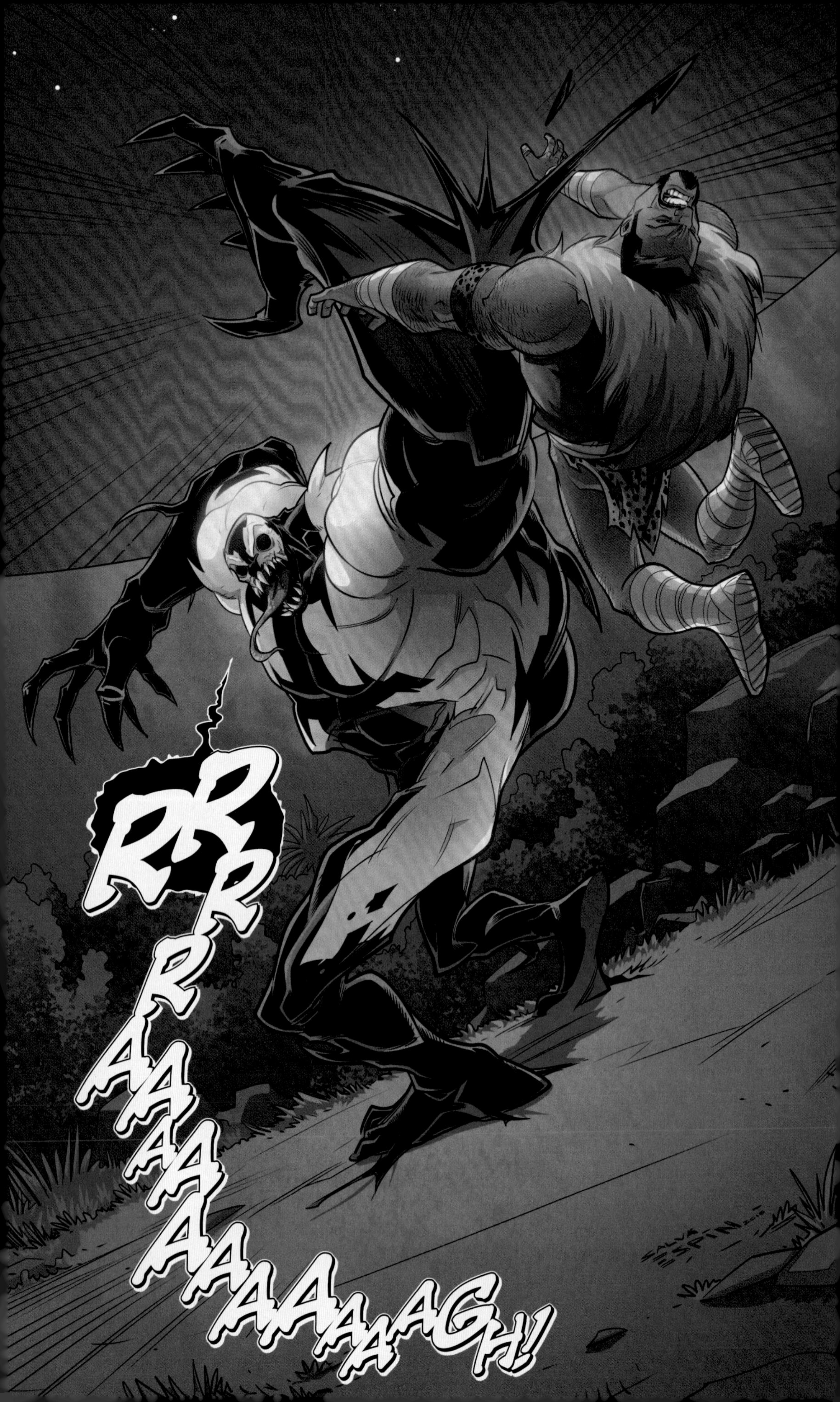
RRRRAAAAAAAAAAAAAGH!

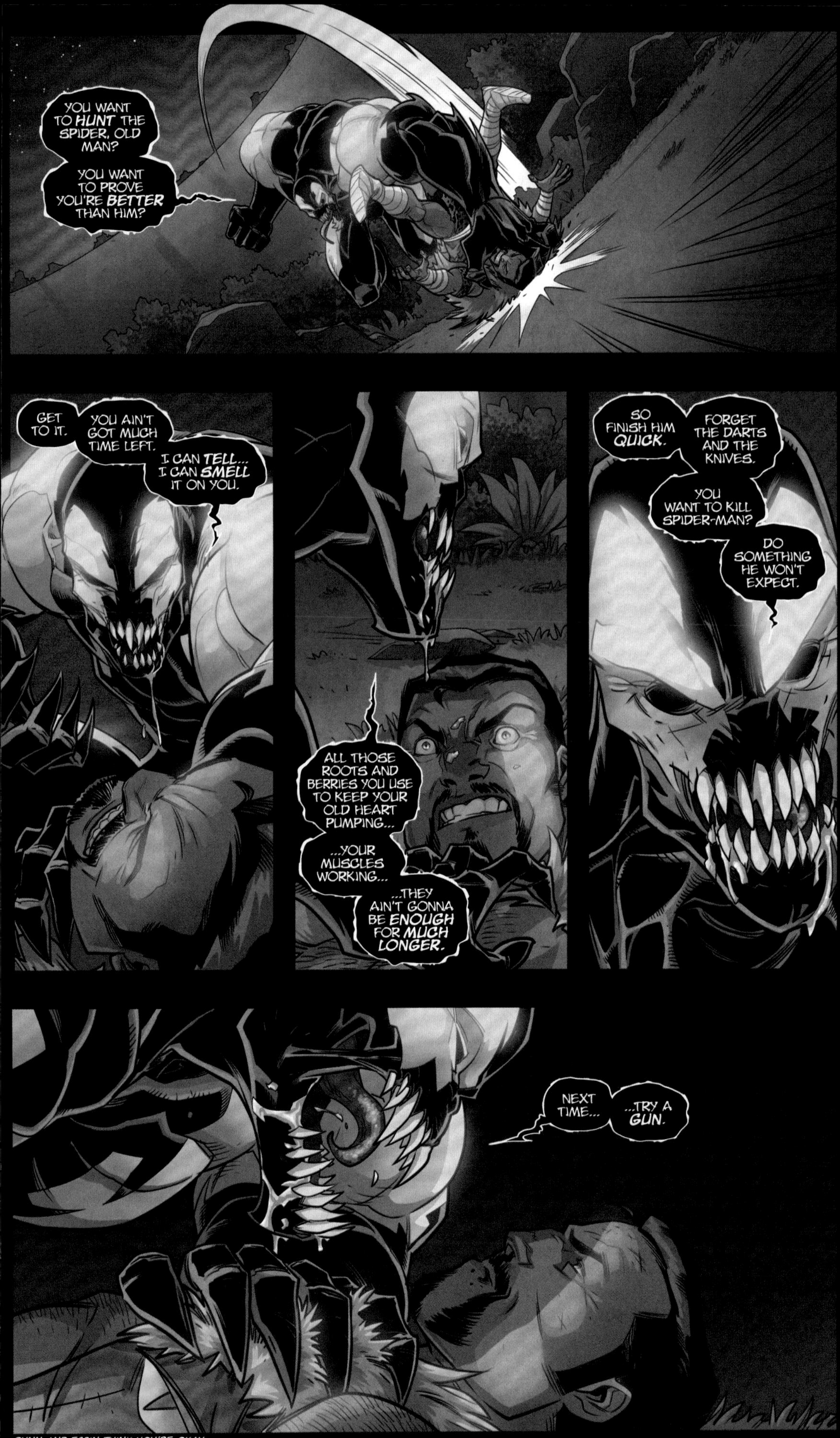
YOU WANT TO HUNT THE SPIDER, OLD MAN?
YOU WANT TO PROVE YOU'RE BETTER THAN HIM?
GET TO IT.
YOU AIN'T GOT MUCH TIME LEFT.
I CAN TELL... I CAN SMELL IT ON YOU.
ALL THOSE ROOTS AND BERRIES YOU USE TO KEEP YOUR OLD HEART PUMPING...
...YOUR MUSCLES WORKING...
...THEY AIN'T GONNA BE ENOUGH FOR MUCH LONGER.
SO FINISH HIM QUICK.
FORGET THE DARTS AND THE KNIVES.
YOU WANT TO KILL SPIDER-MAN?
DO SOMETHING HE WON'T EXPECT.
NEXT TIME...
...TRY A GUN.

BUNN AND ESPIN THINK YOU'RE OKAY

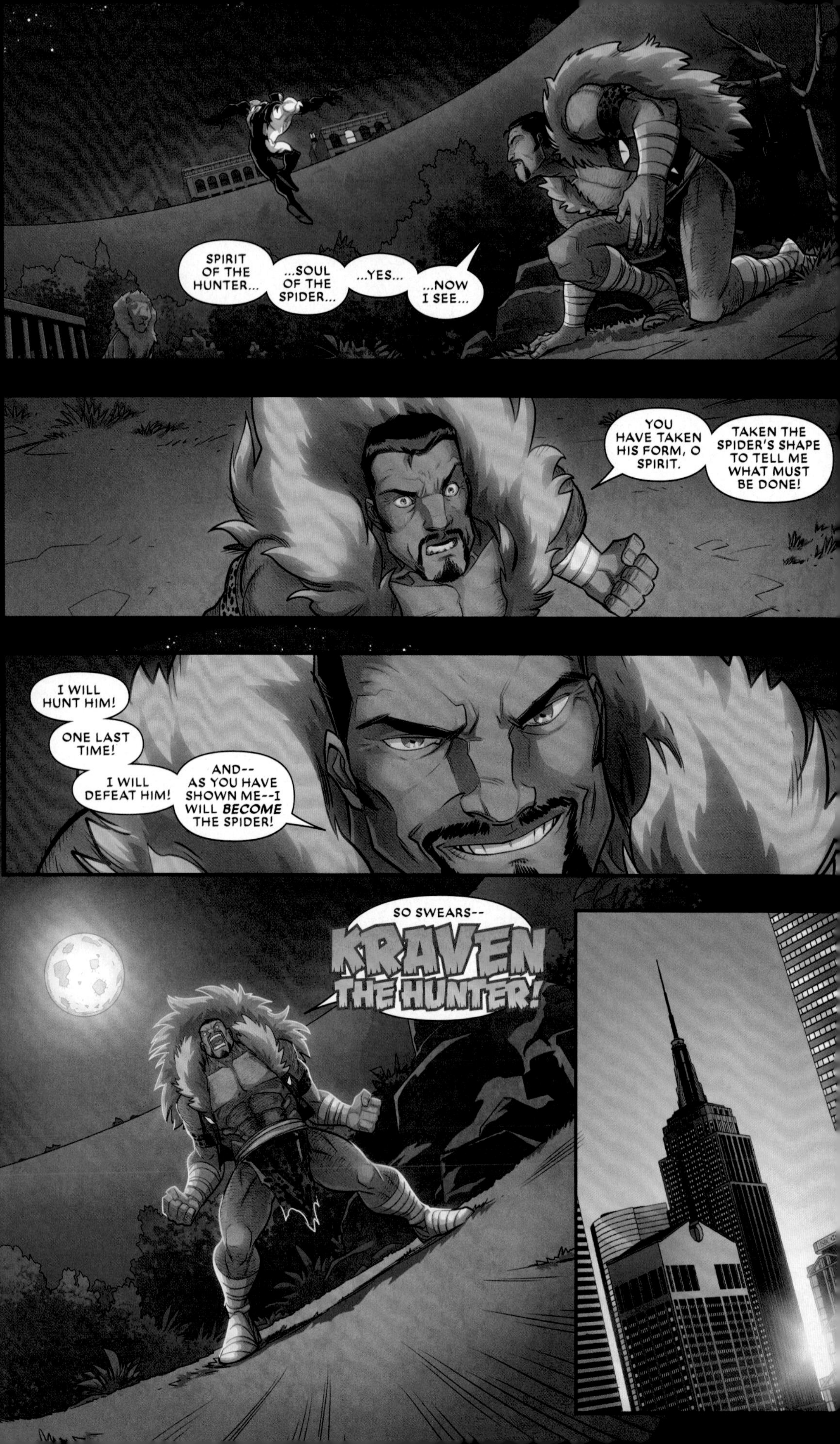
SPIRIT OF THE HUNTER...
...SOUL OF THE SPIDER...
...YES...
...NOW I SEE...
YOU HAVE TAKEN HIS FORM, O SPIRIT.
TAKEN THE SPIDER'S SHAPE TO TELL ME WHAT MUST BE DONE!
I WILL HUNT HIM!
ONE LAST TIME!
I WILL DEFEAT HIM!
AND-- AS YOU HAVE SHOWN ME--I WILL *BECOME* THE SPIDER!
SO SWEARS--
KRAVEN THE HUNTER!

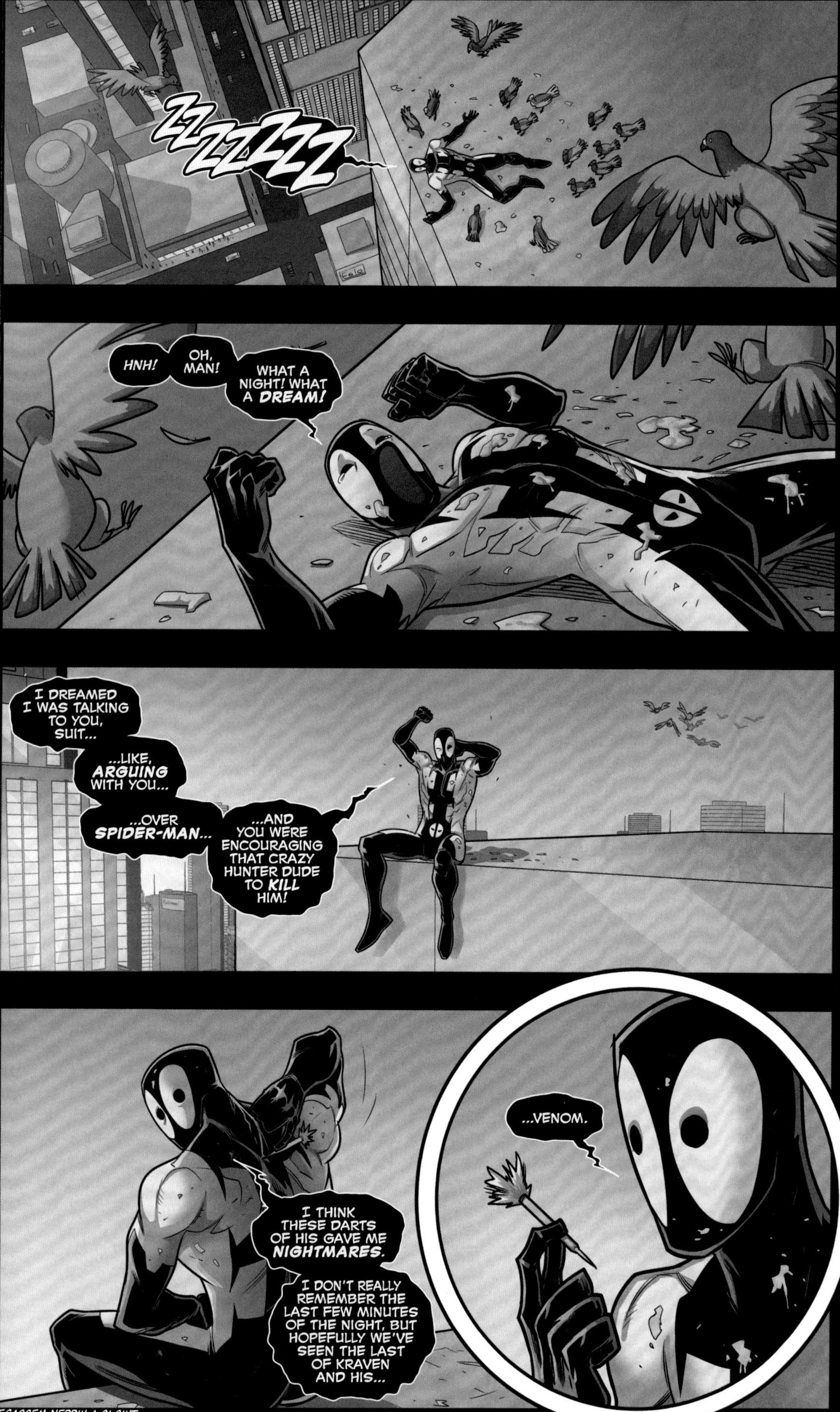
ZZZZZZZ
HNH!
OH, MAN!
WHAT A NIGHT! WHAT A DREAM!
I DREAMED I WAS TALKING TO YOU, SUIT...
...LIKE, ARGUING WITH YOU...
...OVER SPIDER-MAN...
...AND YOU WERE ENCOURAGING THAT CRAZY HUNTER DUDE TO KILL HIM!
I THINK THESE DARTS OF HIS GAVE ME NIGHTMARES.
I DON'T REALLY REMEMBER THE LAST FEW MINUTES OF THE NIGHT, BUT HOPEFULLY WE'VE SEEN THE LAST OF KRAVEN AND HIS...
...VENOM.

EGASSEM NEDDIH A SI SIHT

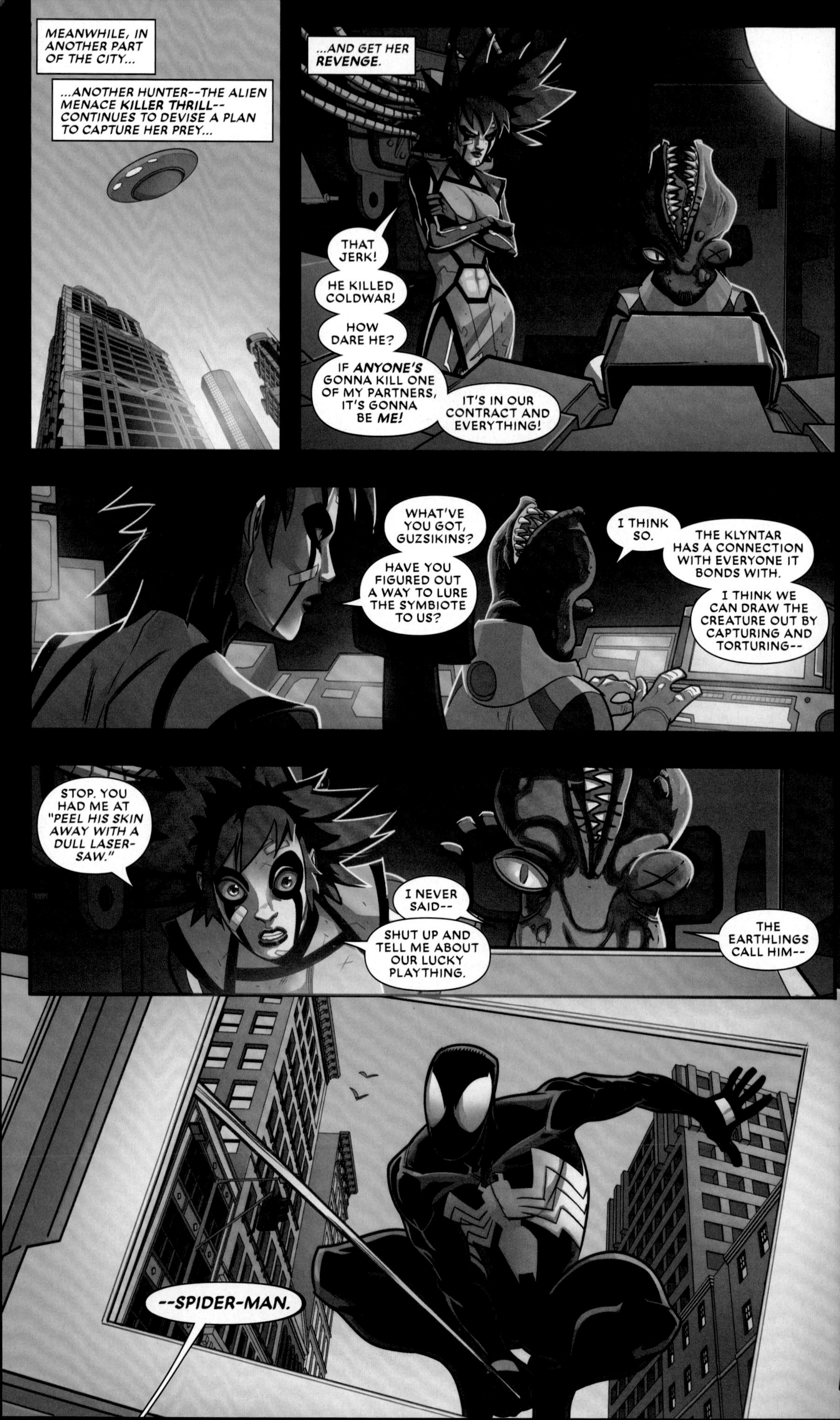
MEANWHILE, IN ANOTHER PART OF THE CITY...
...ANOTHER HUNTER--THE ALIEN MENACE KILLER THRILL--CONTINUES TO DEVISE A PLAN TO CAPTURE HER PREY...
...AND GET HER REVENGE.
THAT JERK!
HE KILLED COLDWAR!
HOW DARE HE?
IF ANYONE'S GONNA KILL ONE OF MY PARTNERS, IT'S GONNA BE ME!
IT'S IN OUR CONTRACT AND EVERYTHING!
WHAT'VE YOU GOT, GUZSIKINS?
HAVE YOU FIGURED OUT A WAY TO LURE THE SYMBIOTE TO US?
I THINK SO.
THE KLYNTAR HAS A CONNECTION WITH EVERYONE IT BONDS WITH.
I THINK WE CAN DRAW THE CREATURE OUT BY CAPTURING AND TORTURING--
STOP. YOU HAD ME AT "PEEL HIS SKIN AWAY WITH A DULL LASER-SAW."
I NEVER SAID--
SHUT UP AND TELL ME ABOUT OUR LUCKY PLAYTHING.
THE EARTHLINGS CALL HIM--
--SPIDER-MAN.

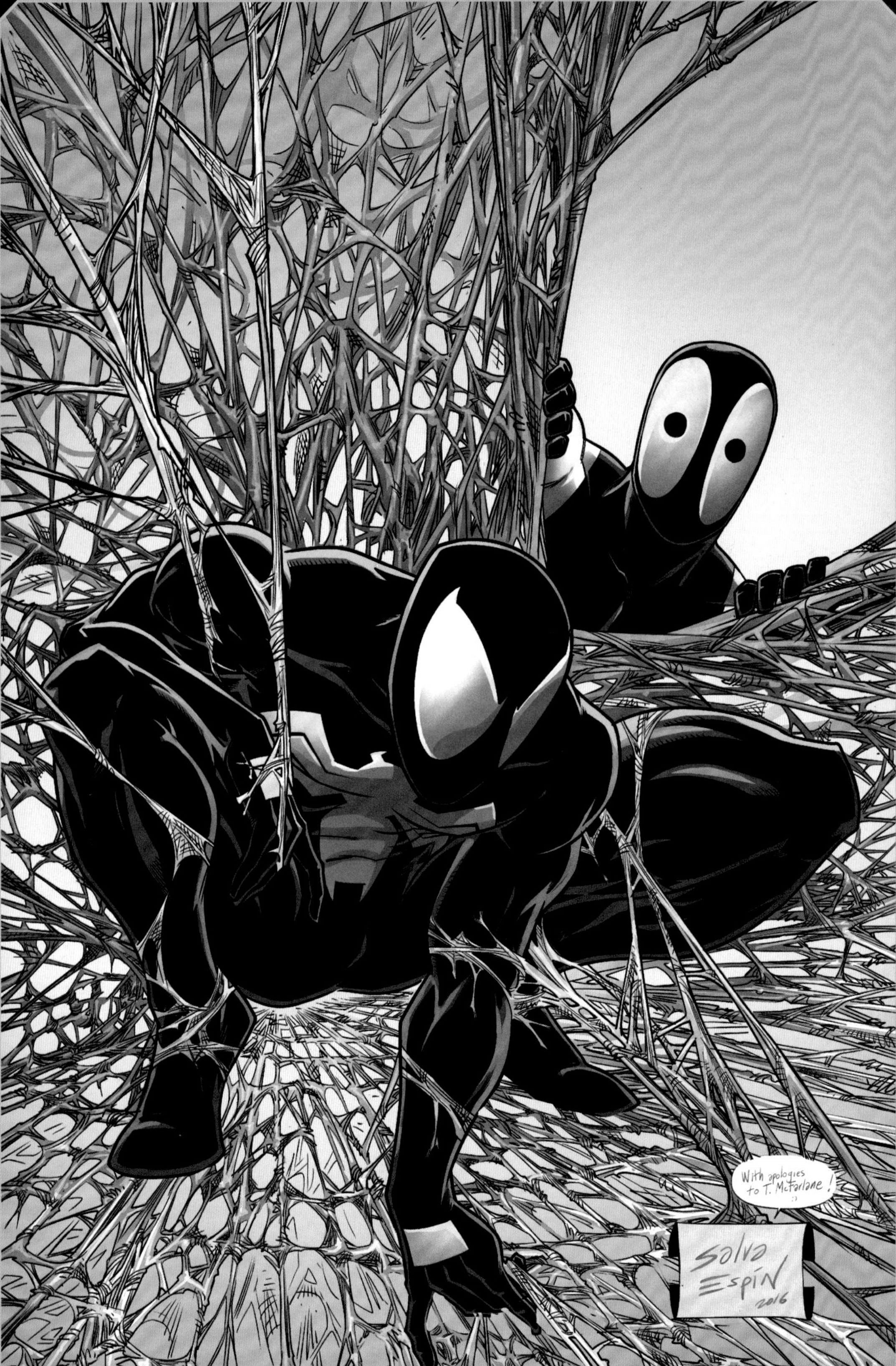
With apologies to T. McFarlane! ;)
Salva Espin 2016

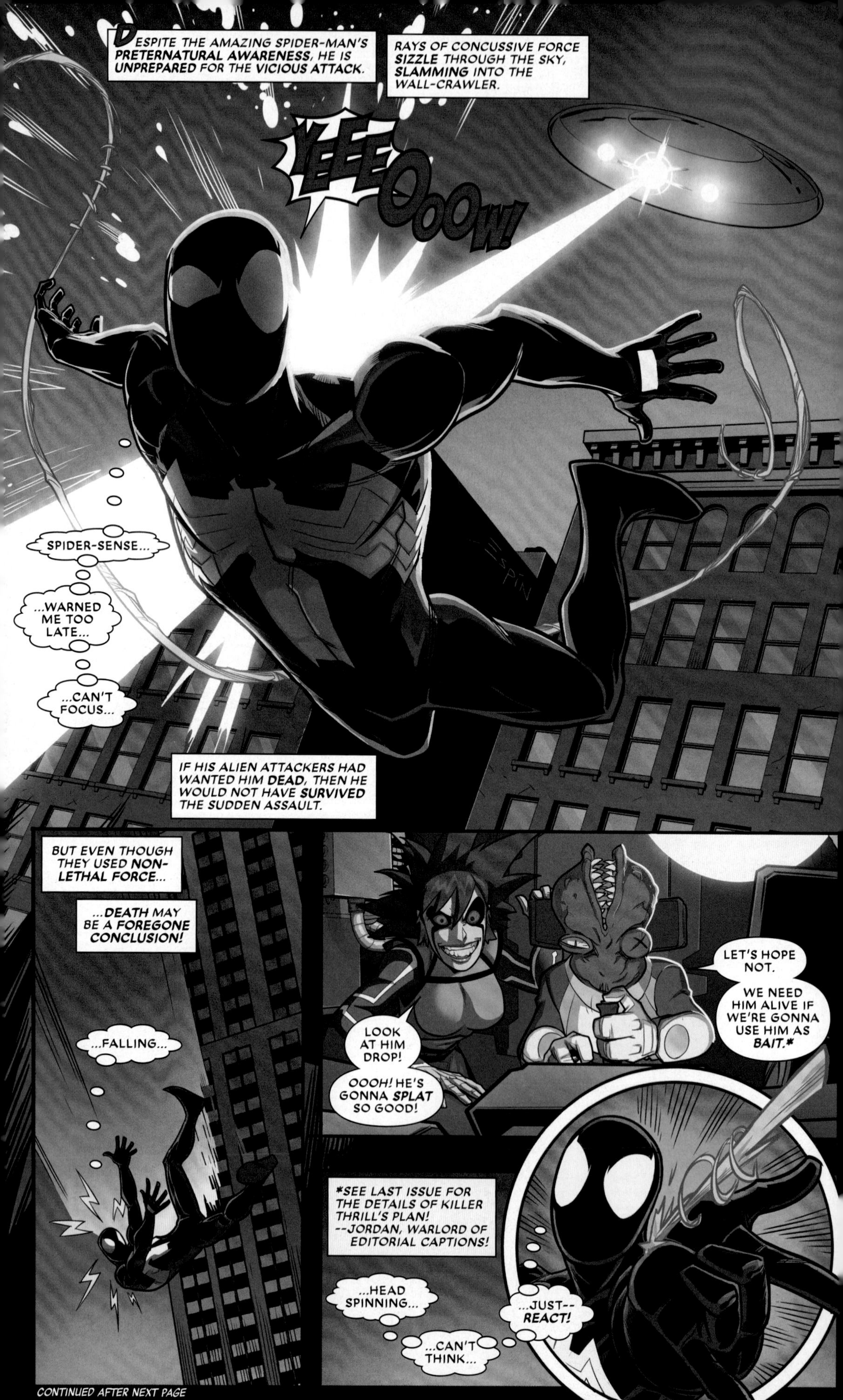

DESPITE THE AMAZING SPIDER-MAN'S PRETERNATURAL AWARENESS, HE IS UNPREPARED FOR THE VICIOUS ATTACK.
RAYS OF CONCUSSIVE FORCE SIZZLE THROUGH THE SKY, SLAMMING INTO THE WALL-CRAWLER.
YEEEOOOOW!
SPIDER-SENSE...
...WARNED ME TOO LATE...
...CAN'T FOCUS...
IF HIS ALIEN ATTACKERS HAD WANTED HIM DEAD, THEN HE WOULD NOT HAVE SURVIVED THE SUDDEN ASSAULT.
BUT EVEN THOUGH THEY USED NON-LETHAL FORCE...
...DEATH MAY BE A FOREGONE CONCLUSION!
...FALLING...
LOOK AT HIM DROP!
OOOH! HE'S GONNA SPLAT SO GOOD!
LET'S HOPE NOT.
WE NEED HIM ALIVE IF WE'RE GONNA USE HIM AS BAIT.*
*SEE LAST ISSUE FOR THE DETAILS OF KILLER THRILL'S PLAN! --JORDAN, WARLORD OF EDITORIAL CAPTIONS!
...HEAD SPINNING...
...CAN'T THINK...
...JUST-- REACT!

CONTINUED AFTER NEXT PAGE

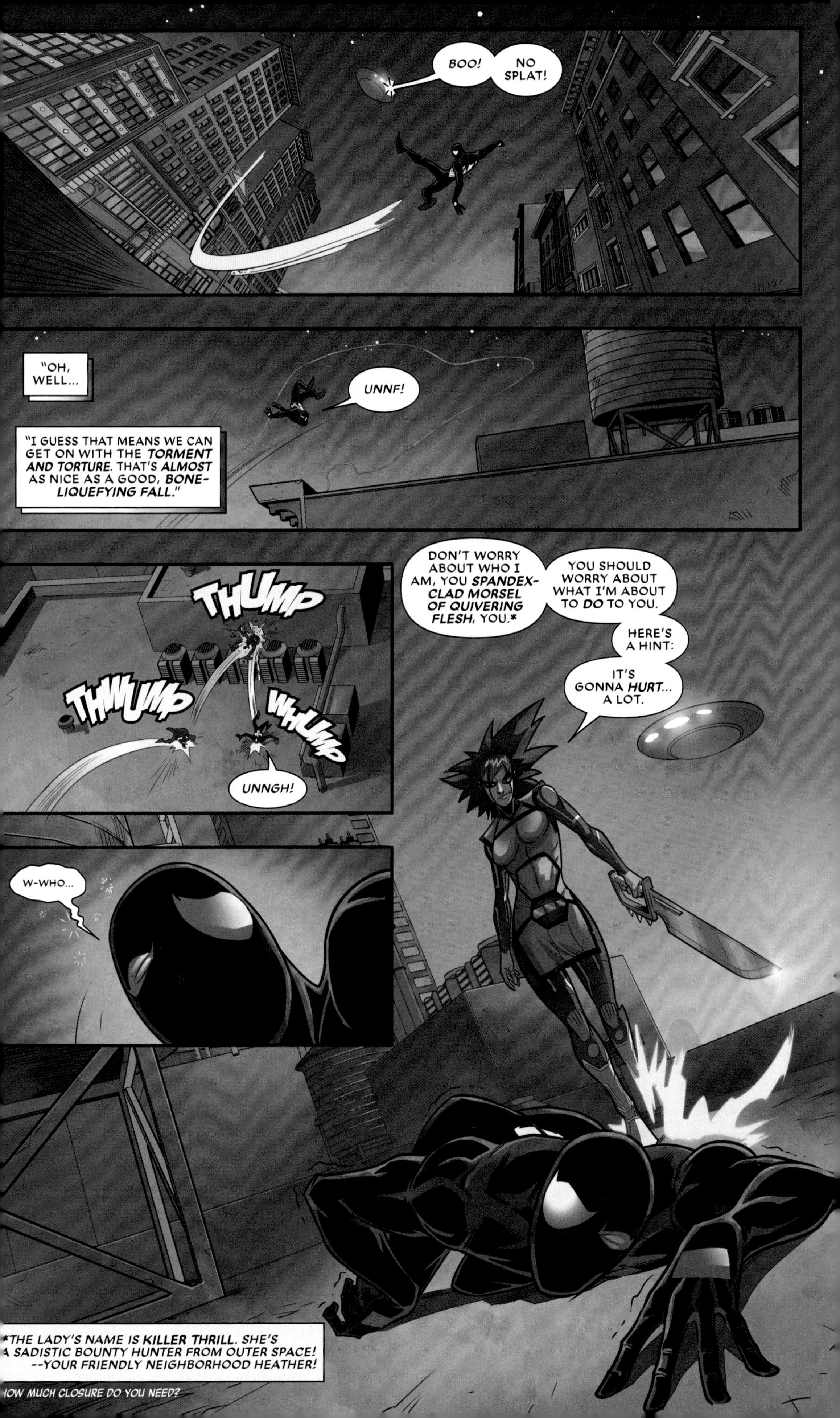
BOO!
NO SPLAT!
"OH, WELL...
UNNF!
"I GUESS THAT MEANS WE CAN GET ON WITH THE TORMENT AND TORTURE. THAT'S ALMOST AS NICE AS A GOOD, BONE-LIQUEFYING FALL."
THUMP
THWUMP
WHUMP
UNNGH!
W-WHO...
DON'T WORRY ABOUT WHO I AM, YOU SPANDEX-CLAD MORSEL OF QUIVERING FLESH, YOU.*
YOU SHOULD WORRY ABOUT WHAT I'M ABOUT TO DO TO YOU.
HERE'S A HINT:
IT'S GONNA HURT... A LOT.
*THE LADY'S NAME IS KILLER THRILL. SHE'S A SADISTIC BOUNTY HUNTER FROM OUTER SPACE! --YOUR FRIENDLY NEIGHBORHOOD HEATHER!
HOW MUCH CLOSURE DO YOU NEED?

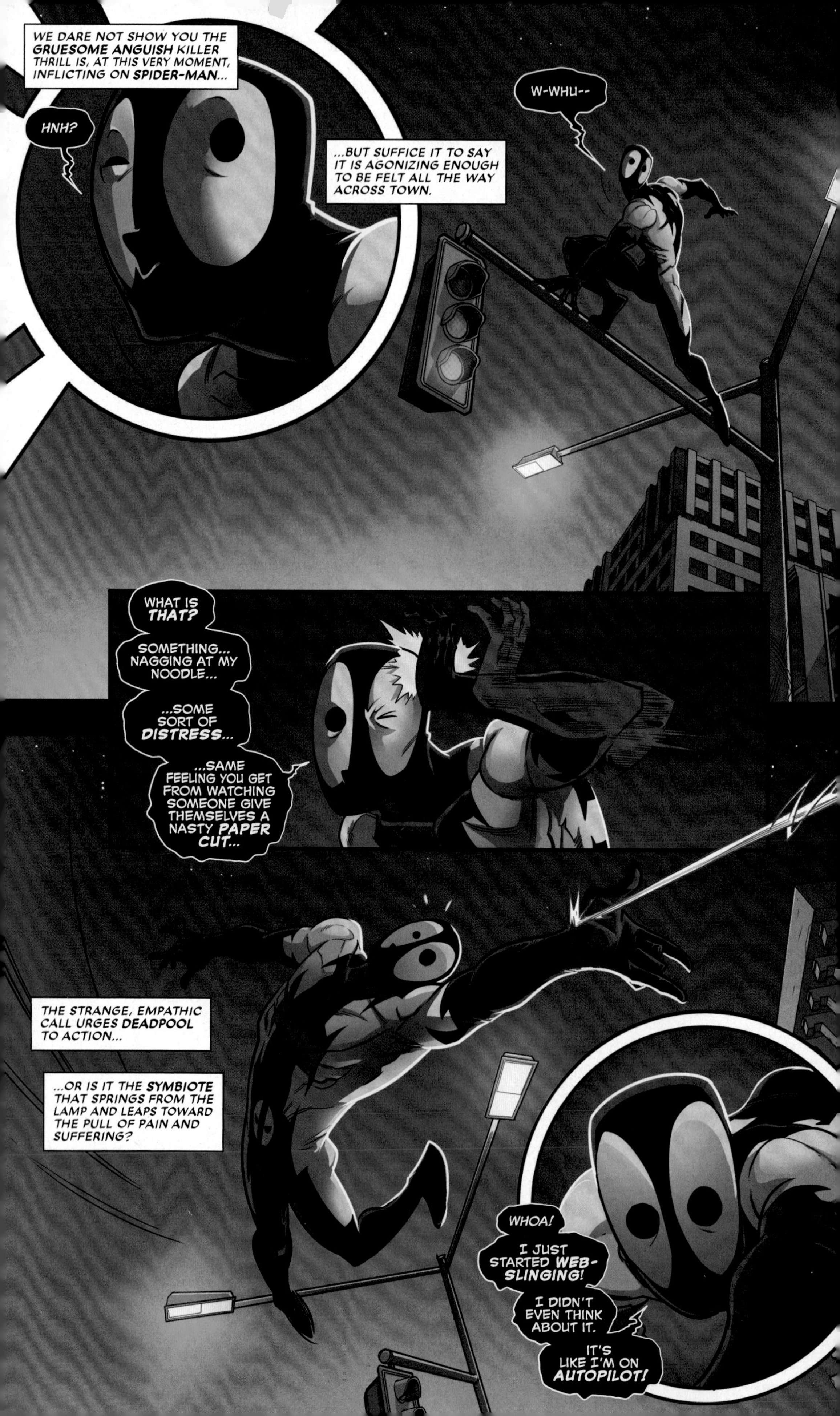
WE DARE NOT SHOW YOU THE GRUESOME ANGUISH KILLER THRILL IS, AT THIS VERY MOMENT, INFLICTING ON SPIDER-MAN...
HNH?
...BUT SUFFICE IT TO SAY IT IS AGONIZING ENOUGH TO BE FELT ALL THE WAY ACROSS TOWN.
W-WHU--
WHAT IS THAT?
SOMETHING... NAGGING AT MY NOODLE...
...SOME SORT OF DISTRESS...
...SAME FEELING YOU GET FROM WATCHING SOMEONE GIVE THEMSELVES A NASTY PAPER CUT...
THE STRANGE, EMPATHIC CALL URGES DEADPOOL TO ACTION...
...OR IS IT THE SYMBIOTE THAT SPRINGS FROM THE LAMP AND LEAPS TOWARD THE PULL OF PAIN AND SUFFERING?
WHOA!
I JUST STARTED WEB-SLINGING!
I DIDN'T EVEN THINK ABOUT IT.
IT'S LIKE I'M ON AUTOPILOT!

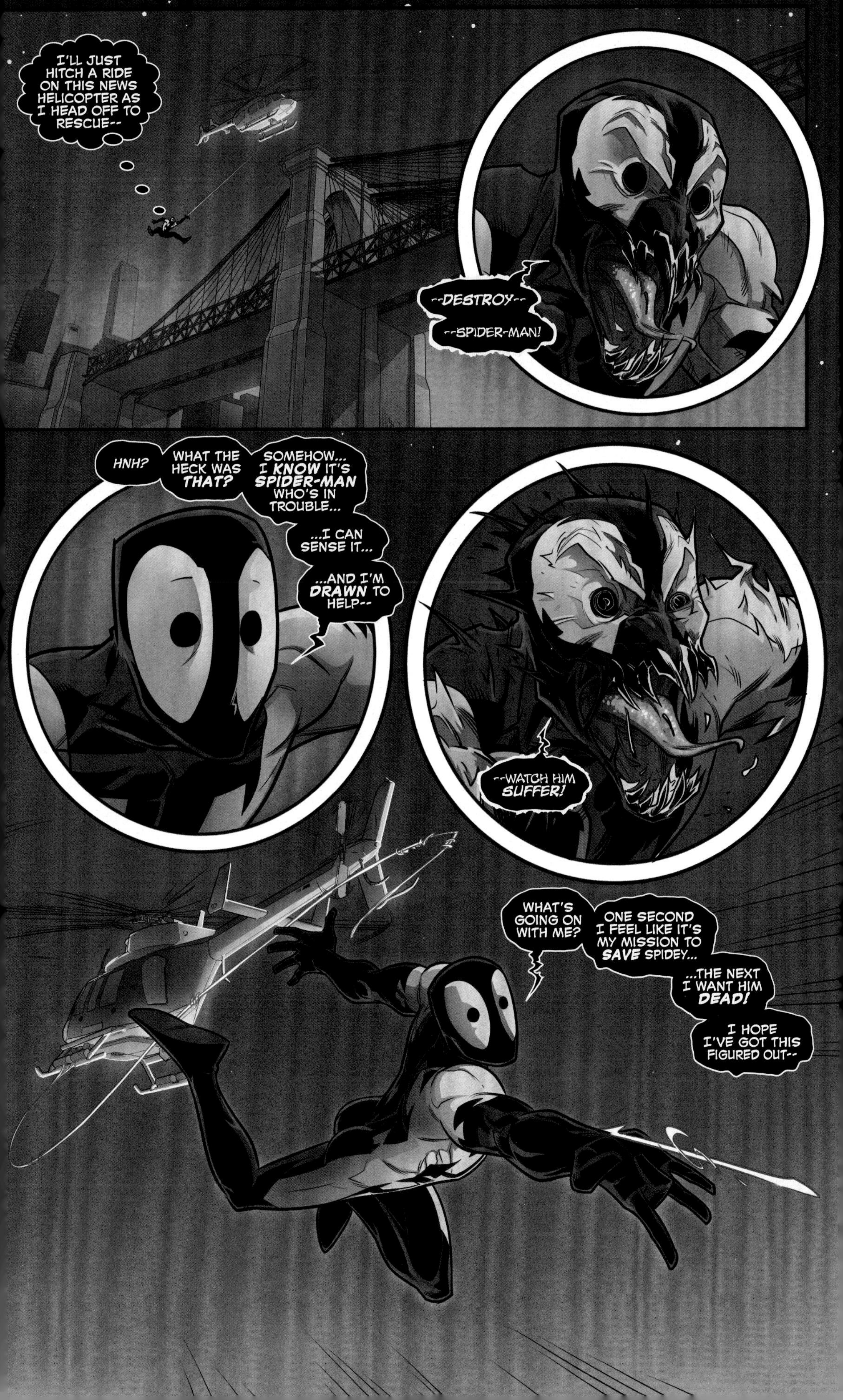
I'LL JUST HITCH A RIDE ON THIS NEWS HELICOPTER AS I HEAD OFF TO RESCUE--
--DESTROY--
--SPIDER-MAN!
HNH?
WHAT THE HECK WAS THAT?
SOMEHOW... I KNOW IT'S SPIDER-MAN WHO'S IN TROUBLE...
...I CAN SENSE IT...
...AND I'M DRAWN TO HELP--
--WATCH HIM SUFFER!
WHAT'S GOING ON WITH ME?
ONE SECOND I FEEL LIKE IT'S MY MISSION TO SAVE SPIDEY...
...THE NEXT I WANT HIM DEAD!
I HOPE I'VE GOT THIS FIGURED OUT--

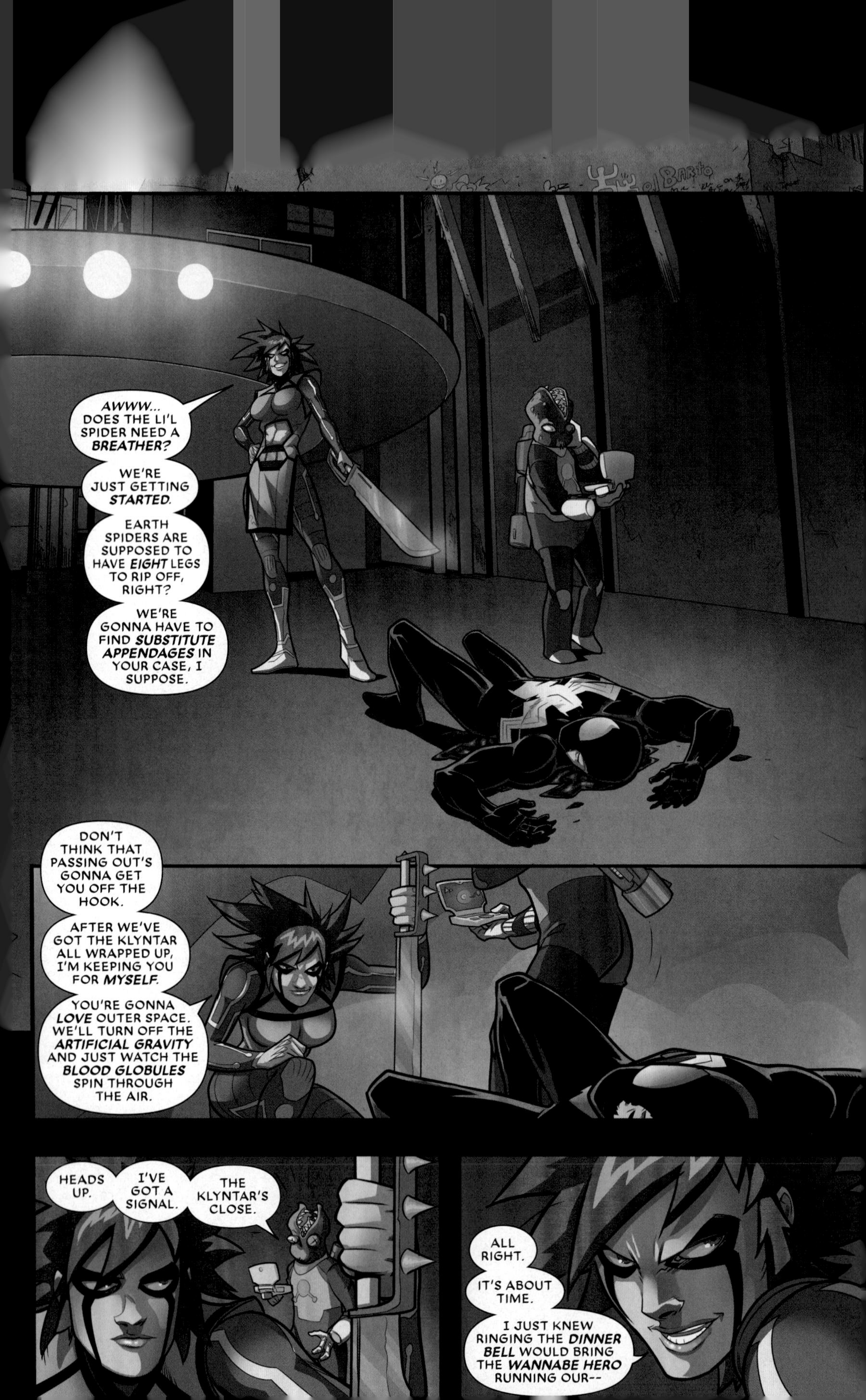
AWWW... DOES THE LI'L SPIDER NEED A BREATHER?
WE'RE JUST GETTING STARTED.
EARTH SPIDERS ARE SUPPOSED TO HAVE EIGHT LEGS TO RIP OFF, RIGHT?
WE'RE GONNA HAVE TO FIND SUBSTITUTE APPENDAGES IN YOUR CASE, I SUPPOSE.
DON'T THINK THAT PASSING OUT'S GONNA GET YOU OFF THE HOOK.
AFTER WE'VE GOT THE KLYNTAR ALL WRAPPED UP, I'M KEEPING YOU FOR MYSELF.
YOU'RE GONNA LOVE OUTER SPACE. WE'LL TURN OFF THE ARTIFICIAL GRAVITY AND JUST WATCH THE BLOOD GLOBULES SPIN THROUGH THE AIR.
HEADS UP.
I'VE GOT A SIGNAL.
THE KLYNTAR'S CLOSE.
ALL RIGHT.
IT'S ABOUT TIME.
I JUST KNEW RINGING THE DINNER BELL WOULD BRING THE WANNABE HERO RUNNING OUR--

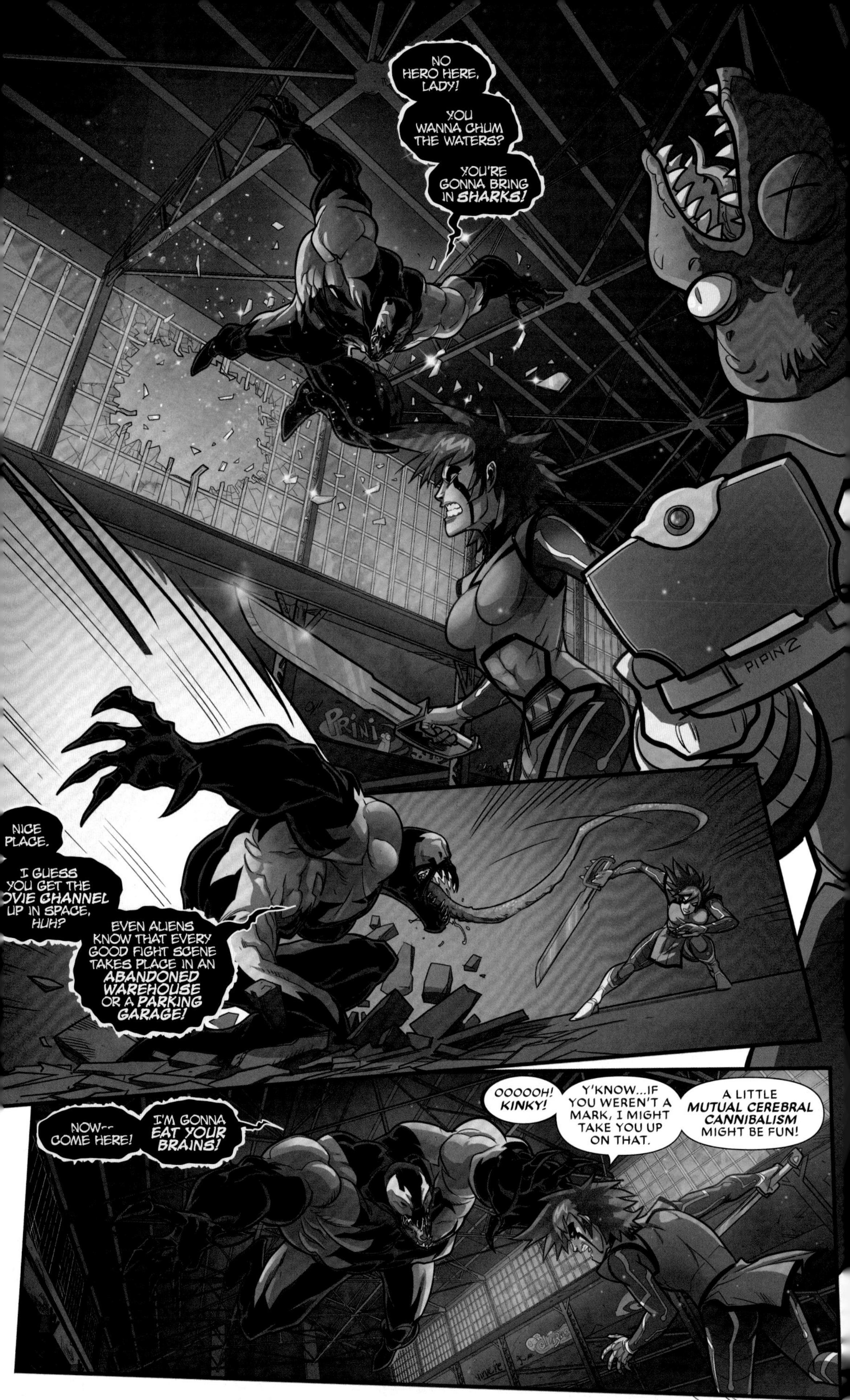

NO HERO HERE, LADY!
YOU WANNA CHUM THE WATERS?
YOU'RE GONNA BRING IN SHARKS!
PIPIN2
NICE PLACE.
I GUESS YOU GET THE OVIE CHANNEL UP IN SPACE, HUH?
EVEN ALIENS KNOW THAT EVERY GOOD FIGHT SCENE TAKES PLACE IN AN ABANDONED WAREHOUSE OR A PARKING GARAGE!
NOW-- COME HERE!
I'M GONNA EAT YOUR BRAINS!
OOOOOH! KINKY!
Y'KNOW...IF YOU WEREN'T A MARK, I MIGHT TAKE YOU UP ON THAT.
A LITTLE MUTUAL CEREBRAL CANNIBALISM MIGHT BE FUN!

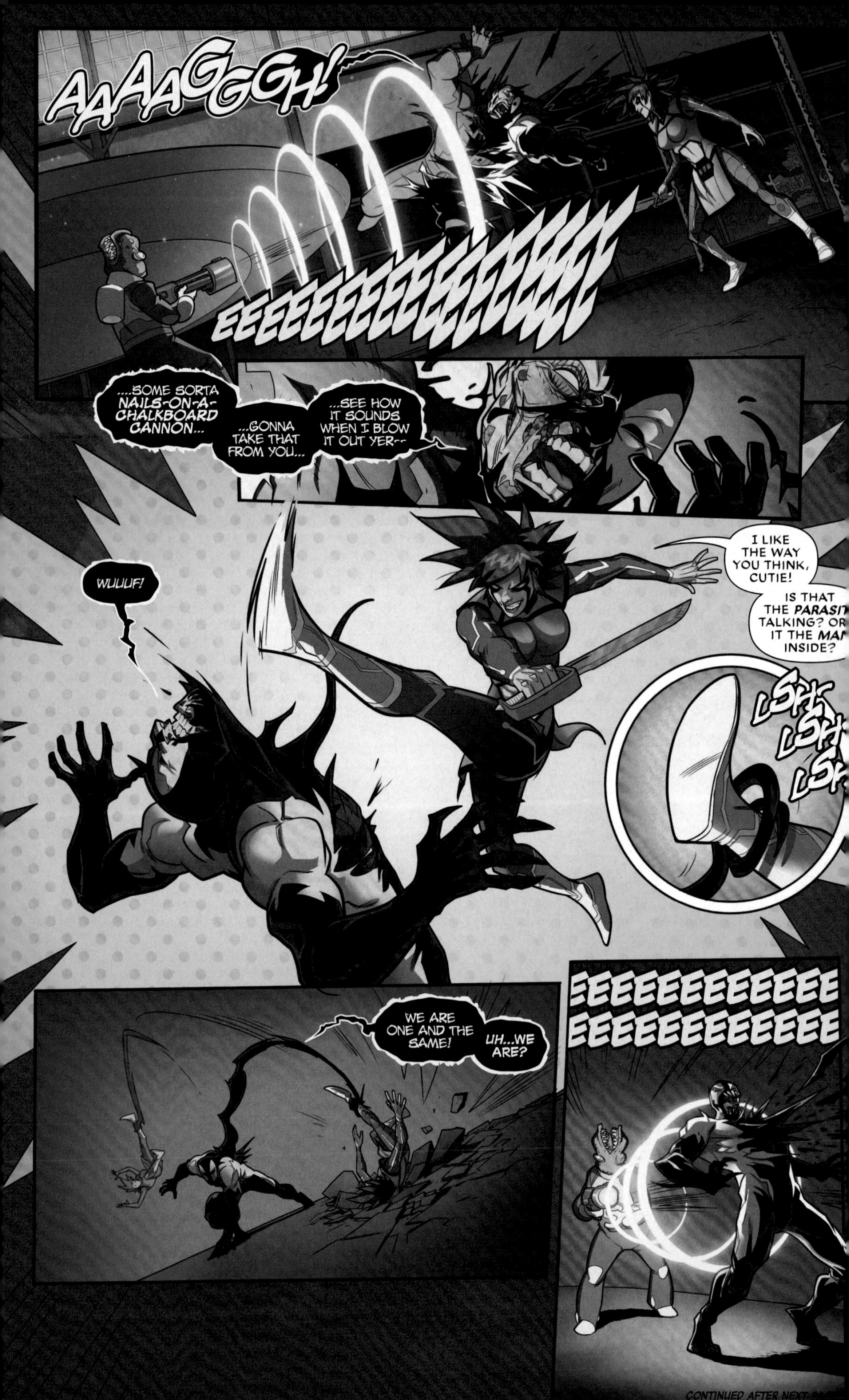
AAAAGGGH!
EEEEEEEEEEEEEEEEEEEE
....SOME SORTA NAILS-ON-A-CHALKBOARD CANNON...
...GONNA TAKE THAT FROM YOU...
...SEE HOW IT SOUNDS WHEN I BLOW IT OUT YER--
WUUUF!
I LIKE THE WAY YOU THINK, CUTIE!
WE ARE ONE AND THE SAME!
UH...WE ARE?
EEEEEEEEEEEEE
EEEEEEEEEEEEE

CONTINUED AFTER NEXT PAGE

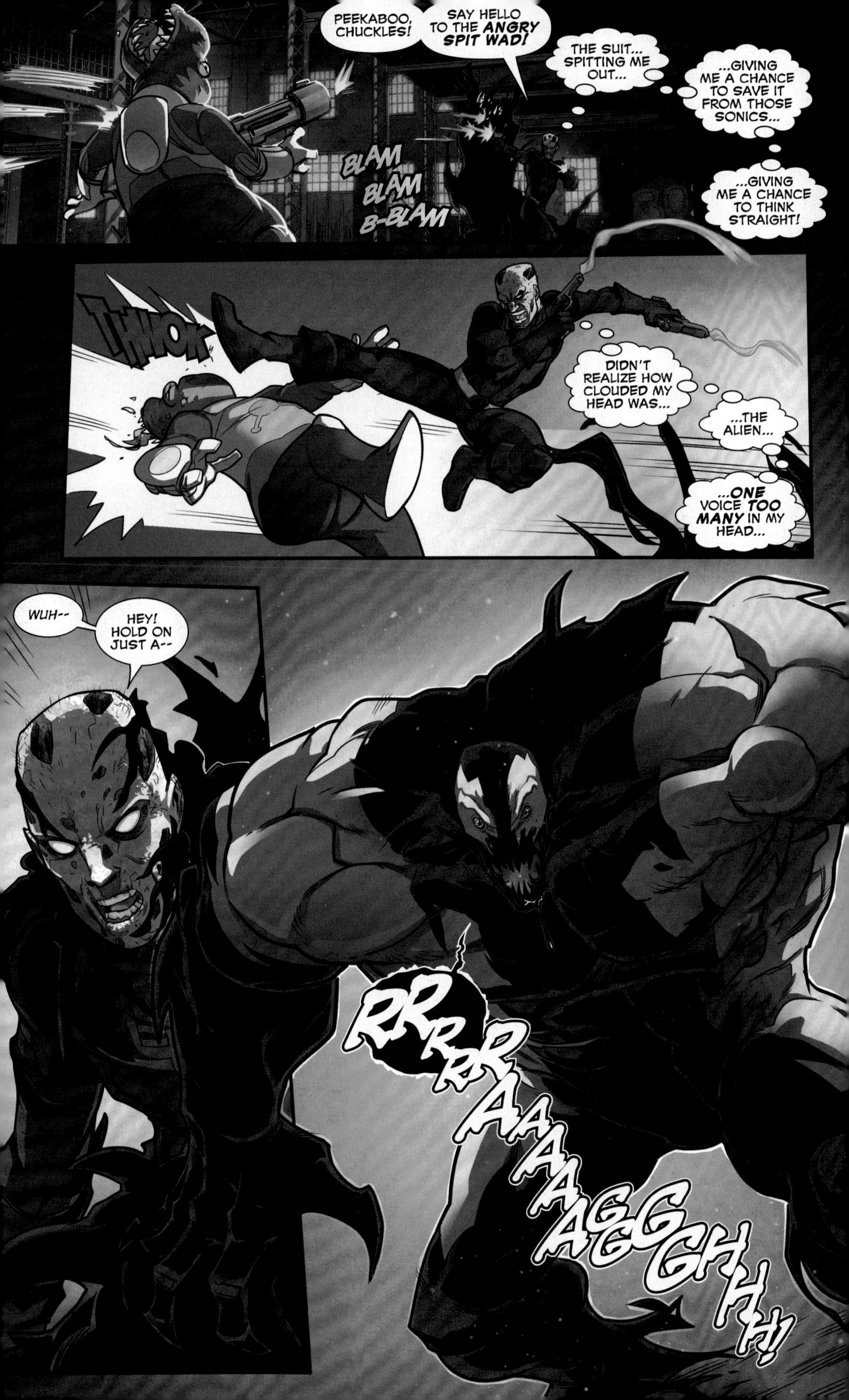

PEEKABOO, CHUCKLES!
SAY HELLO TO THE ANGRY SPIT WAD!
THE SUIT... SPITTING ME OUT...
...GIVING ME A CHANCE TO SAVE IT FROM THOSE SONICS...
...GIVING ME A CHANCE TO THINK STRAIGHT!
BLAM
BLAM
B-BLAM
THWOK
DIDN'T REALIZE HOW CLOUDED MY HEAD WAS...
...THE ALIEN...
...ONE VOICE TOO MANY IN MY HEAD...
WUH--
HEY! HOLD ON JUST A--
RRRRRAAAAAGGGHHH!

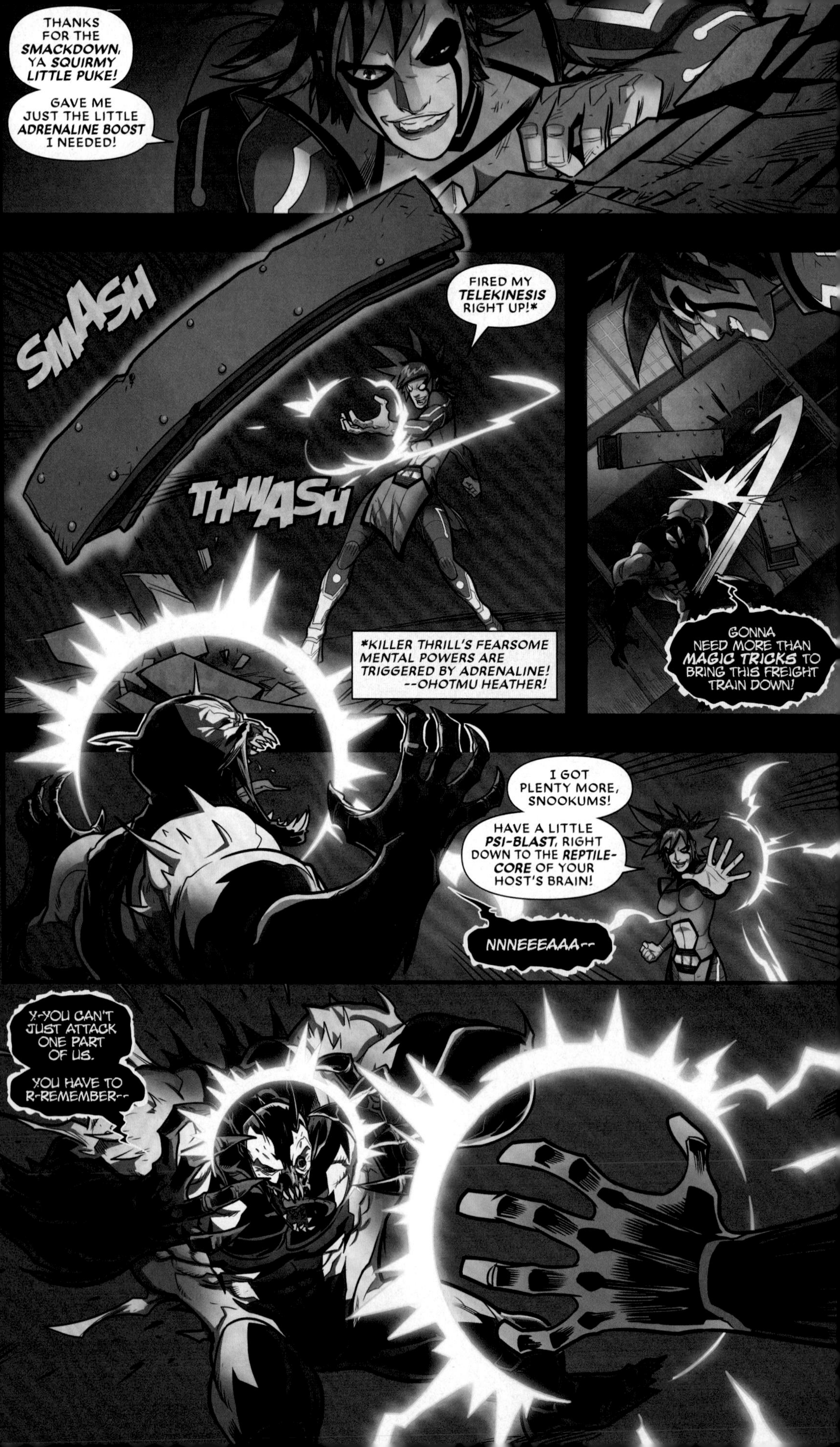
THANKS FOR THE SMACKDOWN, YA SQUIRMY LITTLE PUKE!
GAVE ME JUST THE LITTLE ADRENALINE BOOST I NEEDED!
SMASH
FIRED MY TELEKINESIS RIGHT UP!*
THWASH
*KILLER THRILL'S FEARSOME MENTAL POWERS ARE TRIGGERED BY ADRENALINE! --OHOTMU HEATHER!
GONNA NEED MORE THAN MAGIC TRICKS TO BRING THIS FREIGHT TRAIN DOWN!
I GOT PLENTY MORE, SNOOKUMS!
HAVE A LITTLE PSI-BLAST, RIGHT DOWN TO THE REPTILE-CORE OF YOUR HOST'S BRAIN!
NNNEEEAAA--
Y-YOU CAN'T JUST ATTACK ONE PART OF US.
YOU HAVE TO R-REMEMBER--

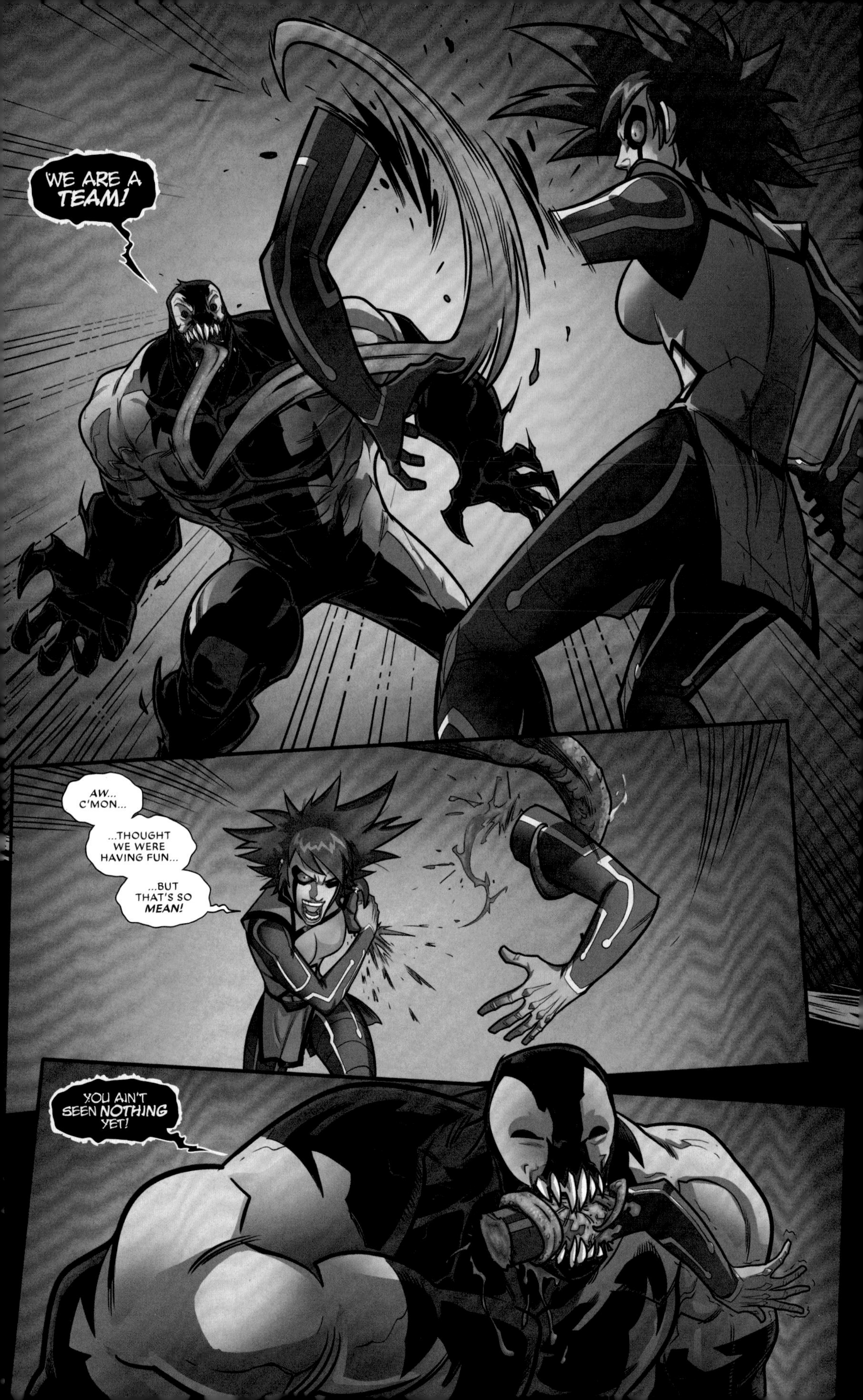
WE ARE A *TEAM!*
AW... C'MON...
...THOUGHT WE WERE HAVING FUN...
...BUT THAT'S SO *MEAN!*
YOU AIN'T SEEN *NOTHING* YET!

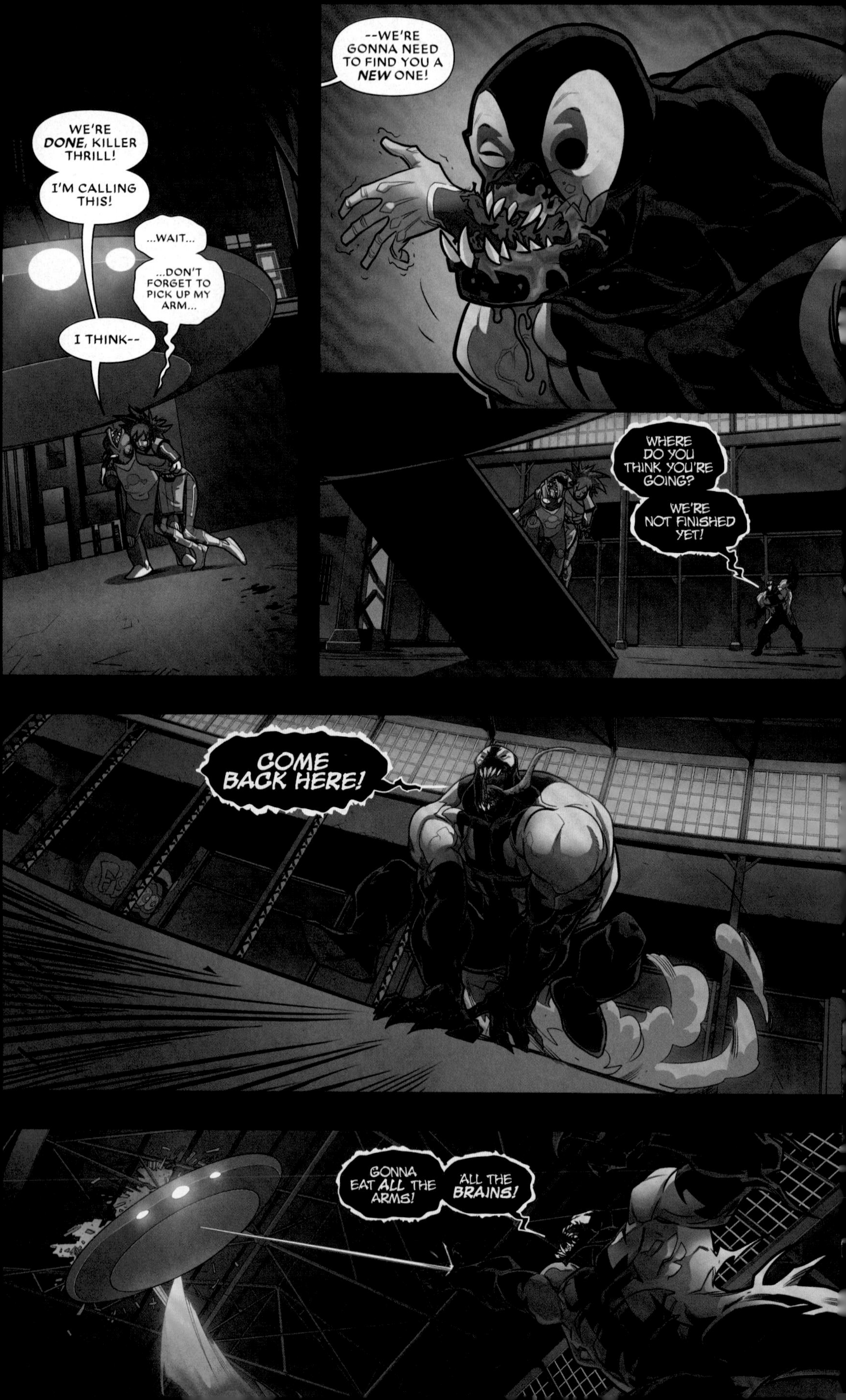
WE'RE *DONE*, KILLER THRILL!
I'M CALLING THIS!
...WAIT...
...DON'T FORGET TO PICK UP MY ARM...
I THINK--
--WE'RE GONNA NEED TO FIND YOU A *NEW* ONE!
WHERE DO YOU THINK YOU'RE GOING?
WE'RE NOT FINISHED YET!
COME BACK HERE!
GONNA EAT *ALL* THE ARMS!
ALL THE *BRAINS!*

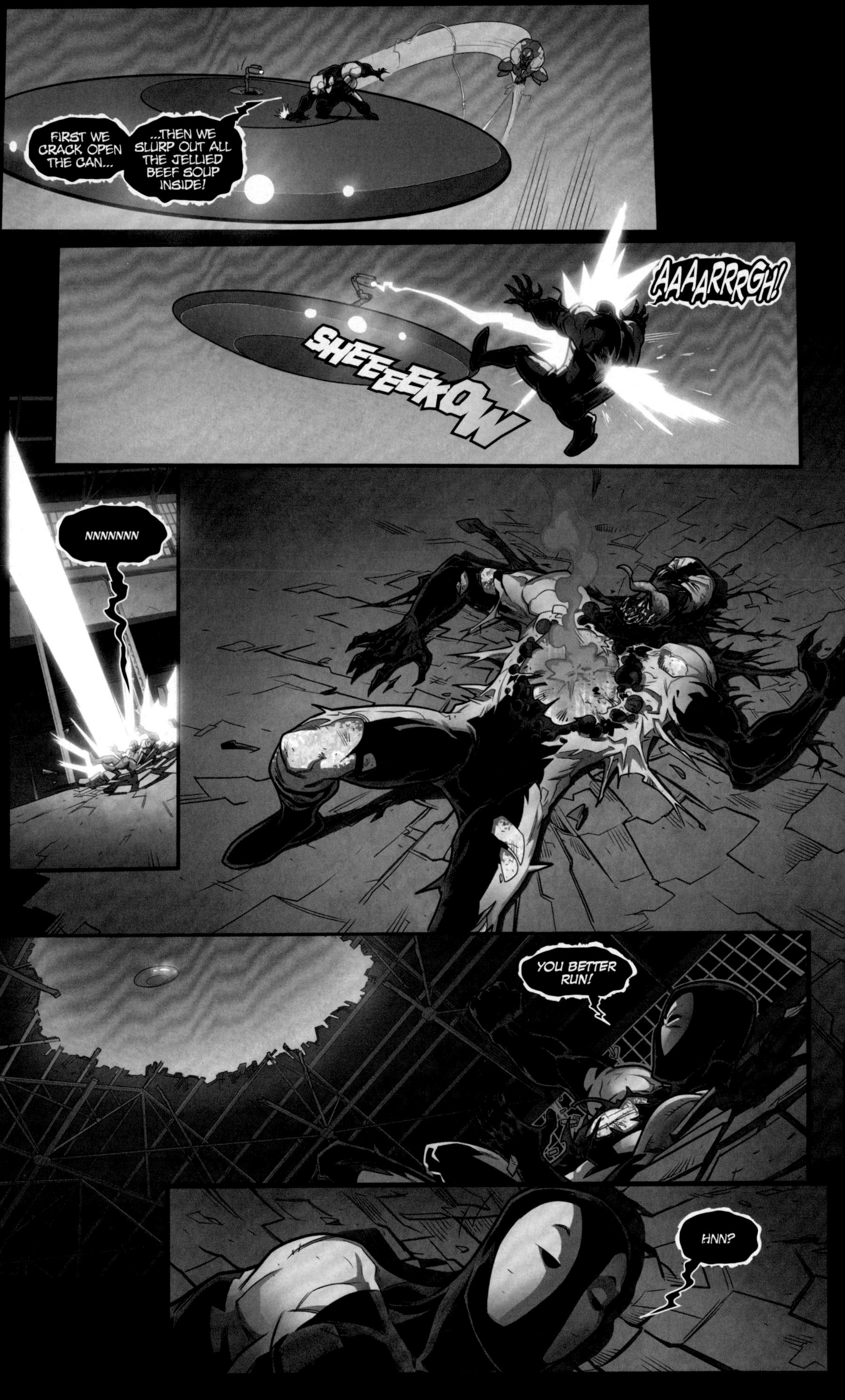
FIRST WE CRACK OPEN THE CAN...
...THEN WE SLURP OUT ALL THE JELLIED BEEF SOUP INSIDE!
AAAARRRGH!
SHEEEEKOW
NNNNNNN
YOU BETTER RUN!
HNN?

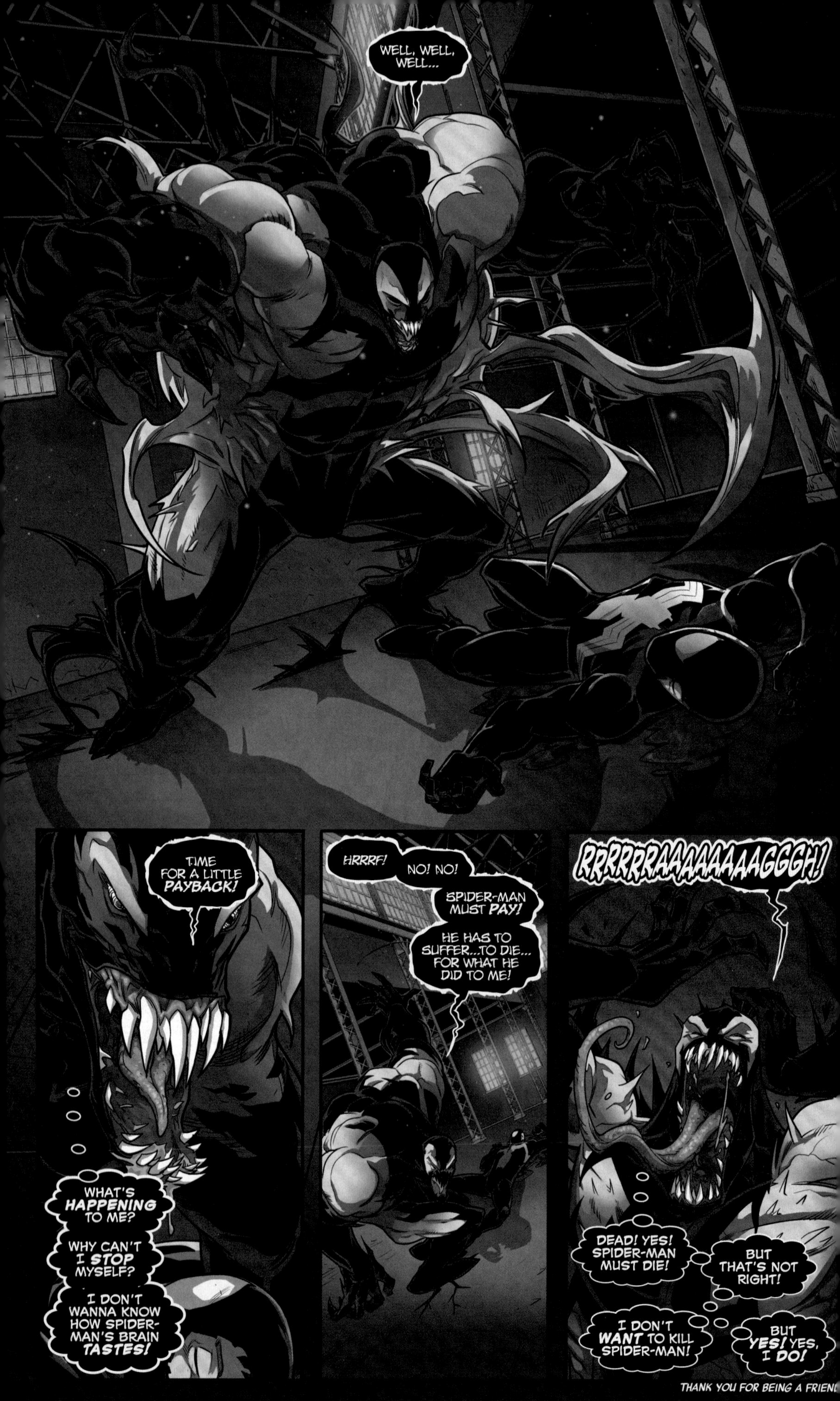
WELL, WELL, WELL...
TIME FOR A LITTLE PAYBACK!
WHAT'S HAPPENING TO ME?
WHY CAN'T I STOP MYSELF?
I DON'T WANNA KNOW HOW SPIDER-MAN'S BRAIN TASTES!
HRRRF!
NO! NO!
SPIDER-MAN MUST PAY!
HE HAS TO SUFFER...TO DIE... FOR WHAT HE DID TO ME!
RRRRRRAAAAAAAAGGGH!
DEAD! YES! SPIDER-MAN MUST DIE!
BUT THAT'S NOT RIGHT!
I DON'T WANT TO KILL SPIDER-MAN!
BUT YES! YES, I DO!

THANK YOU FOR BEING A FRIEN

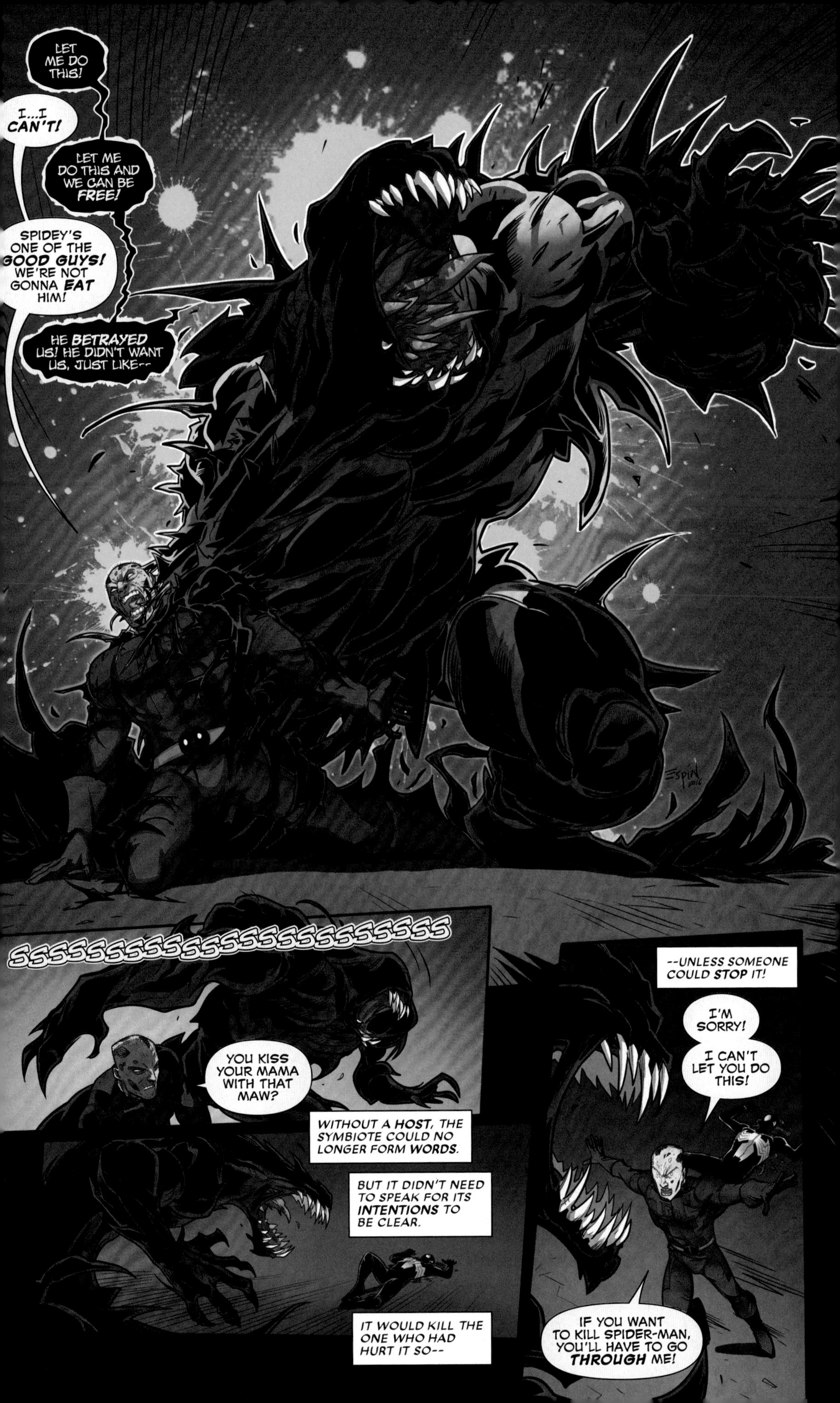
LET ME DO THIS!
I...I CAN'T!
LET ME DO THIS AND WE CAN BE FREE!
SPIDEY'S ONE OF THE GOOD GUYS! WE'RE NOT GONNA EAT HIM!
HE BETRAYED US! HE DIDN'T WANT US, JUST LIKE--
SSSSSSSSSSSSSSSSSSSSSSSSSSSS
YOU KISS YOUR MAMA WITH THAT MAW?
WITHOUT A HOST, THE SYMBIOTE COULD NO LONGER FORM WORDS.
BUT IT DIDN'T NEED TO SPEAK FOR ITS INTENTIONS TO BE CLEAR.
IT WOULD KILL THE ONE WHO HAD HURT IT SO--
--UNLESS SOMEONE COULD STOP IT!
I'M SORRY!
I CAN'T LET YOU DO THIS!
IF YOU WANT TO KILL SPIDER-MAN, YOU'LL HAVE TO GO THROUGH ME!

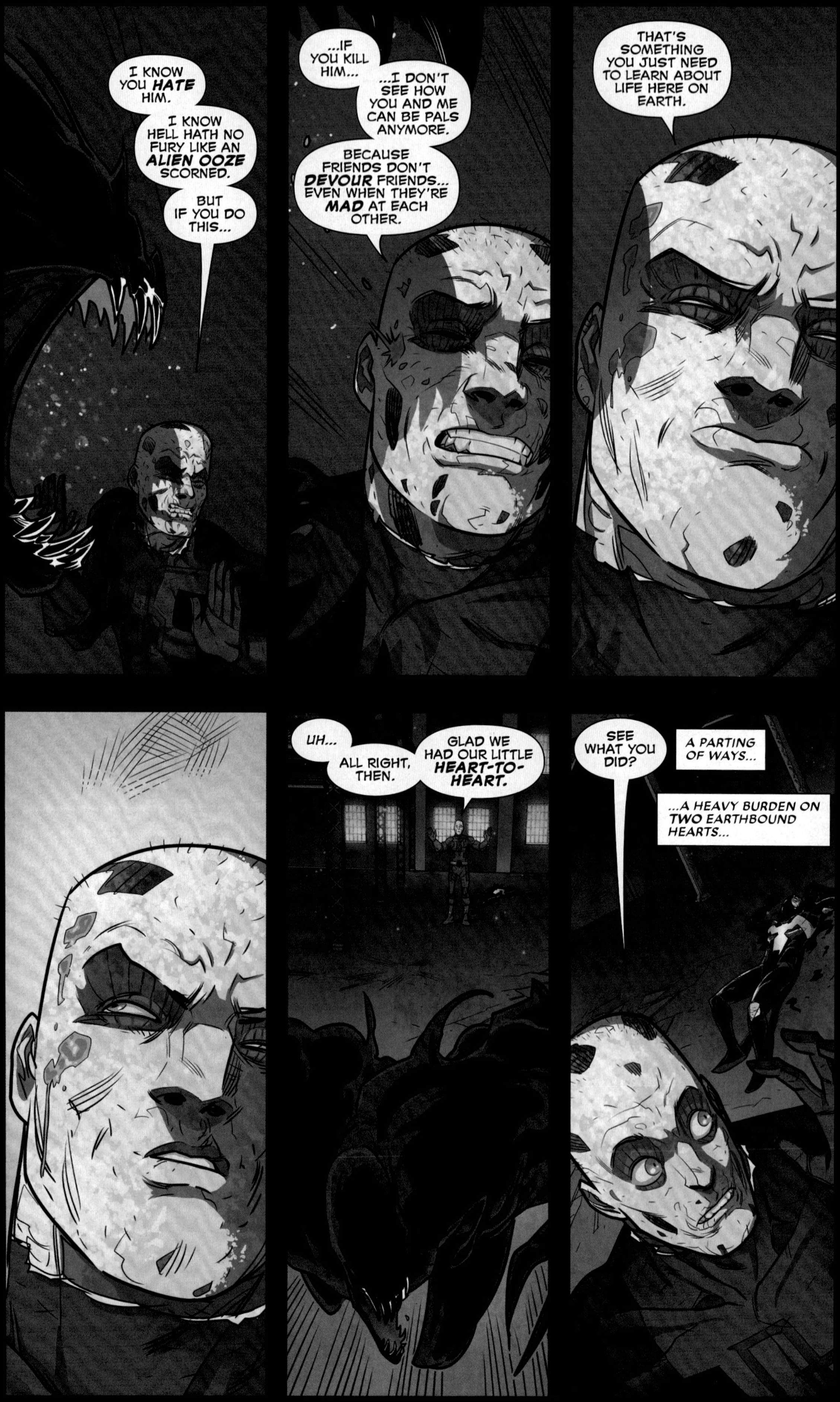
I KNOW YOU **HATE** HIM.
I KNOW HELL HATH NO FURY LIKE AN **ALIEN OOZE** SCORNED.
BUT IF YOU DO THIS...
...IF YOU KILL HIM...
...I DON'T SEE HOW YOU AND ME CAN BE PALS ANYMORE.
BECAUSE FRIENDS DON'T **DEVOUR** FRIENDS... EVEN WHEN THEY'RE **MAD** AT EACH OTHER.
THAT'S SOMETHING YOU JUST NEED TO LEARN ABOUT LIFE HERE ON EARTH.
UH...
ALL RIGHT, THEN.
GLAD WE HAD OUR LITTLE **HEART-TO-HEART.**
SEE WHAT YOU DID?
A PARTING OF WAYS...
...A HEAVY BURDEN ON **TWO** EARTHBOUND HEARTS...

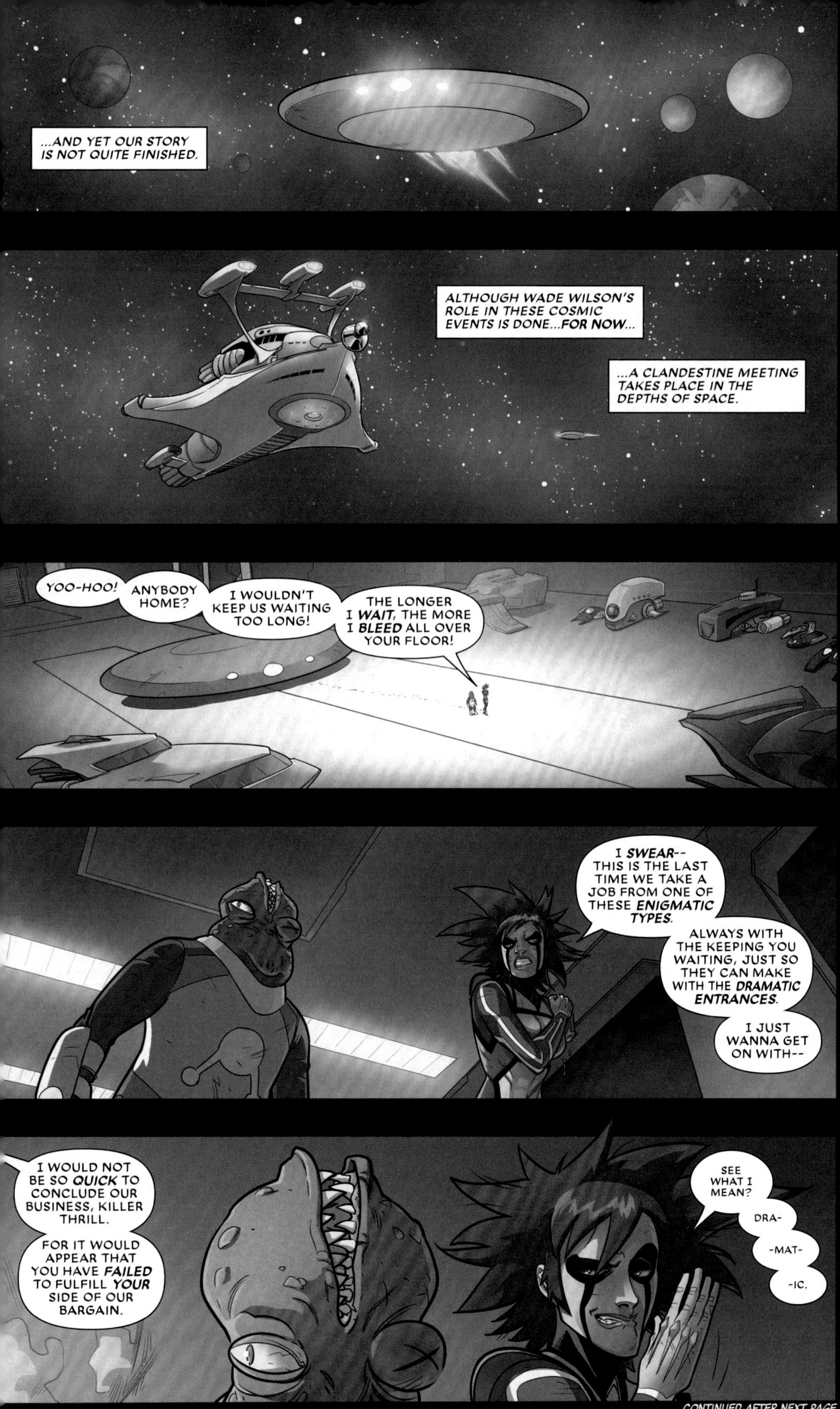
...AND YET OUR STORY IS NOT QUITE FINISHED.
ALTHOUGH WADE WILSON'S ROLE IN THESE COSMIC EVENTS IS DONE...FOR NOW...
...A CLANDESTINE MEETING TAKES PLACE IN THE DEPTHS OF SPACE.
YOO-HOO!
ANYBODY HOME?
I WOULDN'T KEEP US WAITING TOO LONG!
THE LONGER I WAIT, THE MORE I BLEED ALL OVER YOUR FLOOR!
I SWEAR-- THIS IS THE LAST TIME WE TAKE A JOB FROM ONE OF THESE ENIGMATIC TYPES.
ALWAYS WITH THE KEEPING YOU WAITING, JUST SO THEY CAN MAKE WITH THE DRAMATIC ENTRANCES.
I JUST WANNA GET ON WITH--
I WOULD NOT BE SO QUICK TO CONCLUDE OUR BUSINESS, KILLER THRILL.
FOR IT WOULD APPEAR THAT YOU HAVE FAILED TO FULFILL YOUR SIDE OF OUR BARGAIN.
SEE WHAT I MEAN?
DRA-
-MAT-
-IC.

CONTINUED AFTER NEXT PAGE

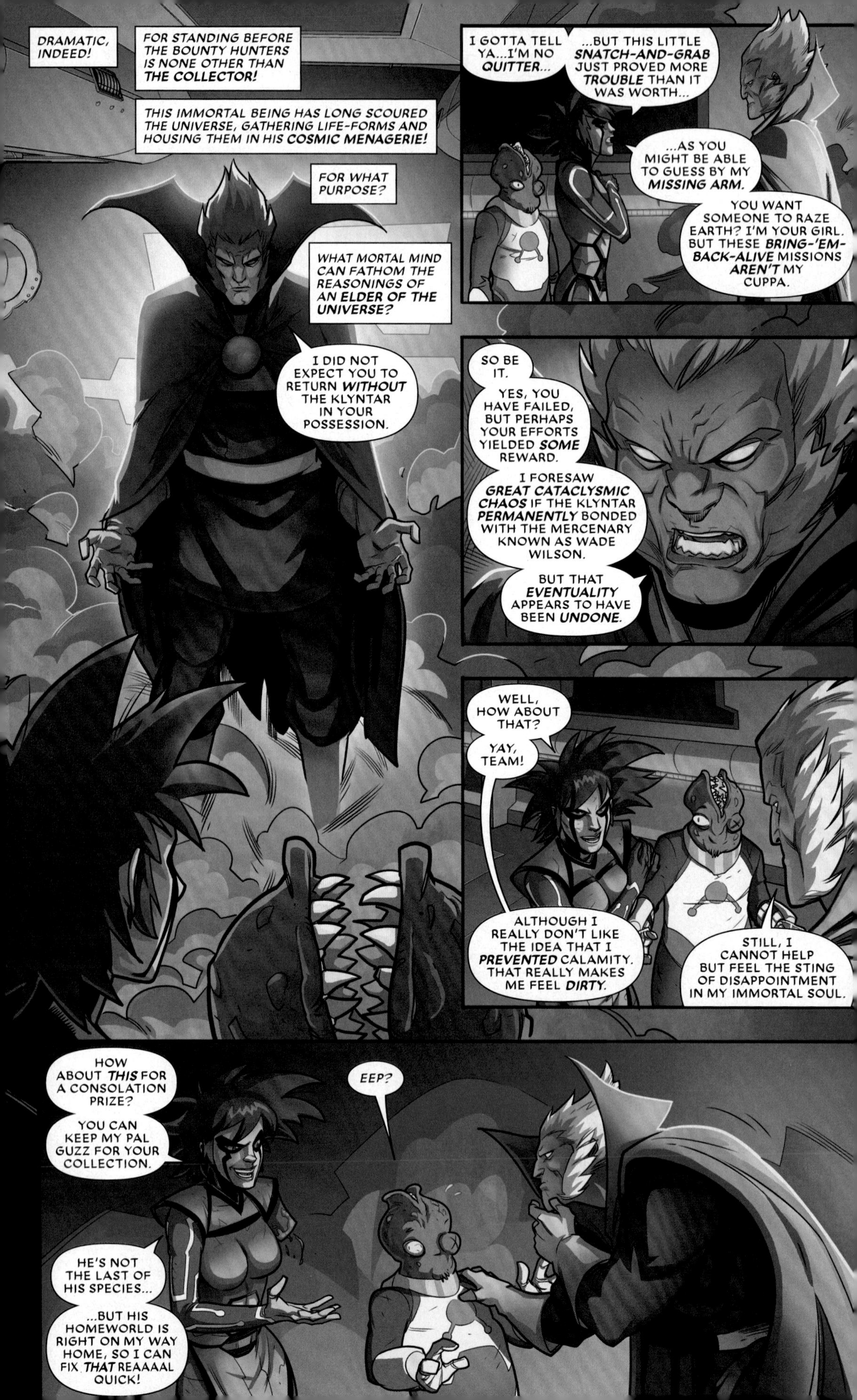
DRAMATIC, INDEED!
FOR STANDING BEFORE THE BOUNTY HUNTERS IS NONE OTHER THAN THE COLLECTOR!
THIS IMMORTAL BEING HAS LONG SCOURED THE UNIVERSE, GATHERING LIFE-FORMS AND HOUSING THEM IN HIS COSMIC MENAGERIE!
FOR WHAT PURPOSE?
WHAT MORTAL MIND CAN FATHOM THE REASONINGS OF AN ELDER OF THE UNIVERSE?
I DID NOT EXPECT YOU TO RETURN WITHOUT THE KLYNTAR IN YOUR POSSESSION.
I GOTTA TELL YA...I'M NO QUITTER...
...BUT THIS LITTLE SNATCH-AND-GRAB JUST PROVED MORE TROUBLE THAN IT WAS WORTH...
...AS YOU MIGHT BE ABLE TO GUESS BY MY MISSING ARM.
YOU WANT SOMEONE TO RAZE EARTH? I'M YOUR GIRL. BUT THESE BRING-'EM-BACK-ALIVE MISSIONS AREN'T MY CUPPA.
SO BE IT.
YES, YOU HAVE FAILED, BUT PERHAPS YOUR EFFORTS YIELDED SOME REWARD.
I FORESAW GREAT CATACLYSMIC CHAOS IF THE KLYNTAR PERMANENTLY BONDED WITH THE MERCENARY KNOWN AS WADE WILSON.
BUT THAT EVENTUALITY APPEARS TO HAVE BEEN UNDONE.
WELL, HOW ABOUT THAT?
YAY, TEAM!
ALTHOUGH I REALLY DON'T LIKE THE IDEA THAT I PREVENTED CALAMITY. THAT REALLY MAKES ME FEEL DIRTY.
STILL, I CANNOT HELP BUT FEEL THE STING OF DISAPPOINTMENT IN MY IMMORTAL SOUL.
HOW ABOUT THIS FOR A CONSOLATION PRIZE?
YOU CAN KEEP MY PAL GUZZ FOR YOUR COLLECTION.
EEP?
HE'S NOT THE LAST OF HIS SPECIES...
...BUT HIS HOMEWORLD IS RIGHT ON MY WAY HOME, SO I CAN FIX THAT REAAAAL QUICK!

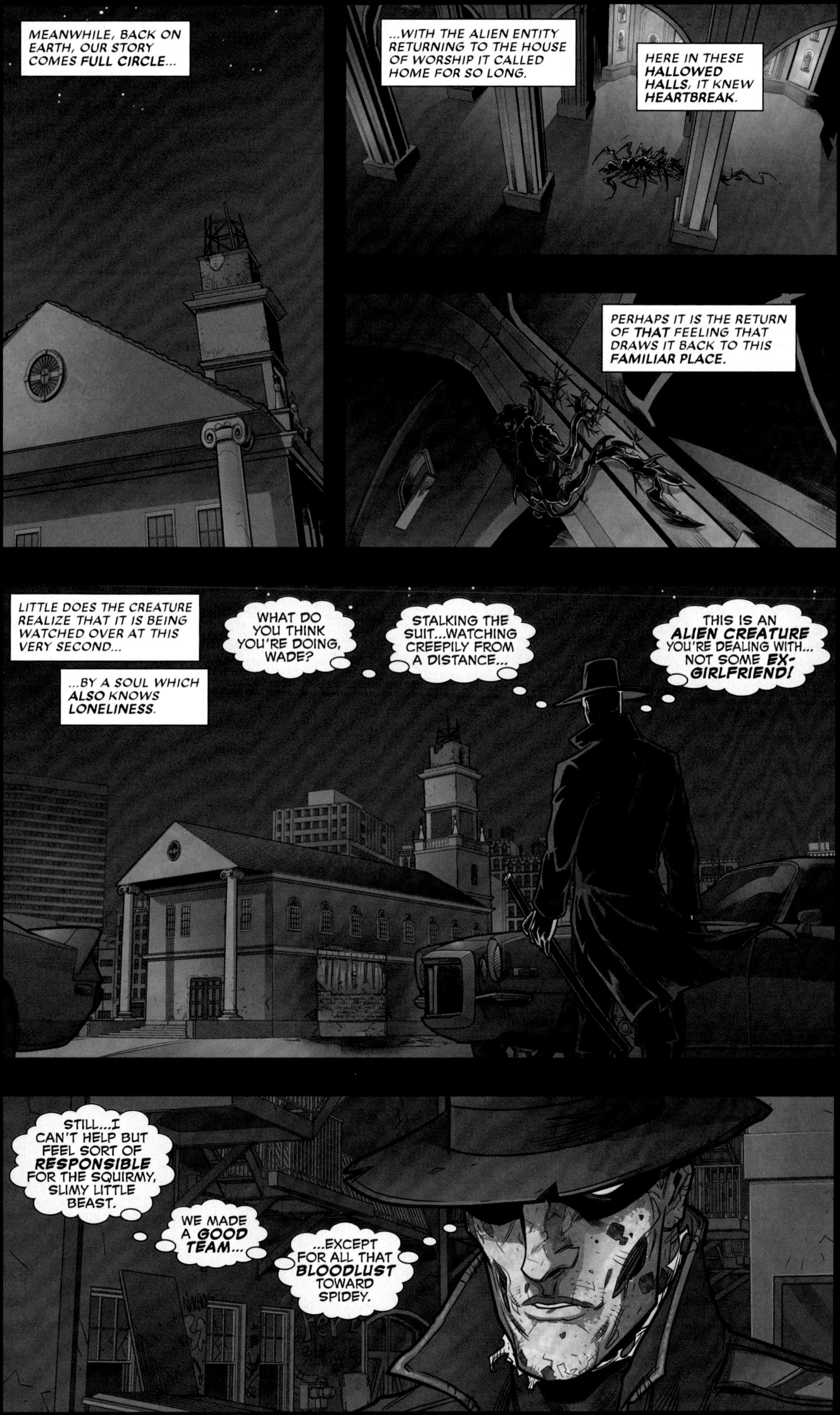

MEANWHILE, BACK ON EARTH, OUR STORY COMES FULL CIRCLE...
...WITH THE ALIEN ENTITY RETURNING TO THE HOUSE OF WORSHIP IT CALLED HOME FOR SO LONG.
HERE IN THESE HALLOWED HALLS, IT KNEW HEARTBREAK.
PERHAPS IT IS THE RETURN OF THAT FEELING THAT DRAWS IT BACK TO THIS FAMILIAR PLACE.
LITTLE DOES THE CREATURE REALIZE THAT IT IS BEING WATCHED OVER AT THIS VERY SECOND...
...BY A SOUL WHICH ALSO KNOWS LONELINESS.
WHAT DO YOU THINK YOU'RE DOING, WADE?
STALKING THE SUIT...WATCHING CREEPILY FROM A DISTANCE...
THIS IS AN ALIEN CREATURE YOU'RE DEALING WITH... NOT SOME EX-GIRLFRIEND!
STILL...I CAN'T HELP BUT FEEL SORT OF RESPONSIBLE FOR THE SQUIRMY, SLIMY LITTLE BEAST.
WE MADE A GOOD TEAM...
...EXCEPT FOR ALL THAT BLOODLUST TOWARD SPIDEY.

DRUIDS & DRAGONS IN POWER MAN AND IRON FIST #118!

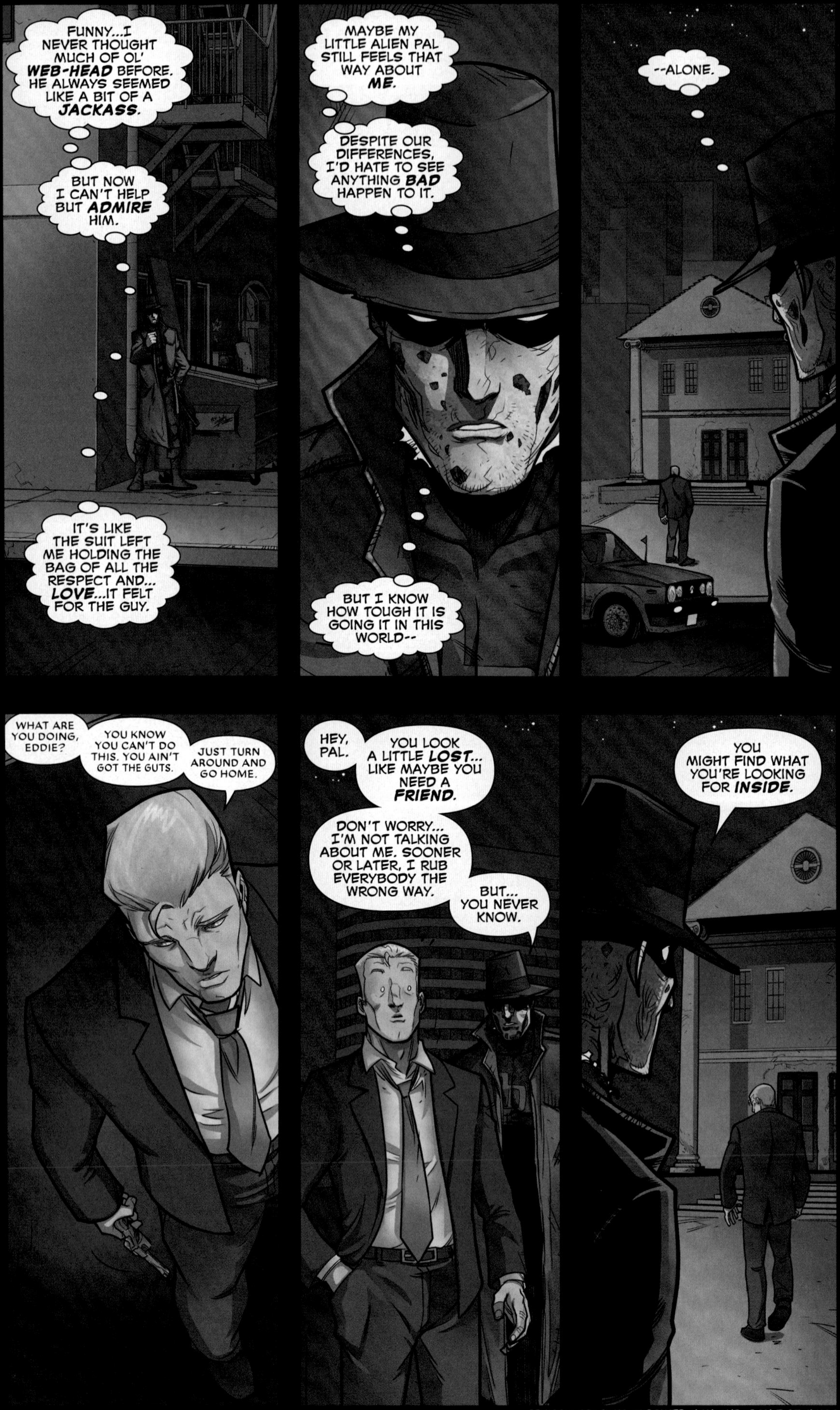
FUNNY...I NEVER THOUGHT MUCH OF OL' WEB-HEAD BEFORE. HE ALWAYS SEEMED LIKE A BIT OF A JACKASS.
BUT NOW I CAN'T HELP BUT ADMIRE HIM.
IT'S LIKE THE SUIT LEFT ME HOLDING THE BAG OF ALL THE RESPECT AND... LOVE...IT FELT FOR THE GUY.
MAYBE MY LITTLE ALIEN PAL STILL FEELS THAT WAY ABOUT ME.
DESPITE OUR DIFFERENCES, I'D HATE TO SEE ANYTHING BAD HAPPEN TO IT.
BUT I KNOW HOW TOUGH IT IS GOING IT IN THIS WORLD--
--ALONE.
WHAT ARE YOU DOING, EDDIE?
YOU KNOW YOU CAN'T DO THIS. YOU AIN'T GOT THE GUTS.
JUST TURN AROUND AND GO HOME.
HEY, PAL.
YOU LOOK A LITTLE LOST... LIKE MAYBE YOU NEED A FRIEND.
DON'T WORRY... I'M NOT TALKING ABOUT ME. SOONER OR LATER, I RUB EVERYBODY THE WRONG WAY.
BUT... YOU NEVER KNOW.
YOU MIGHT FIND WHAT YOU'RE LOOKING FOR INSIDE.

DRUIDS & DRAGONS IN POWER MAN AND IRON FIST #118!

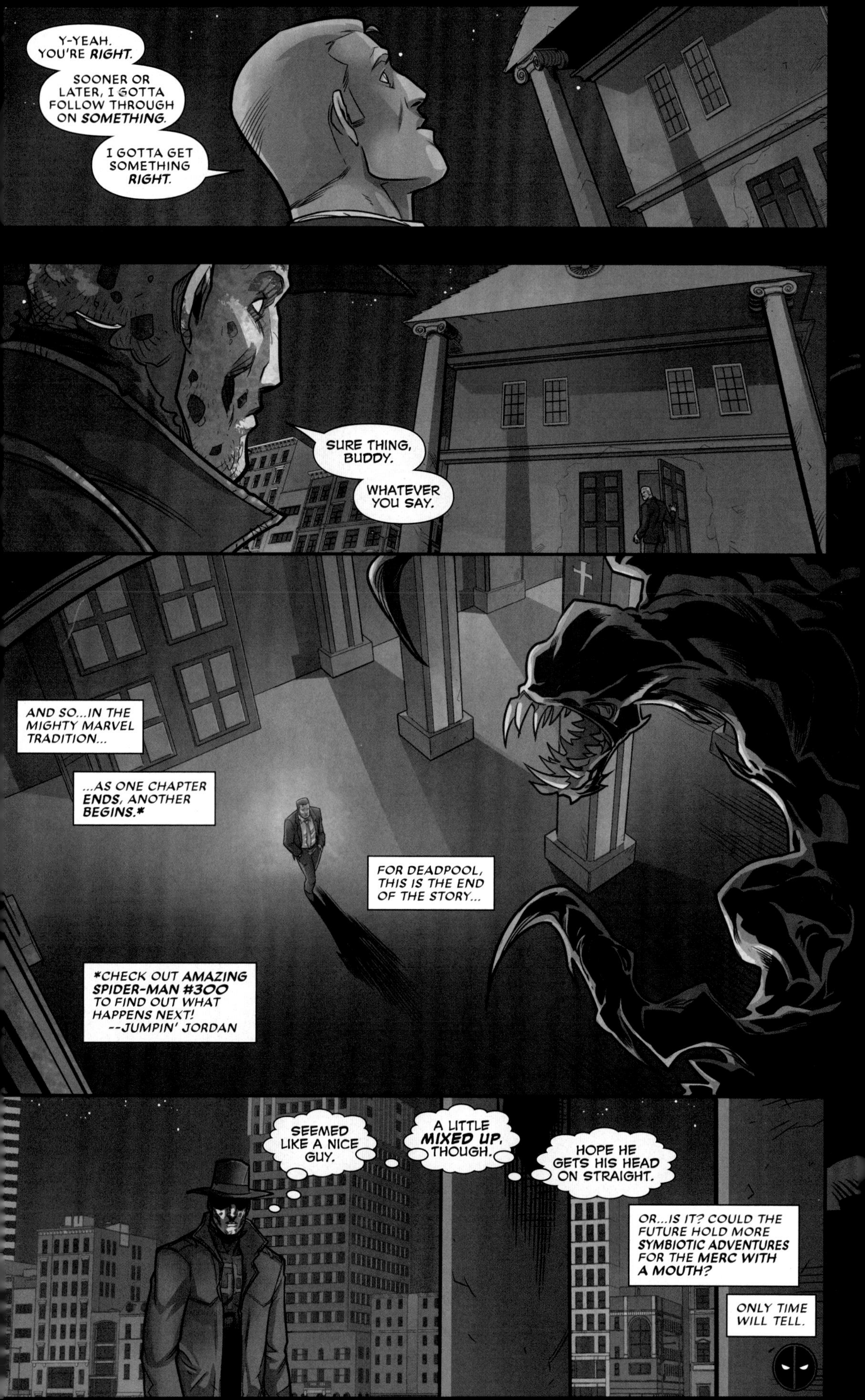
Y-YEAH. YOU'RE RIGHT.
SOONER OR LATER, I GOTTA FOLLOW THROUGH ON SOMETHING.
I GOTTA GET SOMETHING RIGHT.
SURE THING, BUDDY.
WHATEVER YOU SAY.
AND SO...IN THE MIGHTY MARVEL TRADITION...
...AS ONE CHAPTER ENDS, ANOTHER BEGINS.*
FOR DEADPOOL, THIS IS THE END OF THE STORY...
*CHECK OUT AMAZING SPIDER-MAN #300 TO FIND OUT WHAT HAPPENS NEXT! --JUMPIN' JORDAN
SEEMED LIKE A NICE GUY.
A LITTLE MIXED UP, THOUGH.
HOPE HE GETS HIS HEAD ON STRAIGHT.
OR...IS IT? COULD THE FUTURE HOLD MORE SYMBIOTIC ADVENTURES FOR THE MERC WITH A MOUTH?
ONLY TIME WILL TELL.

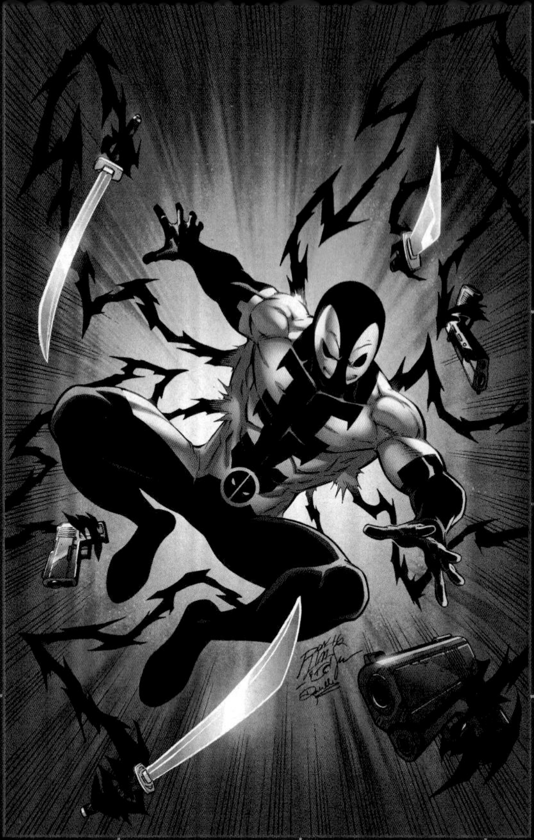

RON LIM, JOHN DELL & RACHELLE ROSENBERG

1 VARIANT

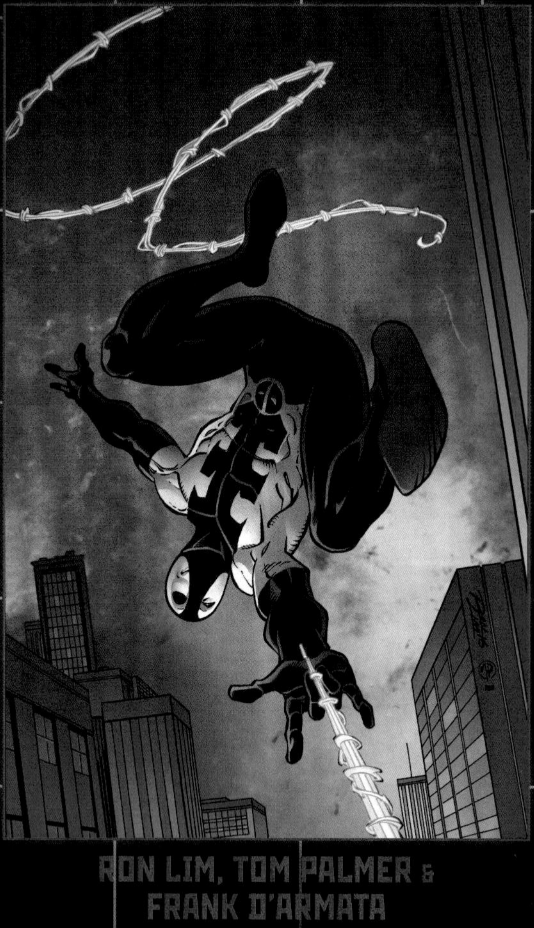

RON LIM, TOM PALMER & FRANK D'ARMATA

2 VARIANT

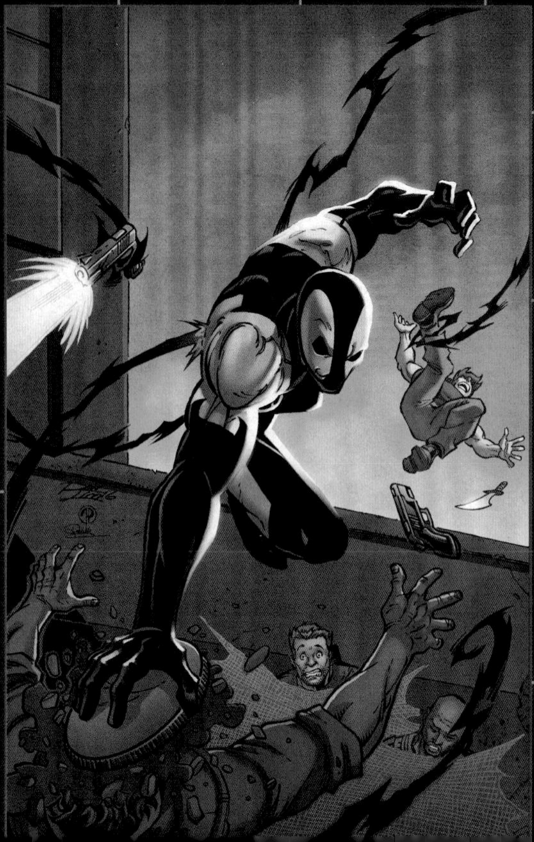

RON LIM, TOM PALMER & RACHELLE ROSENBERG

3 VARIANT

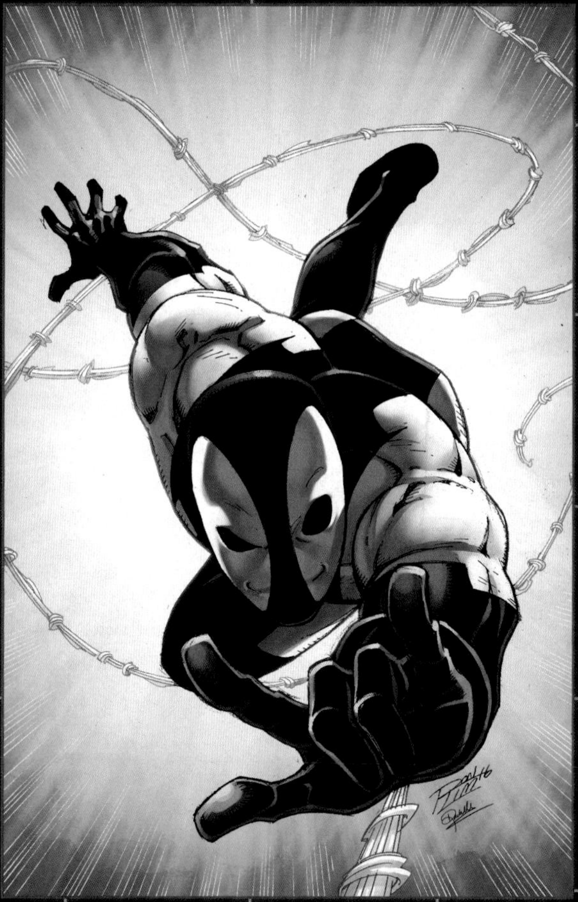

RON LIM &
RACHELLE ROSENBERG
4 VARIANT

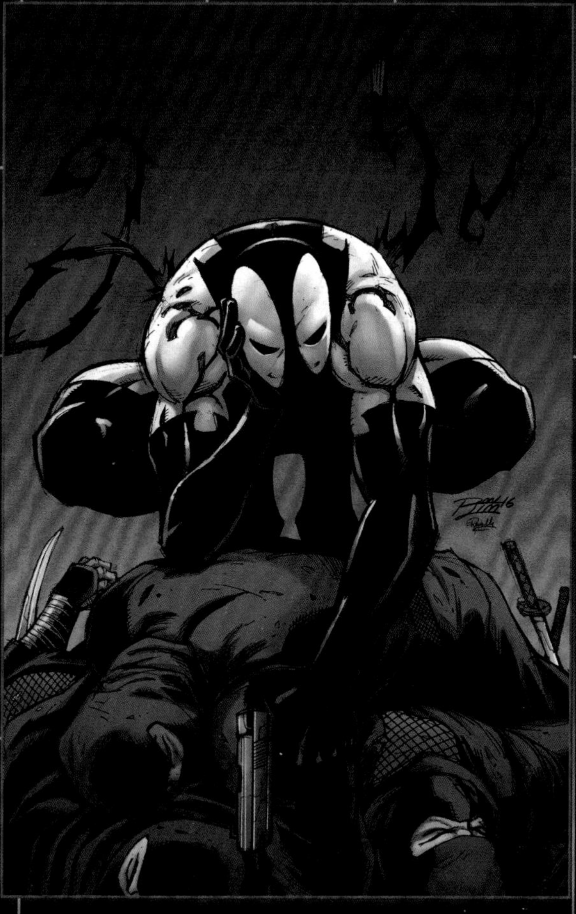

RON LIM &
RACHELLE ROSENBERG
5 VARIANT

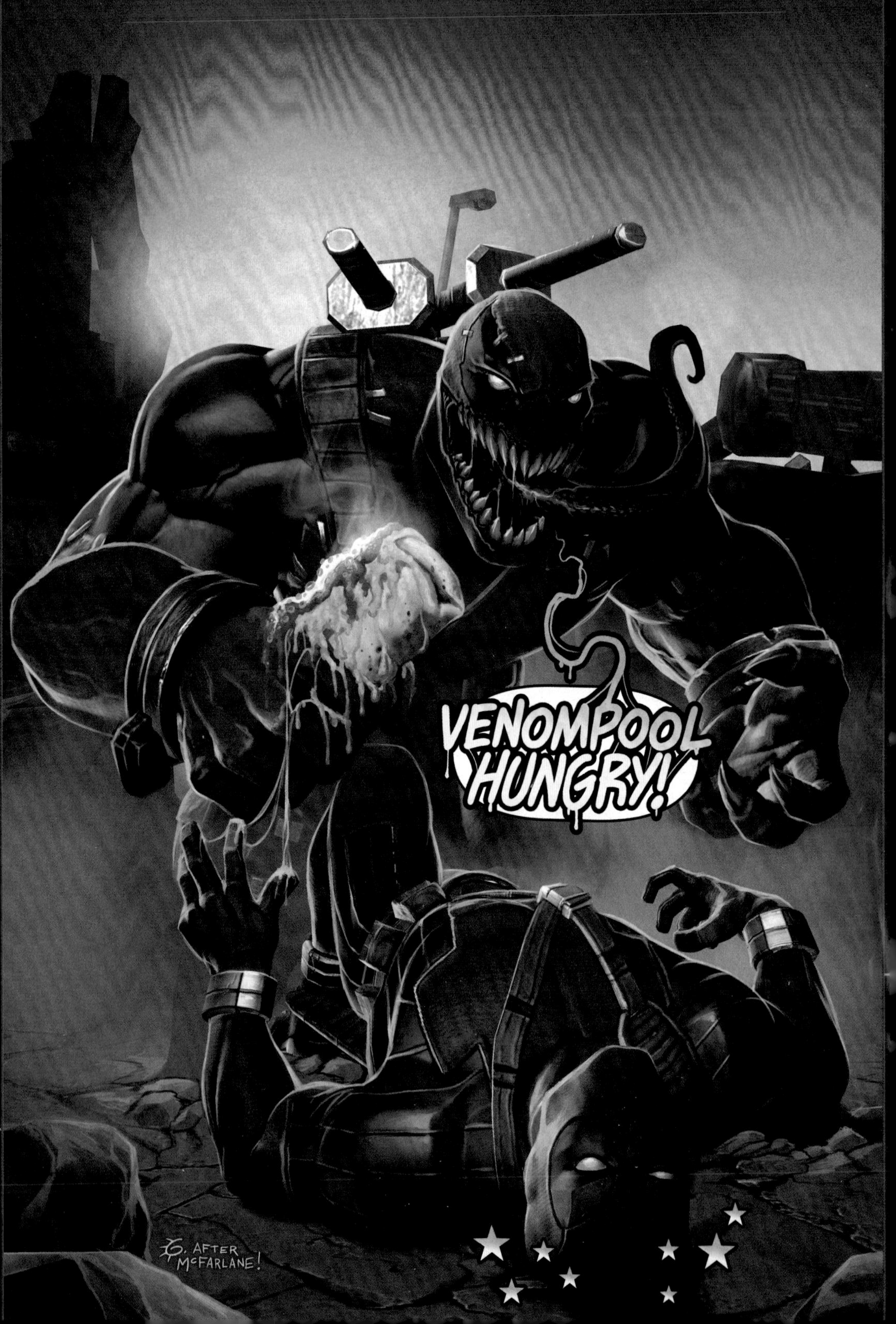
VENOMPOOL HUNGRY!
G. AFTER McFARLANE!